British *Paintings*

1880 - 1980

In memory of Jonathan Black

Edited by Paul Liss and George Richards
Catalogue design by Clémence Godinot

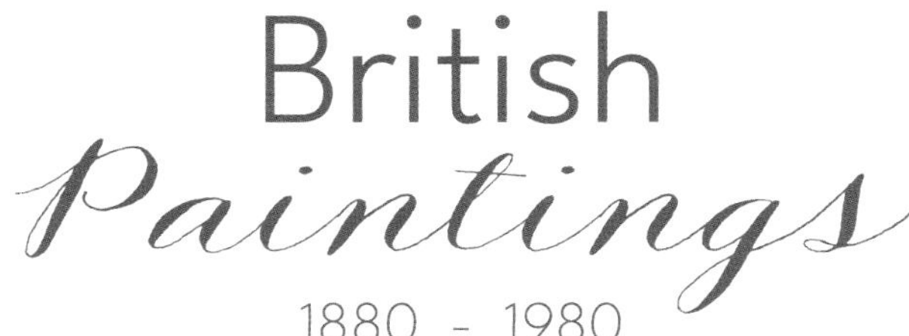

For all enquiries
please contact
George Richards:
george@lissllewellyn.com
+44 (0)7497 492756

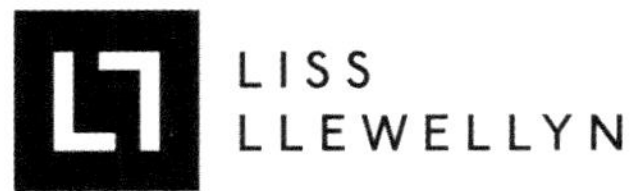

Introduction

This catalogue brings together one hundred years of British Painting, from 1880 - 1980. Women are at the forefront: the essential process of rewriting their work into the narrative continues.

Among the women celebrated here are Marion Adnams, Averil Burleigh, Hilda Carline, Ithell Colquhoun, Evelyn Dunbar, Margaret Gere, Kathleen Guthrie, Winifred Knights, Rachel Reckitt and Paule Vézelay. There is still work to be done: research into Laura Jewis, the creator of the striking 1937 altarpiece (p. 90) is ongoing but has so far yielded little. Frustrating as this may be, it stands as a testament to a reality that is not acknowledged often enough: so many women of extraordinary talent have all but disappeared from view, sometimes completely so. This might have been the result of marriage and the associated name-change, or of their work simply not having been preserved or valued, or a combination of these factors.

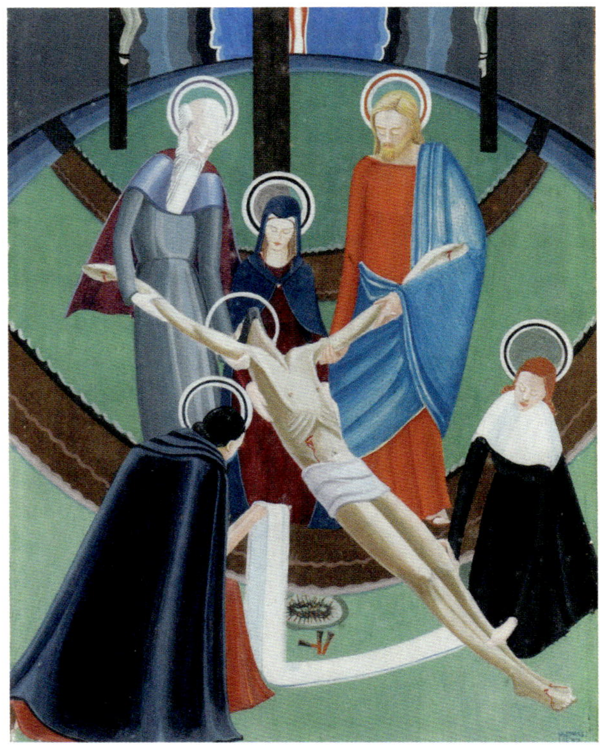

Laura A. Jewis (1896-), Scenes from the Life of Christ, 1937

Working directly with artists' estates can bear rich fruit. Pictures not seen for decades come to light, as is the case with the group of works featured by the Carline family, George, Richard, Hilda and Sidney. This catalogue is dedicated to the memory of the scholar Dr Jonathan Black, who did so much to make their work more visible.

'Masterpiece' is a much-overused word, most likely involving an element of subjectivity and often commercial bias. One must also note the gendered implication of the word and why it is reflective of an outdated view of art history. However in this catalogue there are works of undeniable historical importance, such as Cundall's epic World War II canvas *The British Railways Carry On*. Whatever superlatives might or might not be applied, such works at least bring with them a sense of discovery. Sauter's outstanding triptych *Never More!* is a case in point. Sauter has recently been the subject of a brilliant biography by Jeffrey S. Reznick, (War and Peace in the Worlds of Rudolf H. Sauter: A Cultural History of a Creative Life, Anthem Press, 2022) and the significance of this particular work, which at the time of publication was untraced, occupies a central part of that narrative.

When looking at a major painting by a minor figure, Patrick Elliott, Chief Curator of Modern and Contemporary Art at the National Galleries of Scotland, was once heard to remark 'it might not be a masterpiece, but it certainly is *this artist's* masterpiece'. This might be said of Monnington's *Winter*, on the cover of this catalogue. *Winter* was his winning submission for the coveted British School at Rome Scholarship in 1922. The winner in 1920 was Winifred Knights, whom Monnington married in 1924, and whose iconic painting *The Deluge*, now in the Tate, earned her fame as the first woman to win a Rome Scholarship. Monnington's development as an artist is beautifully illustrated by the four works in this catalogue (pp 104-111). Of his journey from figurative to abstract art he commented: 'Surely what matters is not whether a work is abstract or representative, but whether it has merit. If those who visit exhibitions would come without preconceptions, would apply to art the elementary standards they apply in other spheres, they might glimpse new horizons. They might ask themselves: is this work distinguished or is it commonplace? Fresh and original or uninspired, derivative and dull? Is it modest or pretentious?'

Monnington's yardstick might well be used to judge the dazzling Jack Smith (p. 130); the classic early John Cecil Stephenson, from the collection of the legendary Dr Jeffrey Sherwin (p. 140); the astonishing R.A. Wilson, painted in 1919, a decade earlier than any British artist credited with painting purely abstract works (p. 148); and the outstanding Paule Vézelay (p. 146) who, born Marjorie Watson-Williams, changed her name when she moved in 1926 to Paris. Here she worked on the edge of the *avant garde*, becoming closely associated with André Masson, (with whom she lived for four years), Sophie Taeuber-Arp and Alberto Giacometti.

'Masterpiece' might be too big a word for Fyffe Christie's tender portrait of his wife (p. 46), but is it too much to compare it with a Lucien Freud? Painted just after their marriage, the sitter treasured it all her life. The same quality of intimacy can be seen in Dunbar's touching portrait of her mother Florence (p. 62); equally so in Knights' magical study of a Bertolini's Bee Orchid (p. 94). What all these have in common is their unbroken provenance, passed down without interruption. We are only the guardians of these treasures as they continue their life's journey, but the pleasure of living with them is unquantifiable.

Paul Liss

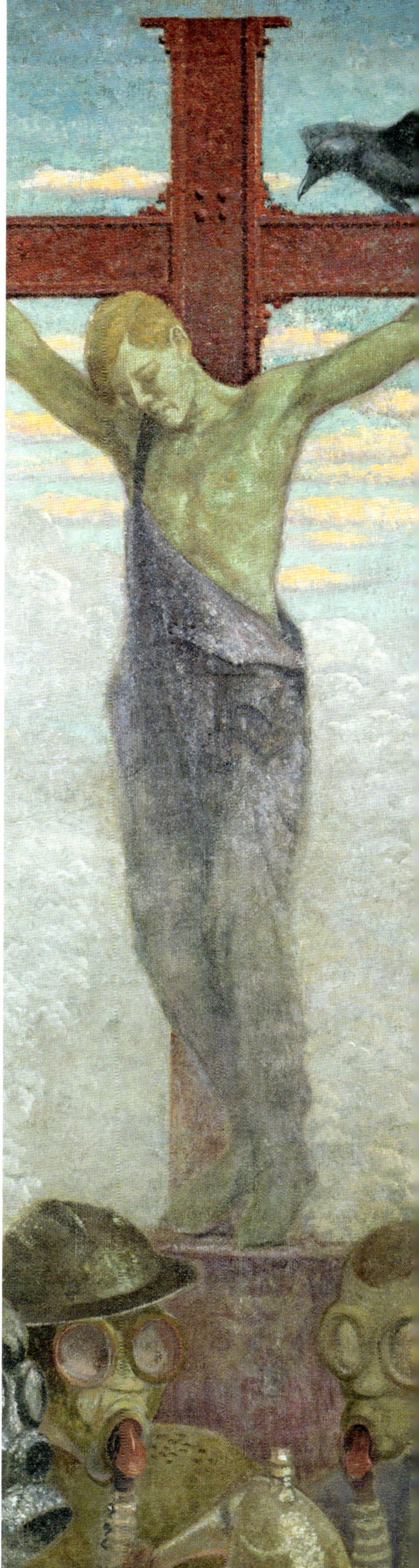

Rudolf Sauter (1895-1977), Never More!

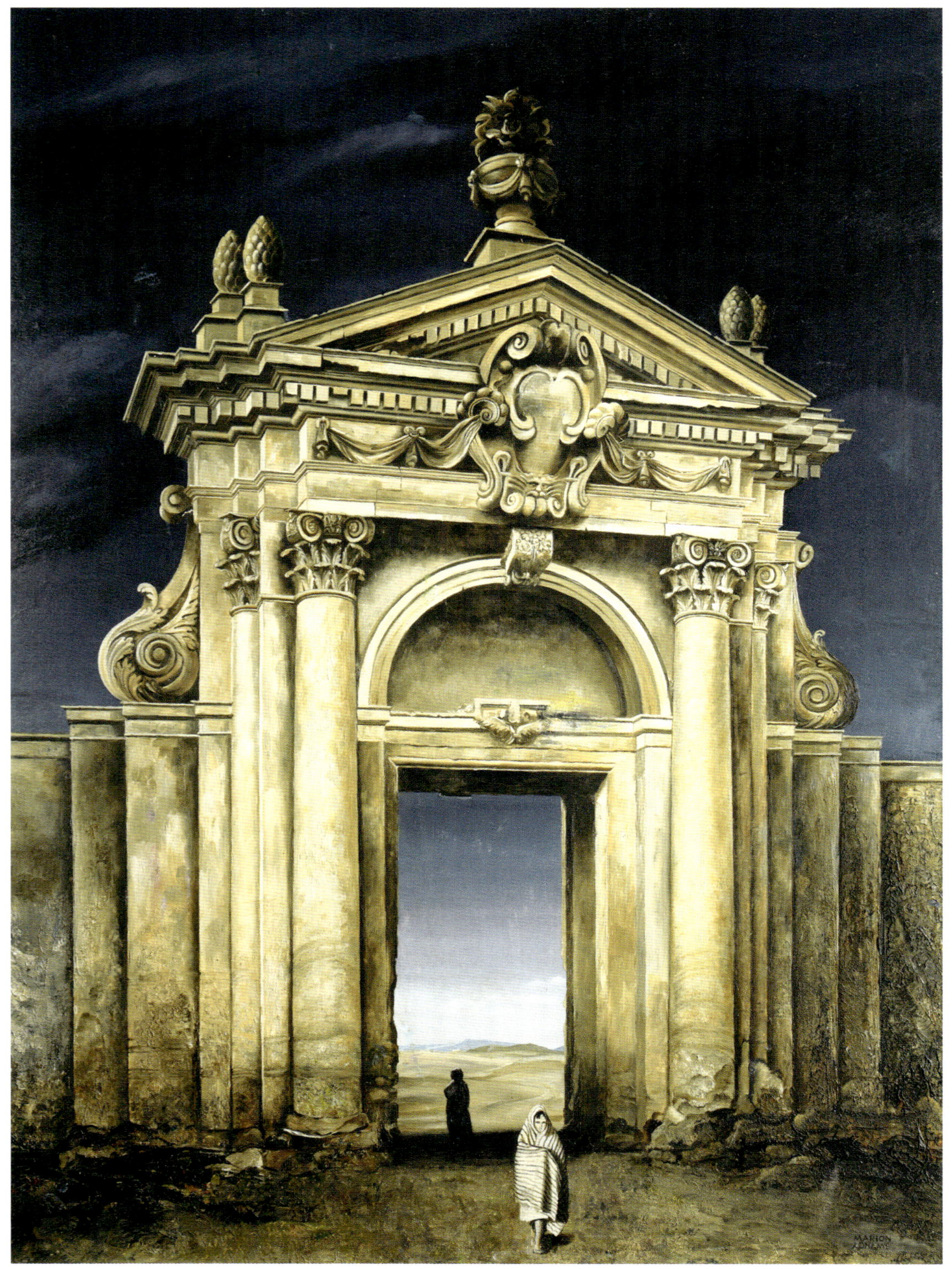

Marion Adnams (1898-1995)

That Same Door, 1962

Oil on hardboard - 78.8 x 58.5 cm.

During her six-decade career, Marion Adnams forged a reputation as a painter of deeply distinctive and dream-like visions inspired by the Surrealist movement. Fascinated by stones, shells and other objects found in the countryside, she created disturbing juxtapositions to produce meditations on life and death. From her home in Derby, painting trips to the South of France provided her main inspiration. Adnam's studio book records that this composition, strongly influenced by the doorway at La Chartreuse Notre-Dame-du-Val-de-Bénédiction, located in Villeneuve-lès-Avignon, in the Occitanie région, was painted in May and June 1962. The monumental portal, by François de Royers de la Valfenière, was inaugurated in 1660 when Louis XIV, accompanied by Cardinal Mazarin, passed though it with great ceremony. Such illustrious associations contrast with the diminutive figure passing through the archway, a subject rich in symbolism enhanced by the motif of the mirror-like shadow in the middle ground, which looks on to a familiar landscape that features in many of Adnam's compositions of this period.

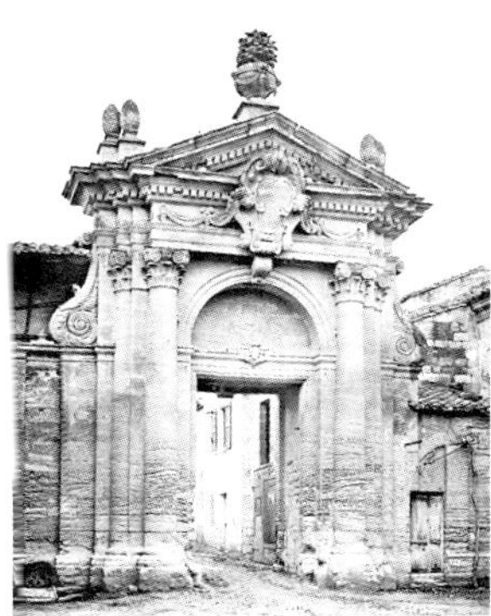

La chartreuse Notre-Dame-du-Val-de-Bénédiction, located in Villeneuve-lès-Avignon

John Banting (1902-1972)

Sylph Melody, 1934

Oil on board, signed and dated 1934 - 35.6 x 27.9 cm.

Banting studied with Meninsky at Westminster School of Art in 1921 and then in Paris. In 1925 he was associated with the Bloomsbury Group and in 1927 he exhibited with the London Group. His early work was influenced by Picasso, Braque and Gris but he quickly evolved his own repertoire of forms and subjects: plants, bones, shells and feathers, often constructed into strange anamorphic figures bearing enigmatic titles not infrequently associated with music. The composition might refer to the classic early novel by Georgina, Duchess of Devonshire, The Sylph, (published anonymously in 1779) in which, desperate for a mentor to guide her through the morass of societal depravity, the heroine Julia Grenville relies on a man who, claiming to be her 'sylph' (an aerial being who knows her every thought and deed), sends her letters warning her against the lures of the city.

Painted in 1934, and exhibited in 1938 at Storran Galleries (one of the three principal London dealers, the others being Wertheim and Cooling) this painting reverberates with Banting's exposure to the Surrealism movement in Paris, where he met with André Breton, Marcel Duchamp, Alberto Giacometti and René Crevel. It anticipates the style that Banting would showcase at the International Surrealist Exhibition in London (1936), New York (1936) and Paris (1938), and includes the amorphous, human-like shapes and disguised profile portraits that can be seen in many of his major works.

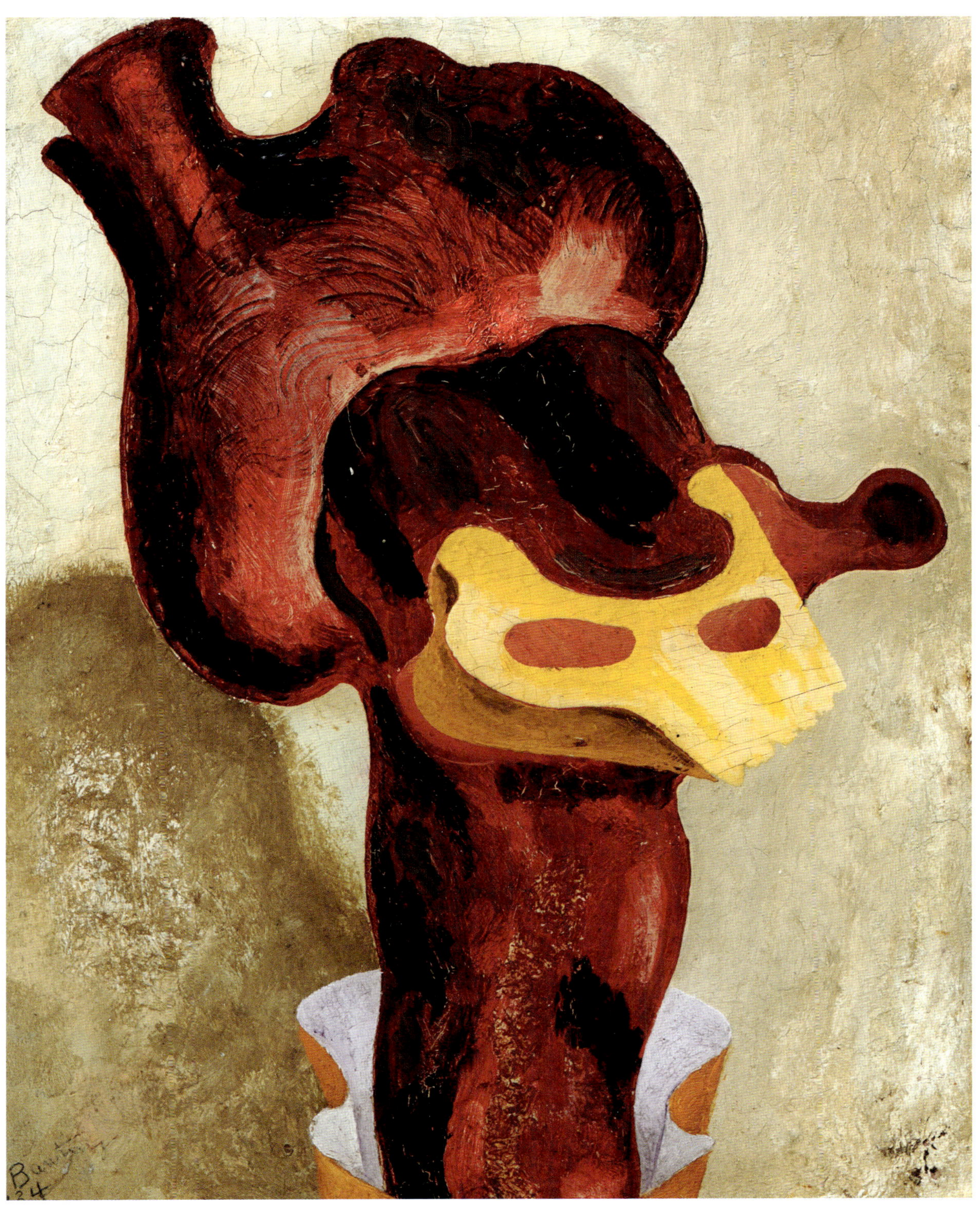

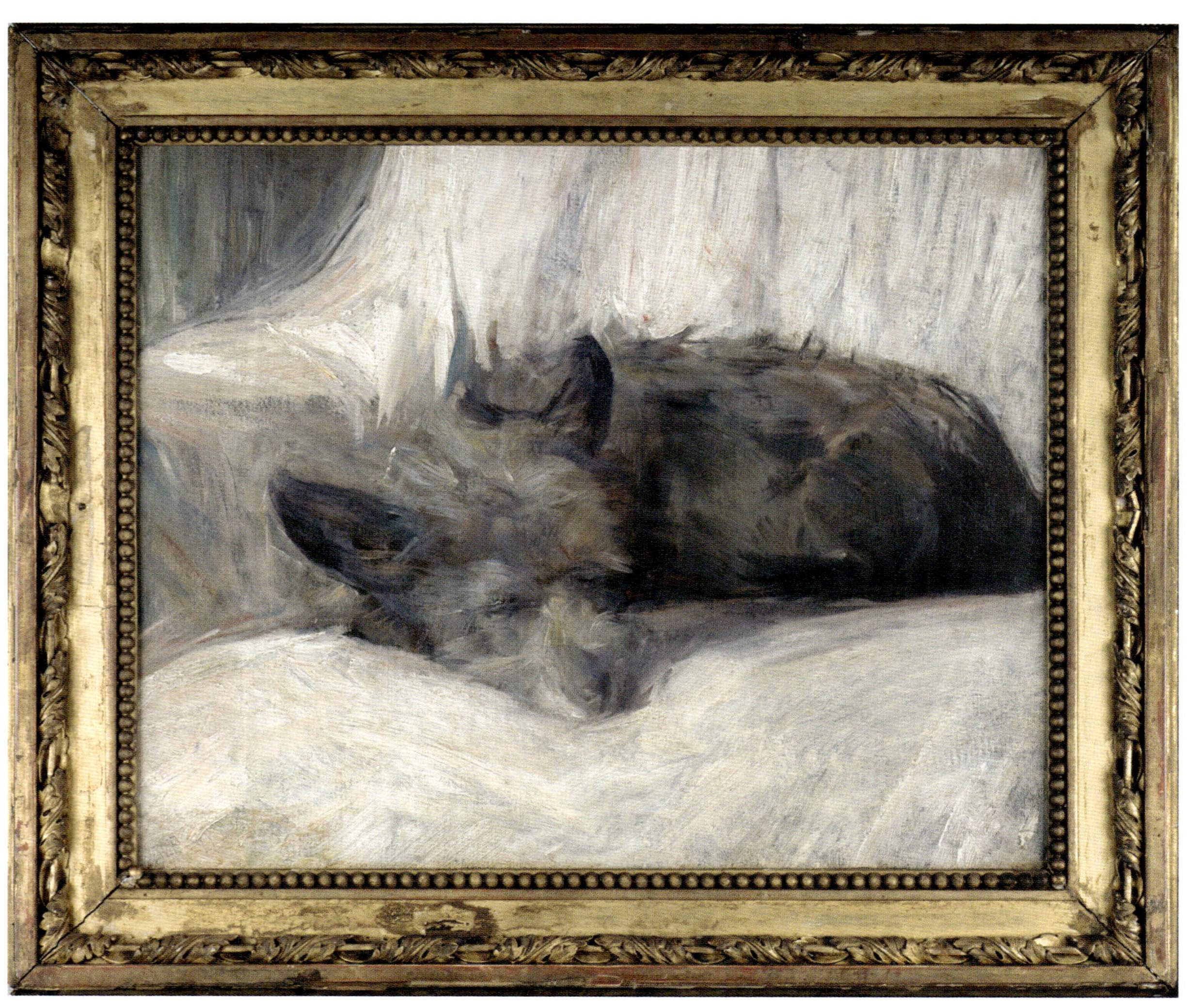

Albert de Belloroche (1864-1944)

Lance at Dunain House, early 1880's

Oil on canvas, signed in pencil - 37.4 x 44.5 cm.

This oil dates to the early 1880s, shortly after Belleroche had enrolled at the atelier of Carolus Duran. Here Belleroche met John Singer Sargent. A life-long friendship ensued, with both the artists sharing studios in Paris and London. Of Belleroche's paintings Frank Brangwyn commented: 'His still-life pictures - with the glimmer of light on silver and other objects, the shadows full of rich and reflected tones - has bought a new note into this kind of painting. One might say that he had carried the tradition of Chardin a step further, giving immediacy to his effects of light and colour, crystallizing the emotion of a particular moment [...] one feels that, with his lively and nervous handling of paint, he makes the objects before him live in the moving light that plays on them, and it is not surprising that Degas thought so highly of these works.' (Apollo, 1935, XXI 124 April).

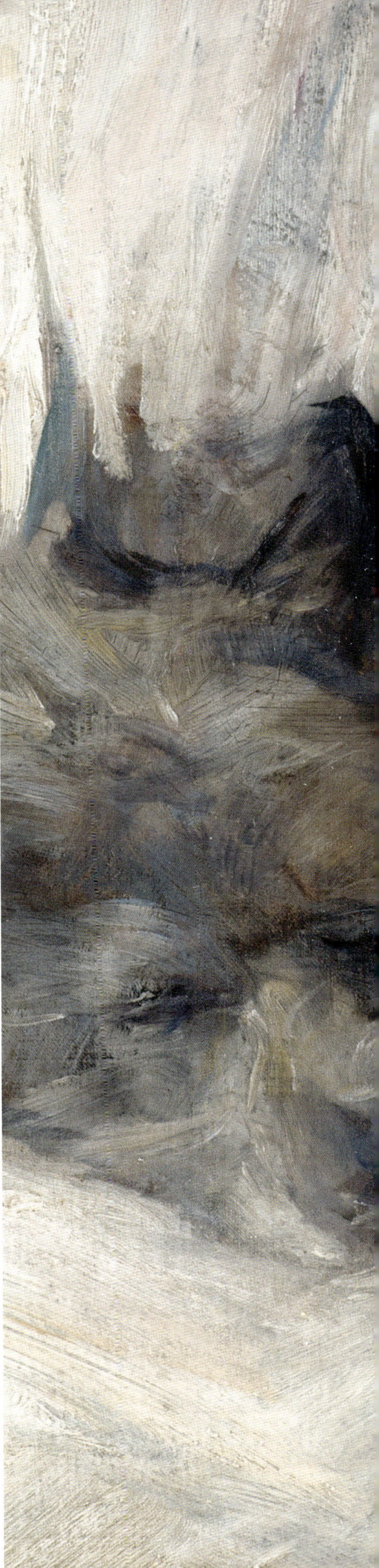

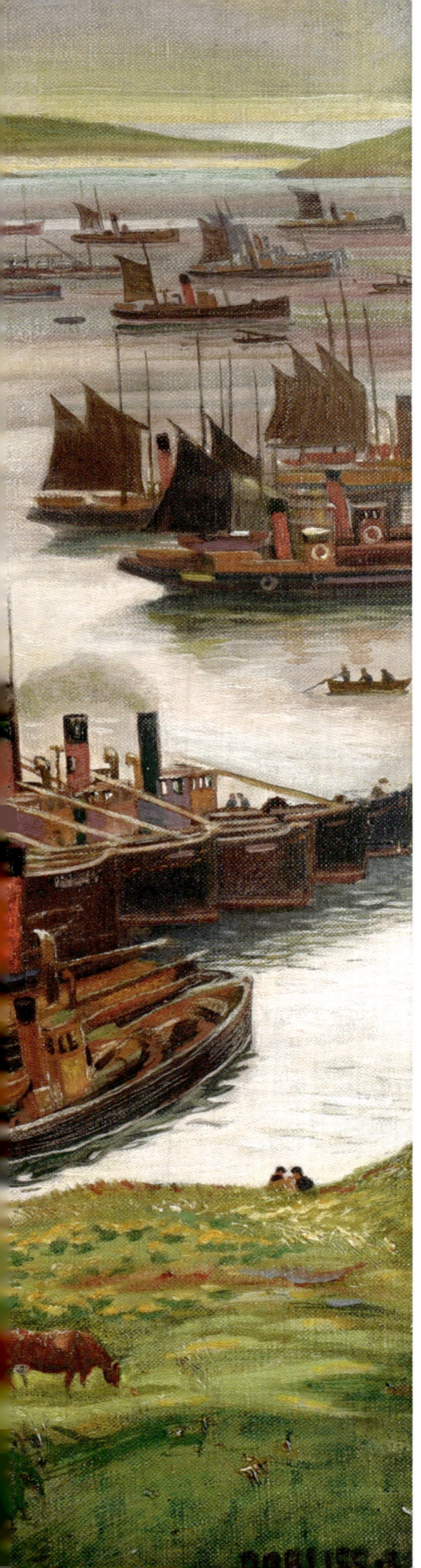

Douglas Percy Bliss (1900-1984)

Castlebay, Barra, (Barraigh), 1933

Oil on canvas, signed and dated - 51 x 61 cm.

Bliss' first series of paintings of Barra were made in 1927 for an exhibition at the St George's Gallery in Hanover Square, a joint show with his friends and fellow Royal College of Art students, Eric Ravilious and Edward Bawden. On this occasion Bliss produced nineteen watercolours of Scottish subjects. He returned to Barra whenever the chance arose, producing predominantly works on paper but also a few oils. According to Simon Lawrence 'the Barra paintings collectively rank among Douglas's finest work'. (Gargoyles and Tattie-Bogles, The Lives and Works of Douglas Percy Bliss & Phyllis Dodd, p. 244).

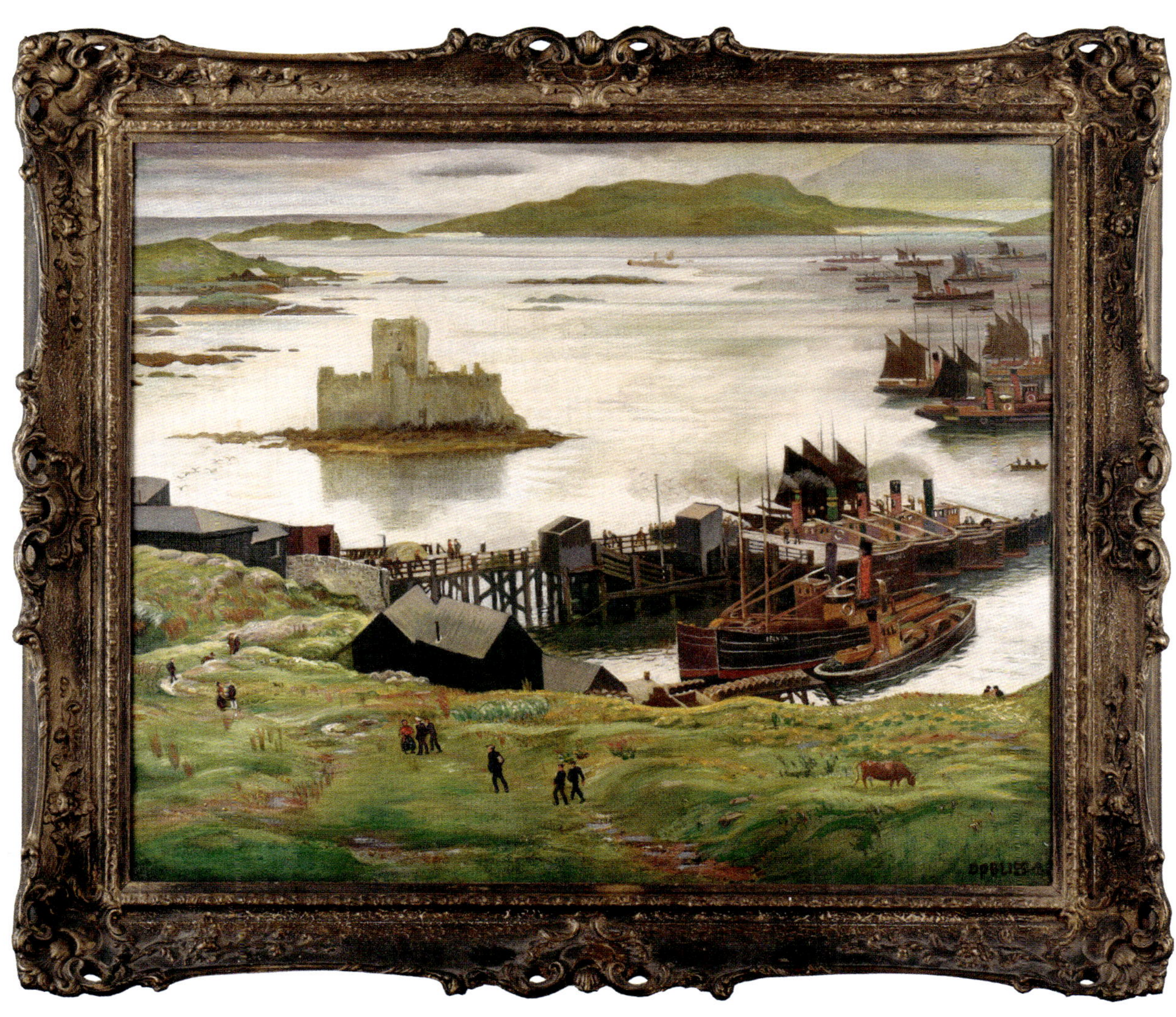

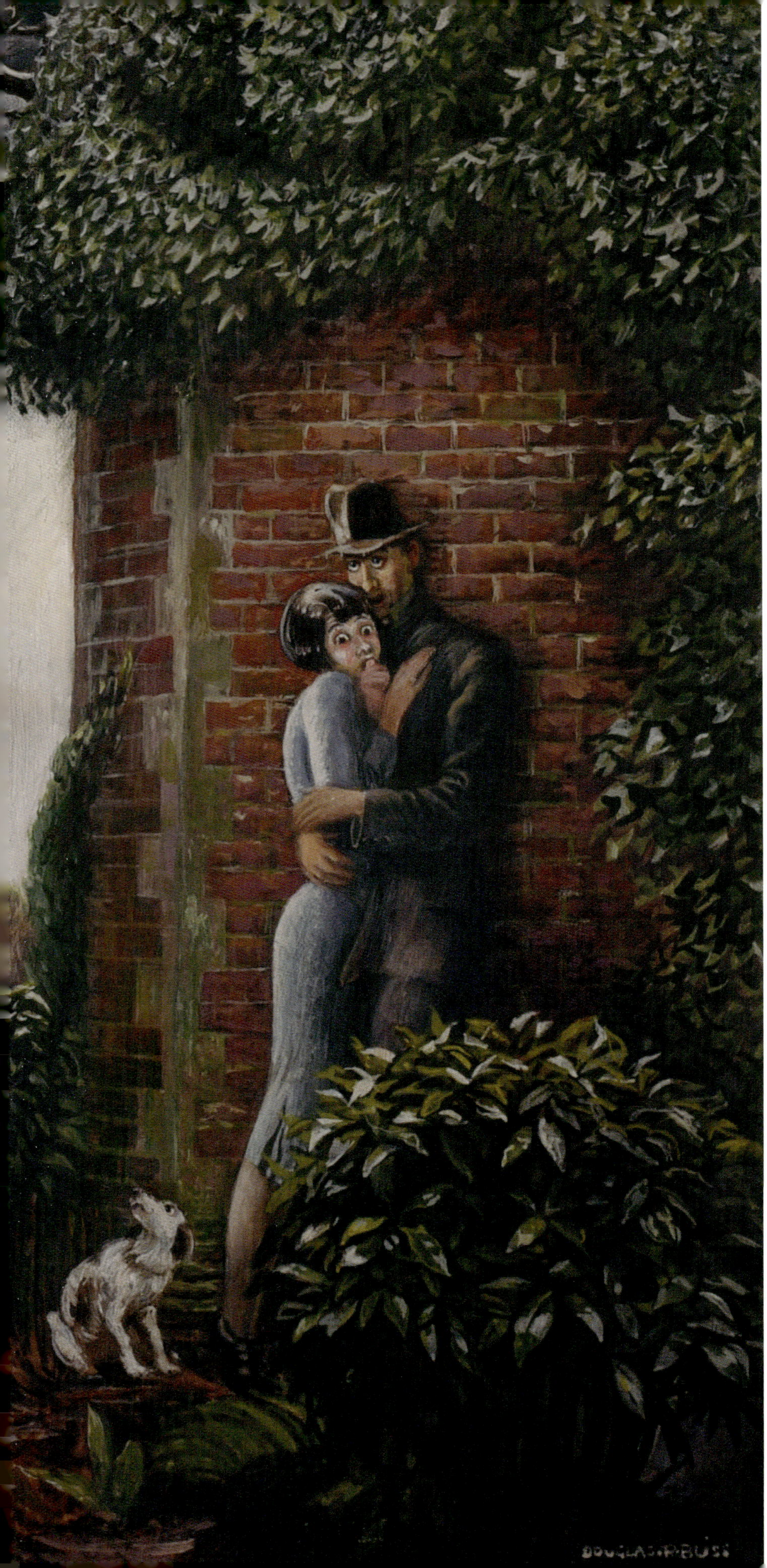

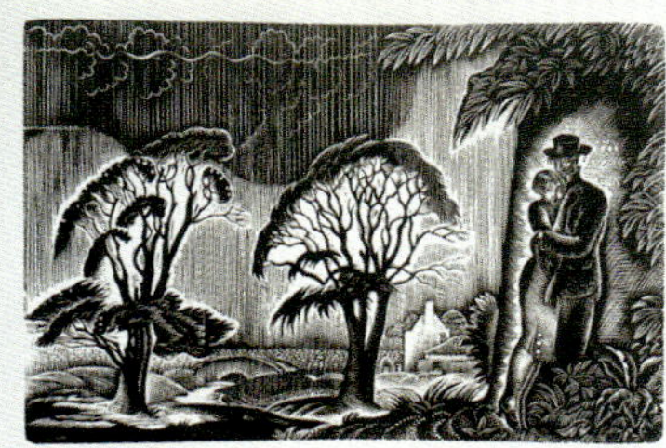

Lovers Sheltering from the Storm, wood-engraving, 4 1/2 x 3 1/4 in. (10.6 x 15.9 cm).

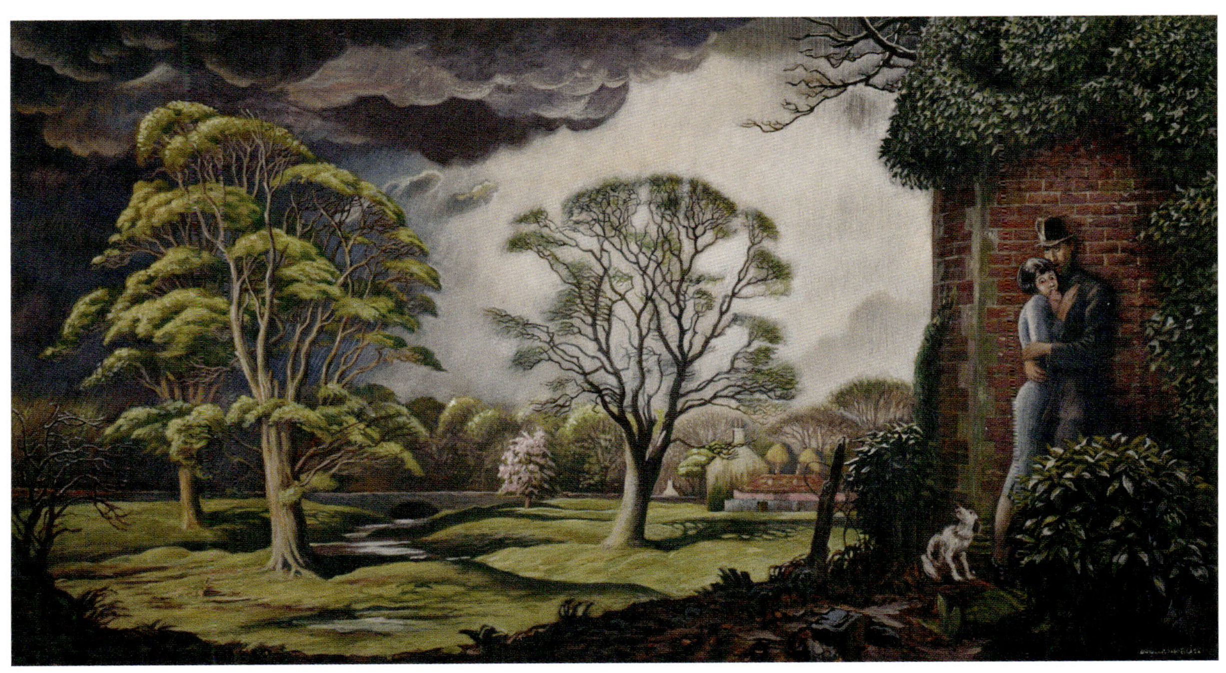

Douglas Percy Bliss (1900-1984)

Lovers sheltering from a storm, 1936

Oil on canvas, signed - 51 x 91.5 cm.

Lovers Sheltering from a Storm was first shown at the Royal Academy Summer Exhibition in 1936 (no. 55). Chosen as one of the highlights by the Illustrated London News, the painting featured in a special editorial entitled Contrasts Between Reality and Imagination. This seems apt, and the picture might credibly be described as hyper-real, for it shows an enhanced reality whereby the colours of the trees and foliage feel all the more acute, while the expressions of the lovers is heightened and cartoonish.

The technique of Lovers Sheltering from a Storm also reveals Bliss' training as a wood-engraver in his postgraduate year at the Royal College of Art. Led by Frank Short and Paul Nash, Bliss would have been taught to meticulously cover the entire block with marks and undulating lines. In fact, a wood-engraving by Bliss of the same subject was produced for Studio Magazine, 1929. The art critic of The Times praised Bliss' wood-engravings for concentrating 'a world of imagination in an inch or two of space', and the same can be said for his painting from this period.

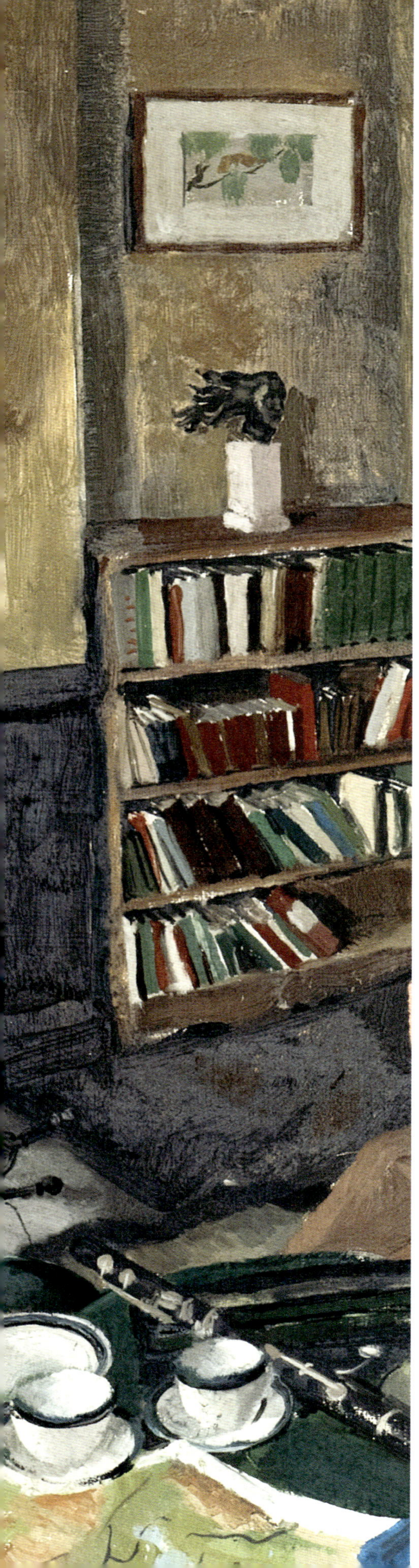

Stephen Bone (1904-1958)

Gavin in his study at St John's, early 1920's

Oil on canvas, signed - 47 x 60 cm.

Gavin Bone was an undergraduate at St John's College, Oxford, matriculating in 1925 and graduating with First Class Honours in 1928. Shortly after, Bone was elected a Fellow of the College in 1931 and began to lecture for the University and tutor St John's undergraduates (most famously these included Philip Larkin and Kingsley Amis) until his premature death from chronic illness on 8 April 1942, aged 34. From records of his academic engagement during his lifetime (such as his publications, essays and lecture notes), Bone's specialism was Later Medieval and Early Modern verse. Yet, after his death there were published two volumes of Old English poetic translations: Anglo-Saxon Poetry (Oxford: Clarendon Press, 1943) and Beowulf (Oxford: Blackwell, 1945). Bone had published some of his translations in his lifetime, but it is clear that in the final years of his life he was passionately occupied with transforming poetry from previous millennium into bold and willful contemporary poems. His Beowulf is accompanied by striking illustrations of key events from the epic poem's narrative, and these attest to Bone's own talent as a visual artist among a family of professional draughtsmen and painters and his lifelong relationship to the arts.

The present oil painting shows Bone, aged between 18 and 20, in his undergraduate rooms at St John's, surrounded by indicators of his great loves: multiple bookcases packed with a great many volumes; and walls abundant in framed illustrations. Two maps feature among them: to the right is a map of the British Isles, likely to remind him of his much-loved Scottish family heritage, and more central is a map of Spain, where he and his family often travelled. A flute is laid out on the table, which Bone was known to play. The picture above the fireplace appears to show a bouquet of flowers, and a vase of flowers appears on the mantle next to it. Orchids were another lifelong interest of Bone's, and his illustrations of orchids (completed by his father and brother) would be posthumously published as The Wild Orchids of Great Britain in 1950 alongside commentary from his childhood friend and novelist Jocelyn Brooke. This intricately detailed setting of Gavin Bone thus encapsulates many of the prominent aspects of Bone's of his tragically short but vibrant and fruitful life.

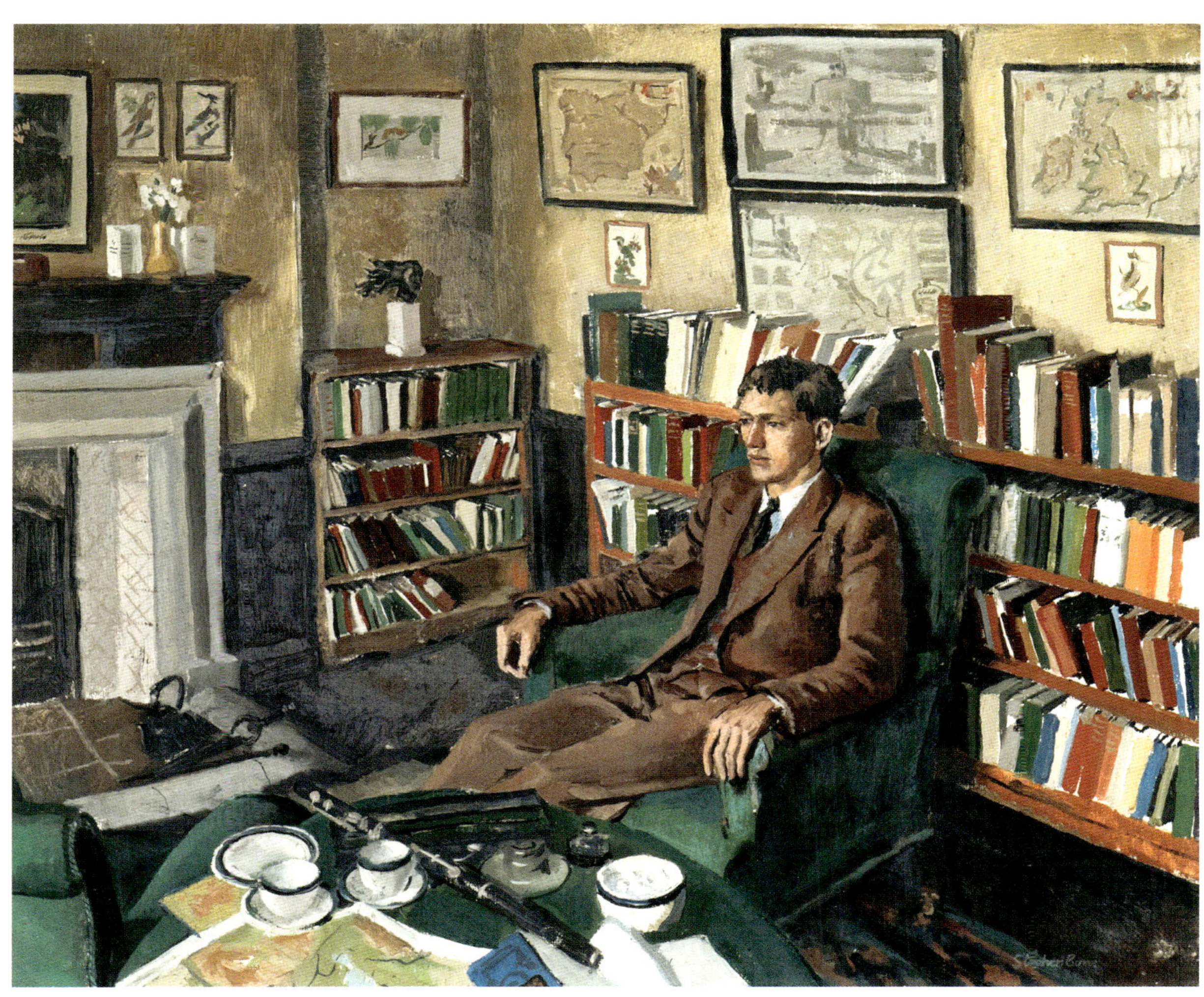

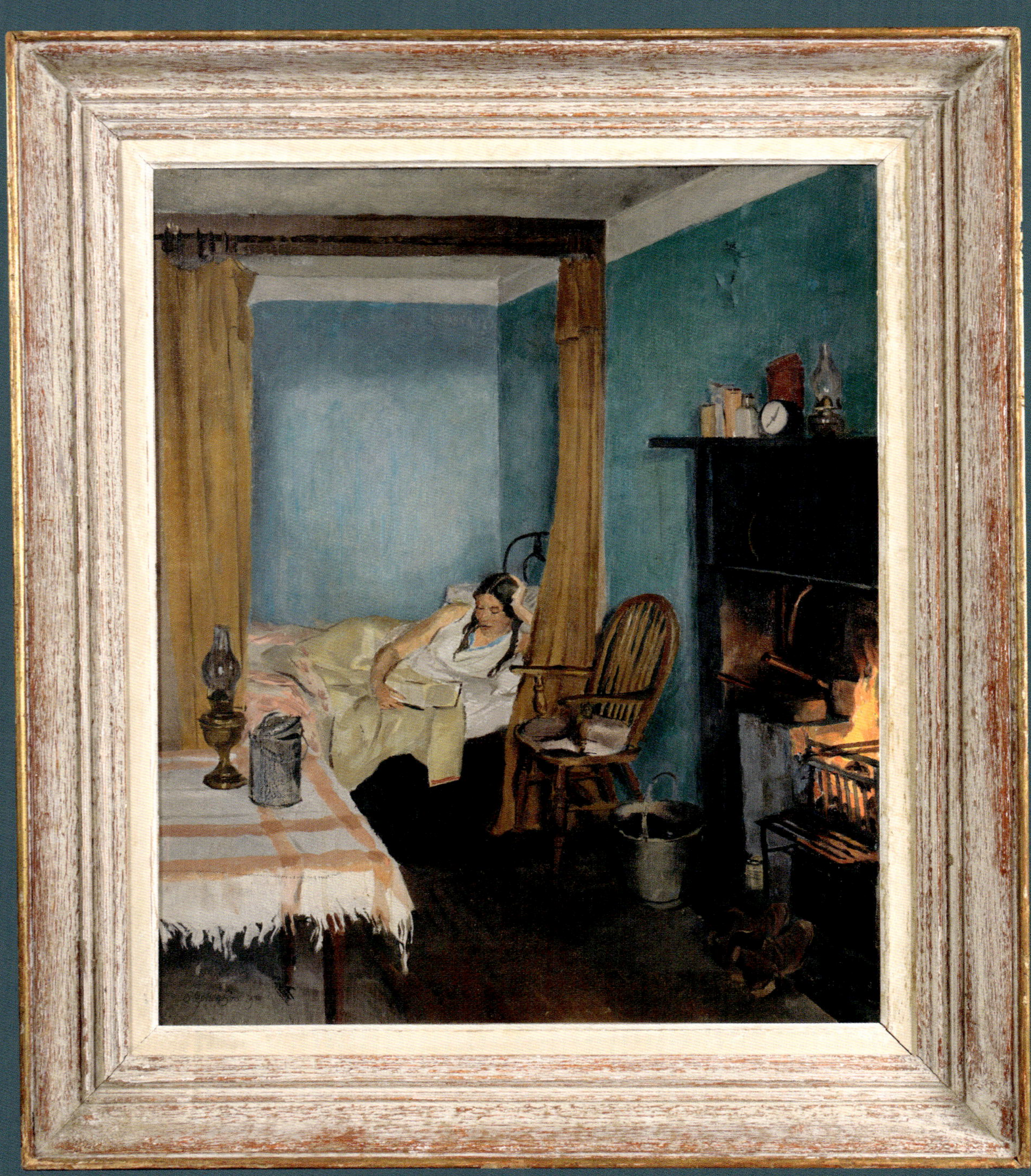

Stephen Bone (1904-1958)

Mary Adshead in bed, 1930

Oil on canvas, signed and dated 1930 - 61 x 51 cm.

Mary Adshead was an English painter, muralist, illustrator and designer. Born in Bloomsbury, London, she was able to enrol at the Slade School of Art in 1921, aged just sixteen. There Henry Tonks recognised her ability and arranged her first mural commission, for a boys' club in Wapping, working with Rex Whistler.

This composition was painted in the first year of Bone's marriage to Adshead, who, although still in her mid 20s was already enjoying considerable success. This painting was included in her first solo exhibition at the Goupil Gallery, and, touchingly, purchased by her father in law, Sir Muirhead Bone. From the same exhibition the Tate acquired 'The Flood'. In the same year she was elected a member of the New English Art Club. Bone and Adshead collaborated on a number of mural schemes and illustrated books together, but her career was longer than her husband's and more successful in terms of commissions and recognition. After Bone's death in 1958, Adshead travelled widely in both Europe and the United States.

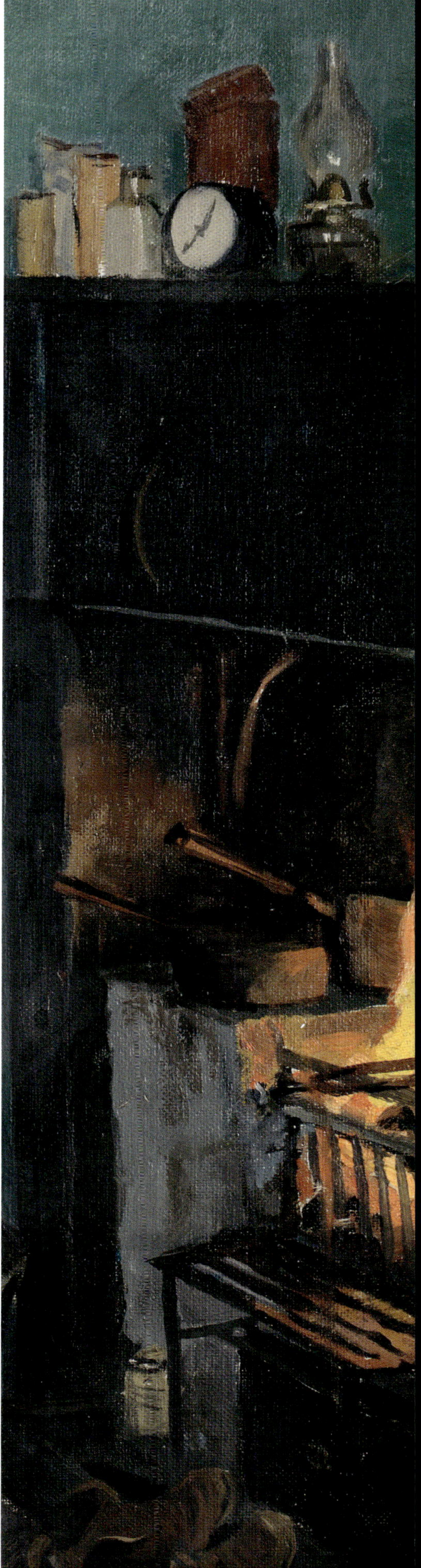

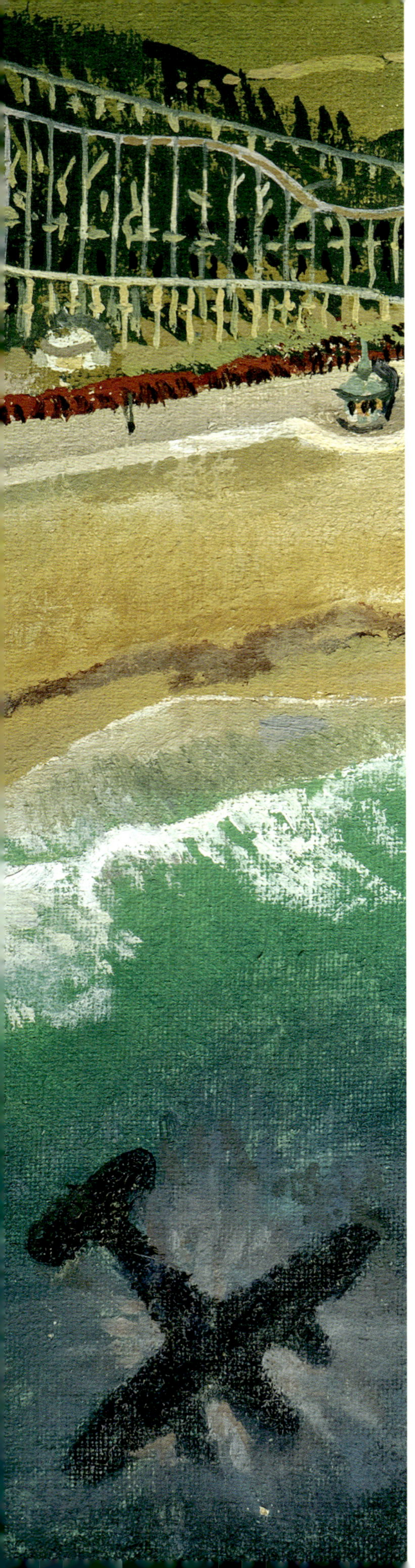

Stephen Bone (1904-1958)

Land, Sea and Air - WW2, c. 1940

Oil on canvas, signed - 51 x 61 cm.

During WW2 Stephen Bone served as a War Artist attached to the Admiralty. The Imperial War Museum hold a number of his works including remarkable paintings of the 1944 Normandy landings.

This imaginative composition is based on a view of Great Yarmouth, where its rollercoaster, opened in 1932 and still in operation, was built parallel to the beach.

With its adventurous aerial perspective, this composition captures a curious juxtaposition of the ornamental kiosks with 'pillboxes' or machine gun emplacements behind, part of the coastal defences during WW2. A German bomber, possibly a Dornier, lies ditched under the waves, close to a half-submerged fishing vessel, possibly a steam drifter. Has the German aircraft bombed the drifter and then been shot down?

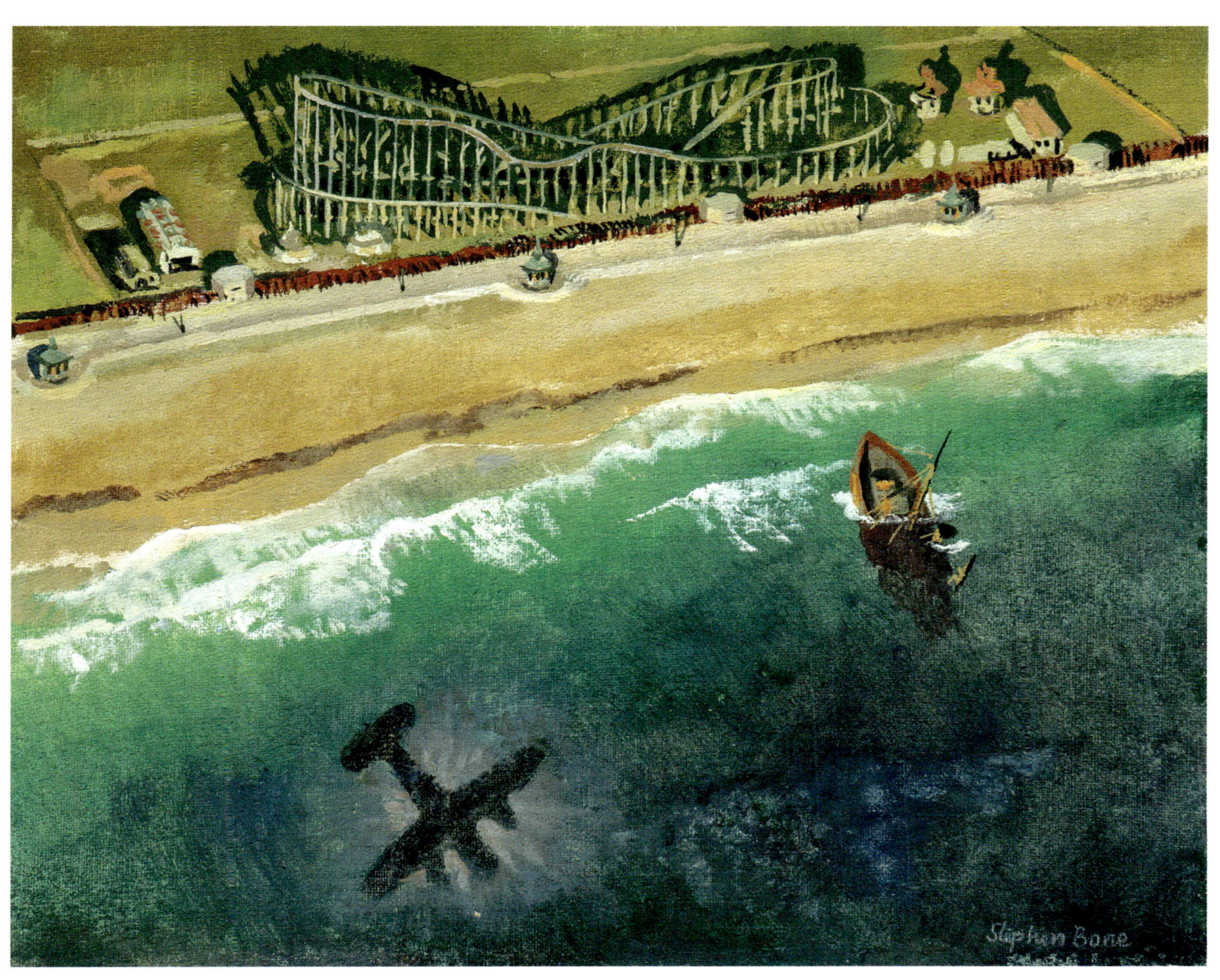
Stephen Bone

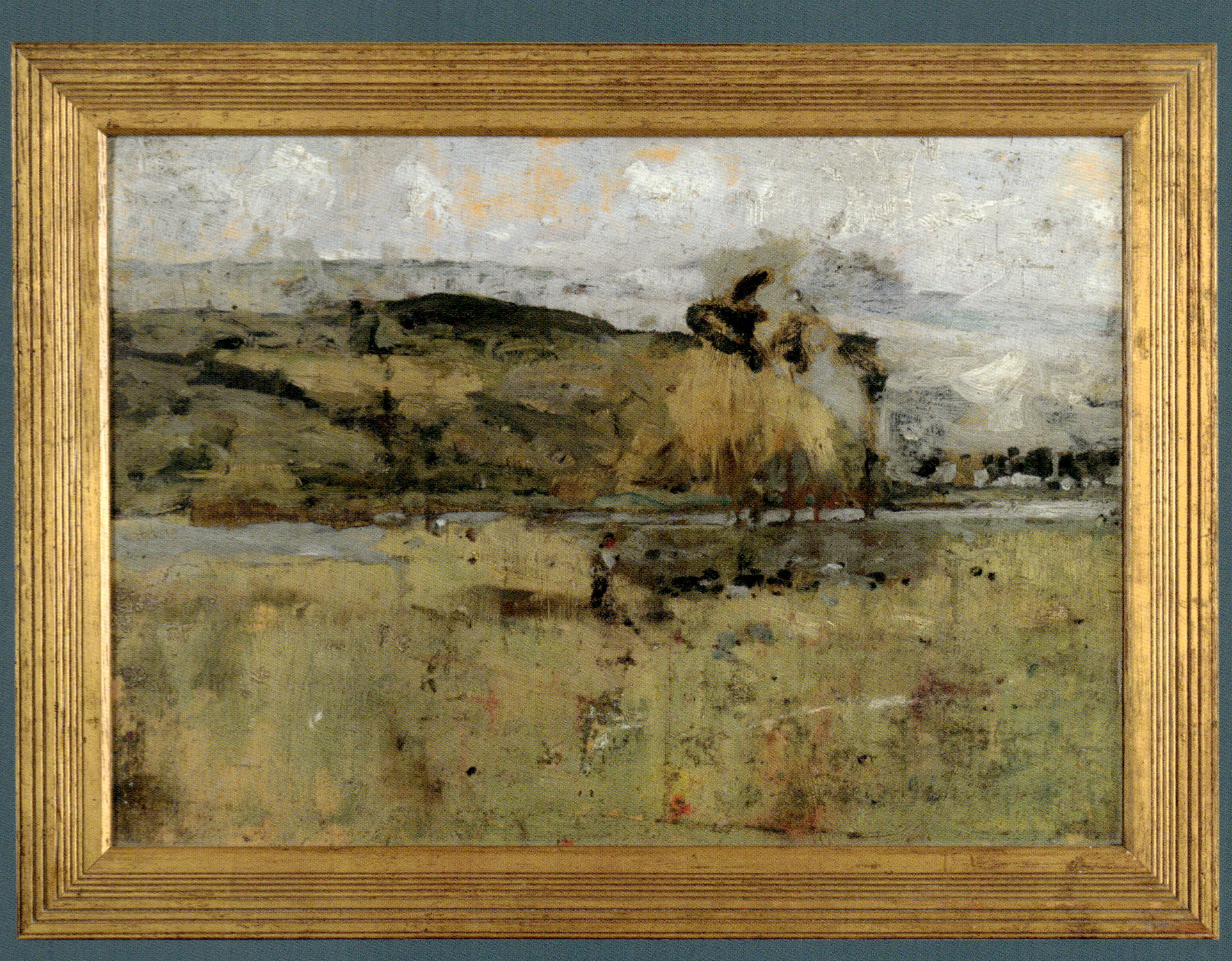

Frank Brangwyn (1867-1956)

Landscape, South Africa, 1891

Oil on panel, signed with monogram - 38 x 49.5 cm.

Embarking on a painting trip early in 1891 Brangwyn sailed to South Africa with William Hunt. This trip proved a turning point for the 24 year-old Brangwyn, where in response to saturated light effects, he painted in an increasingly direct manner with layers of oil applied in the Impressionist technique of 'wet on wet'. The paintings produced in South Africa, which were typically panels which measure 12 x 17 inches (30 x 42cm), are particularly prized : this panel was retained by Brangywn until gifted to 'Count' William de Belleroche towards the end of Brangwyn's life.

This oil will appear as reference number O - 2570 in Dr Libby Horner's forthcoming Catalogue Raisonné of Brangwyn.

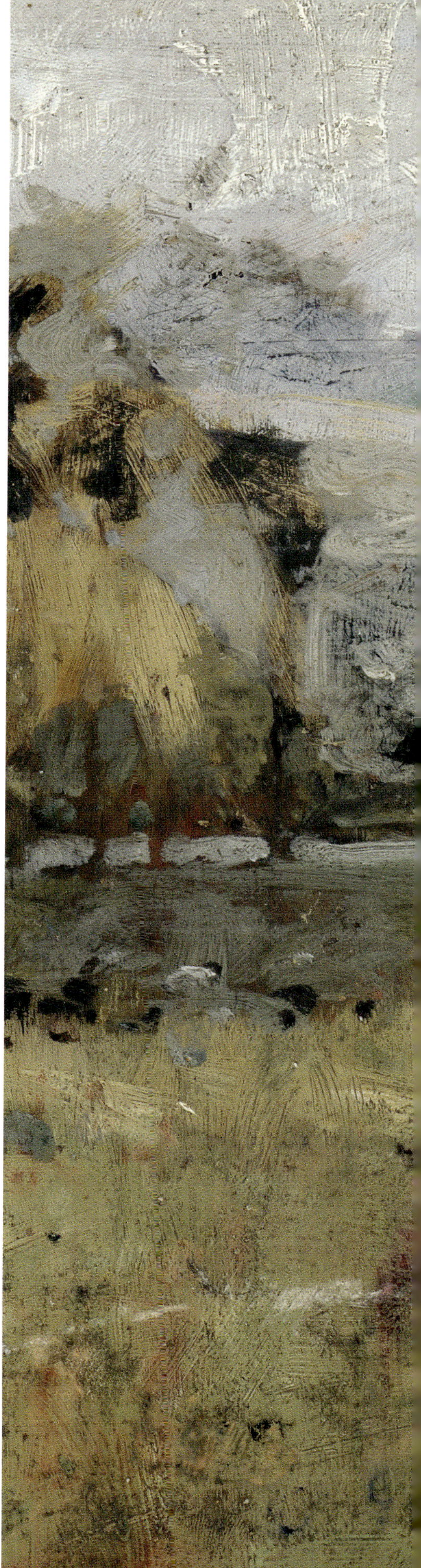

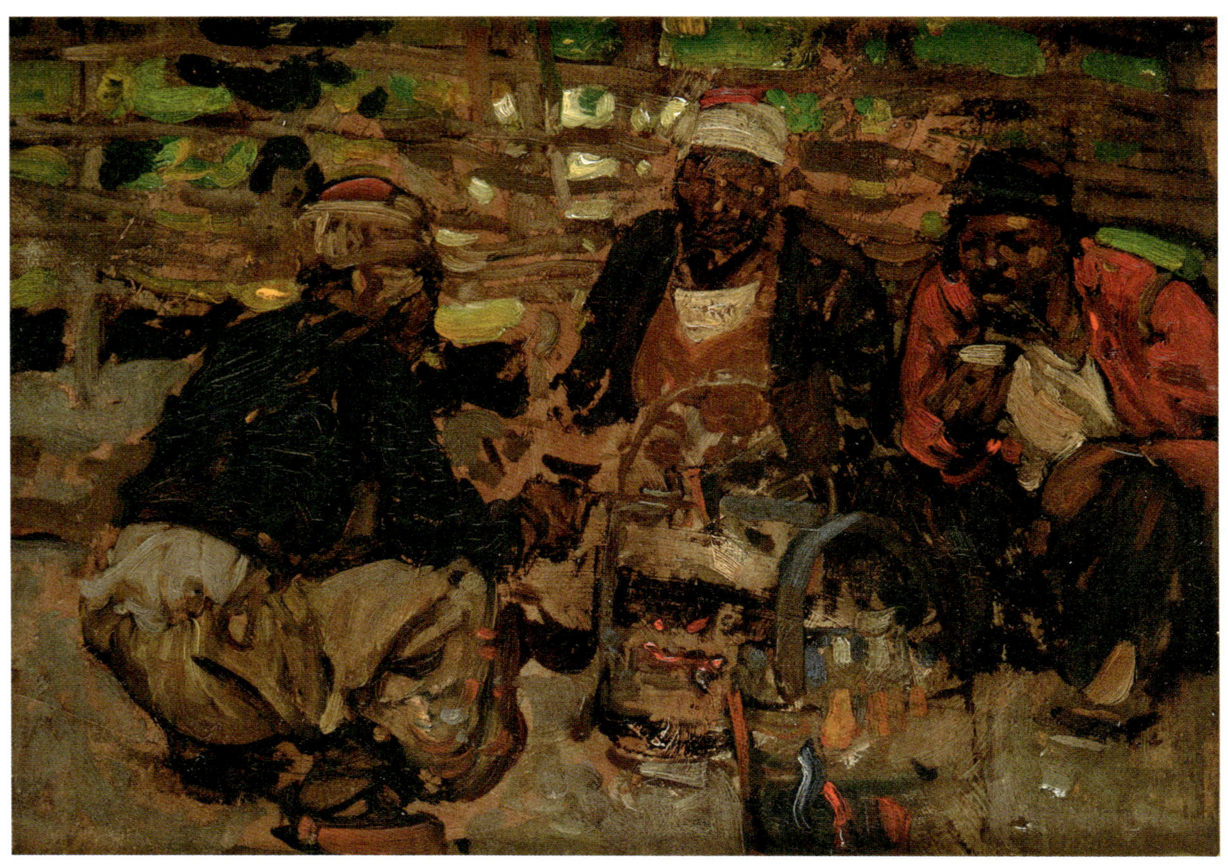

Frank Brangwyn (1867-1956)

Three Men Sitting by a Brazier, c. 1891

Oil on canvas - 31.7 x 42 cm.

Brangwyn's 1891 trip to South Africa resulted in a marked change of palette, the sun-drenched colours inspiring vibrant combinations especially of blue and red, which later led Kandinsky to suggest that Brangwyn was one of the first artists to use such colours in a truly modern way. Brangwyn's work became increasingly sought-after during this period, being bought by prominent collectors such as Shchukin, better known today as a key patron of Gauguin, Picasso and Matisse.
Brangwyn visited Madeira on his return voyage and may have visited east Africa. He may also have visited east Africa, Spain and Italy.
This oil will appear as reference number O-1163 in Dr Libby Horner's forthcoming Catalogue Raisonné of Brangwyn.

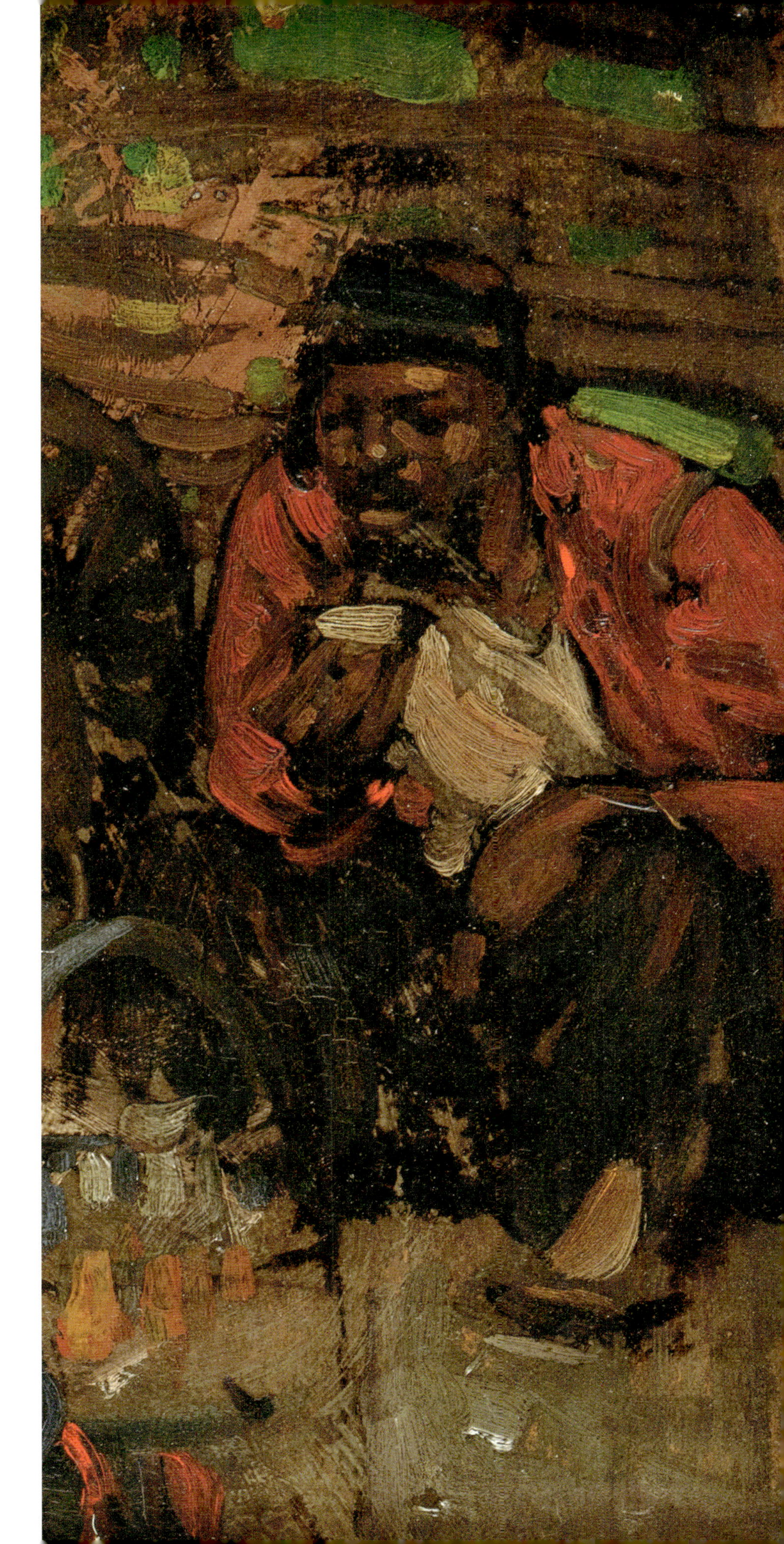

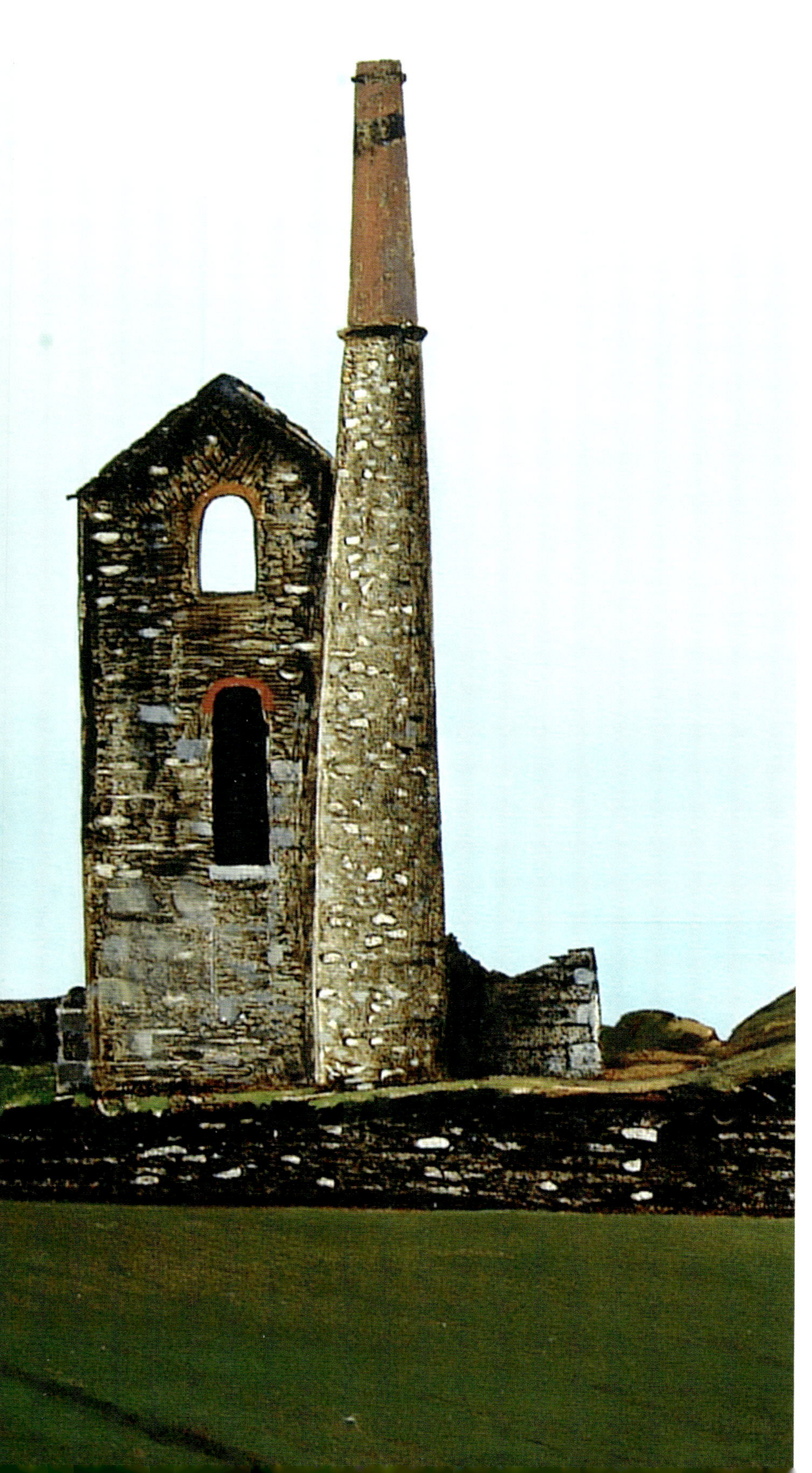

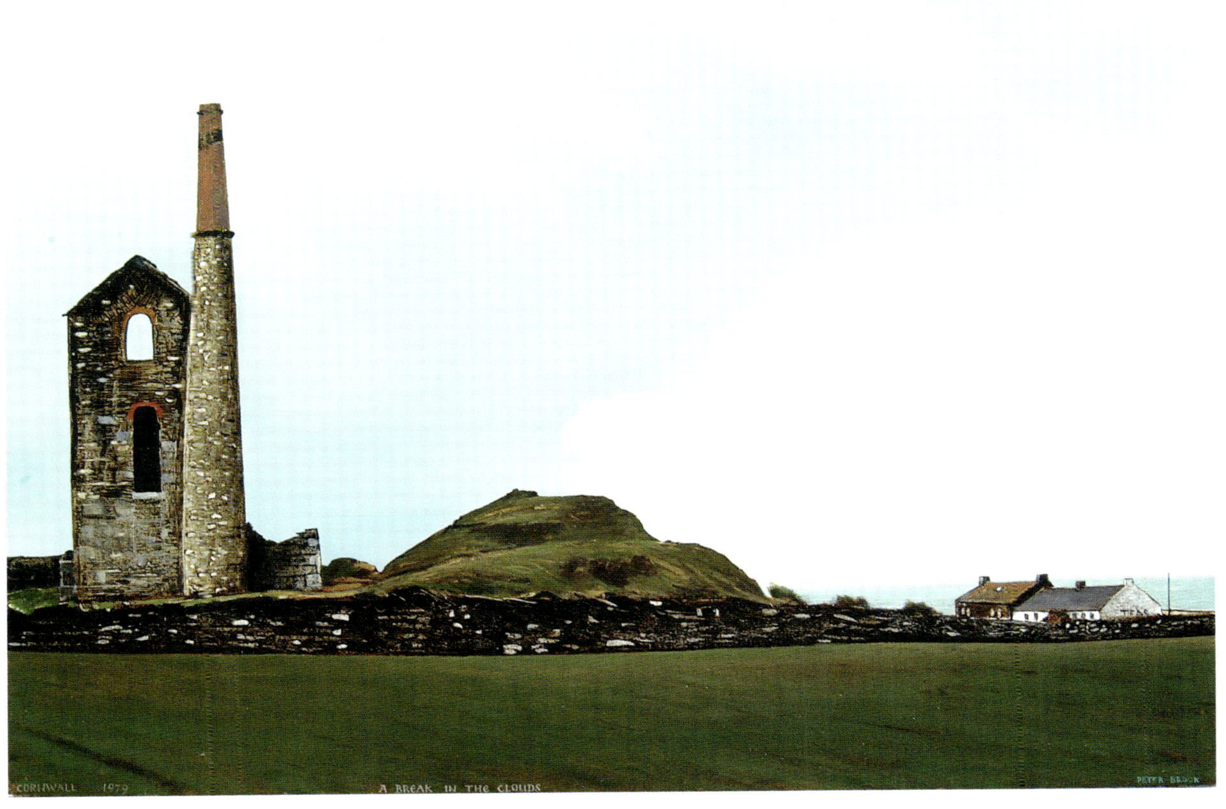

Peter Brook (1927-2009)

A Break in the Clouds, 1979

Oil on canvas, signed, titled and dated - 71 x 100 cm.

In the 1970s Rodney Bewes (best known as Bob Ferris in the hit T.V. sitcom The Likely Lads) frequently lent Brook his cottage on the Lizard in Cornwall. From there Brook produced a remarkable cycle of paintings. 'I loved the sea and when I saw the remains of the Tin Mines with their tall chimneys I felt I must record them. For two or three years we returned, and I thought it was a wonderful area for an artist brought up in the Industrial West Riding'. (Letter to Paul Liss, 14 December 2003). Throughout his life, Peter Brook remained entirely consistent in his vision. While comparison is sometimes made with Lowry and with Brook's friend and fellow artist Carel Weight, the technique he developed of using a variety of rollers and tools for scratching out and his personal involvement with landscape set his works apart.

Averil Mary Burleigh (1883-1949)

Rest by the Way, 1933

Signed, Tempera on panel, in its original James Bourlet sixteenth-century style black and gold frame - 37 x 40 cm.

Averil Burleigh was a long-standing member of the Society of Painters in Tempera. Between 1930 and 1935 she had 17 exhibits at the RA and all are listed as tempera. Burleigh specialised in tempera painting and her work is characterised by a bright palette underpinned with a bold sense of graphic design. Her compositions are usually dominated by female figures In the summer of 1933, Burleigh exhibited three painting at the Royal Academy, hung in galleries specifically set aside for displaying watercolours and temperas. The 1933 exhibition was a family affair with both her husband Charles and daughter Veronica exhibiting works.

The term tempera refers to any painting medium consisting of coloured pigments mixed with a water-soluble binder. Egg tempera, the most common form, consists of pigments bound by egg yolk. On account of its binder, tempera tends to have a matt surface, and, unlike oil, is usually not varnished when finished. Typically painted on a panel prepared with gesso (rather than a canvas), tempera paintings often have sharper defined contours and smoother surfaces. Unlike oil, tempera does not afford areas of impasto (textured paint). Tempera dries fast and therefore colours cannot be blended. Modelling is achieved by laying down innumerable individual brushstrokes of graduated colour adjacent to each other. Many artists working in tempera felt attracted to the labour intensive idea of preparing their own colours, grinding raw pigments with a mortar and pestle.

Although Tempera had been out of favour since the end of the Renaissance, when it was gradually replaced by oil paint, British artists such as William Blake (1757-1827) and the Pre-Raphaelites were passionate advocates of the medium.

Exhibited: The Annual Autumn Exhibition, Walker Galleries, Liverpool, 1933; Walker Art Gallery, Liverpool; The Fine Art Society, March 1934.

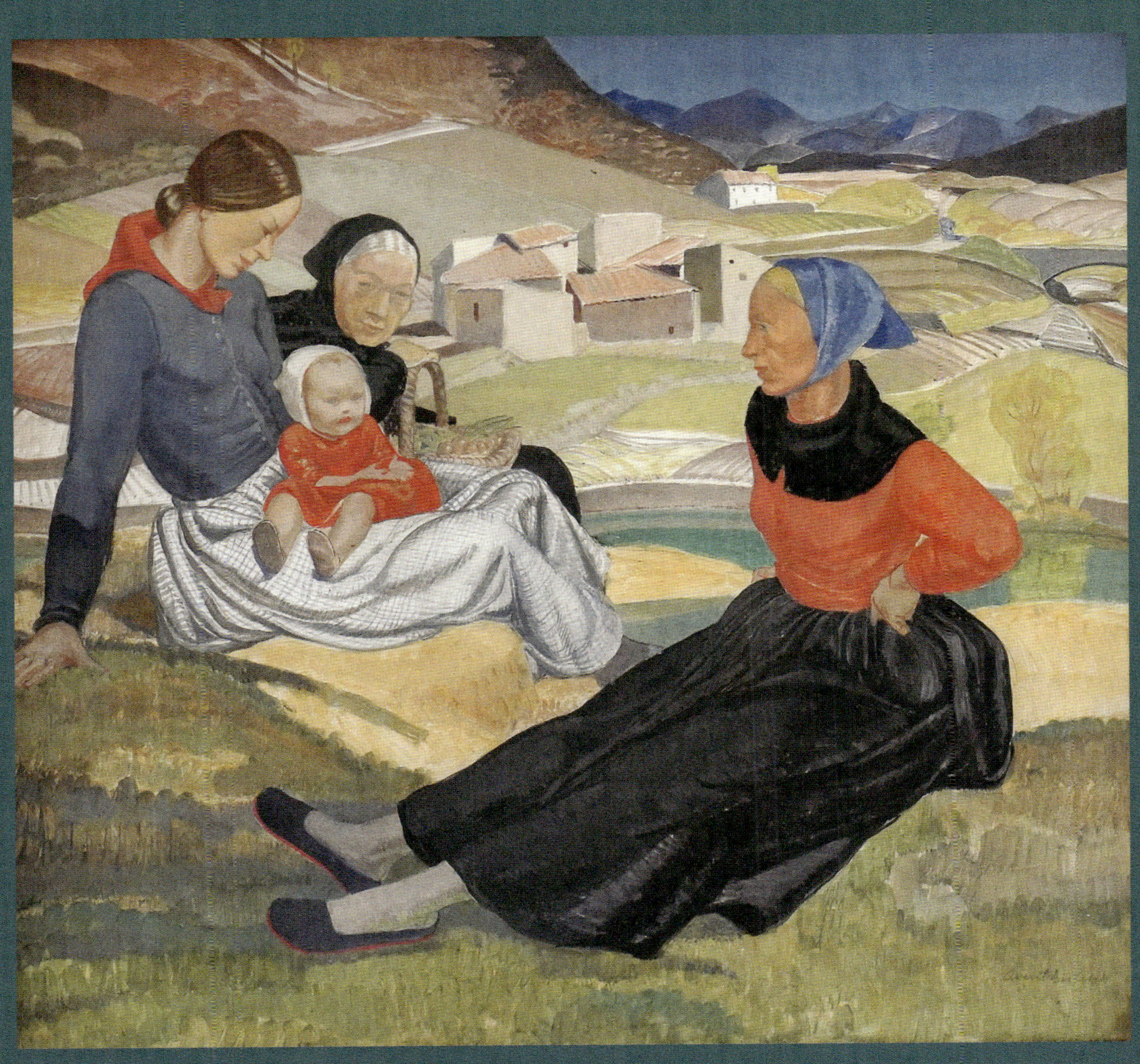

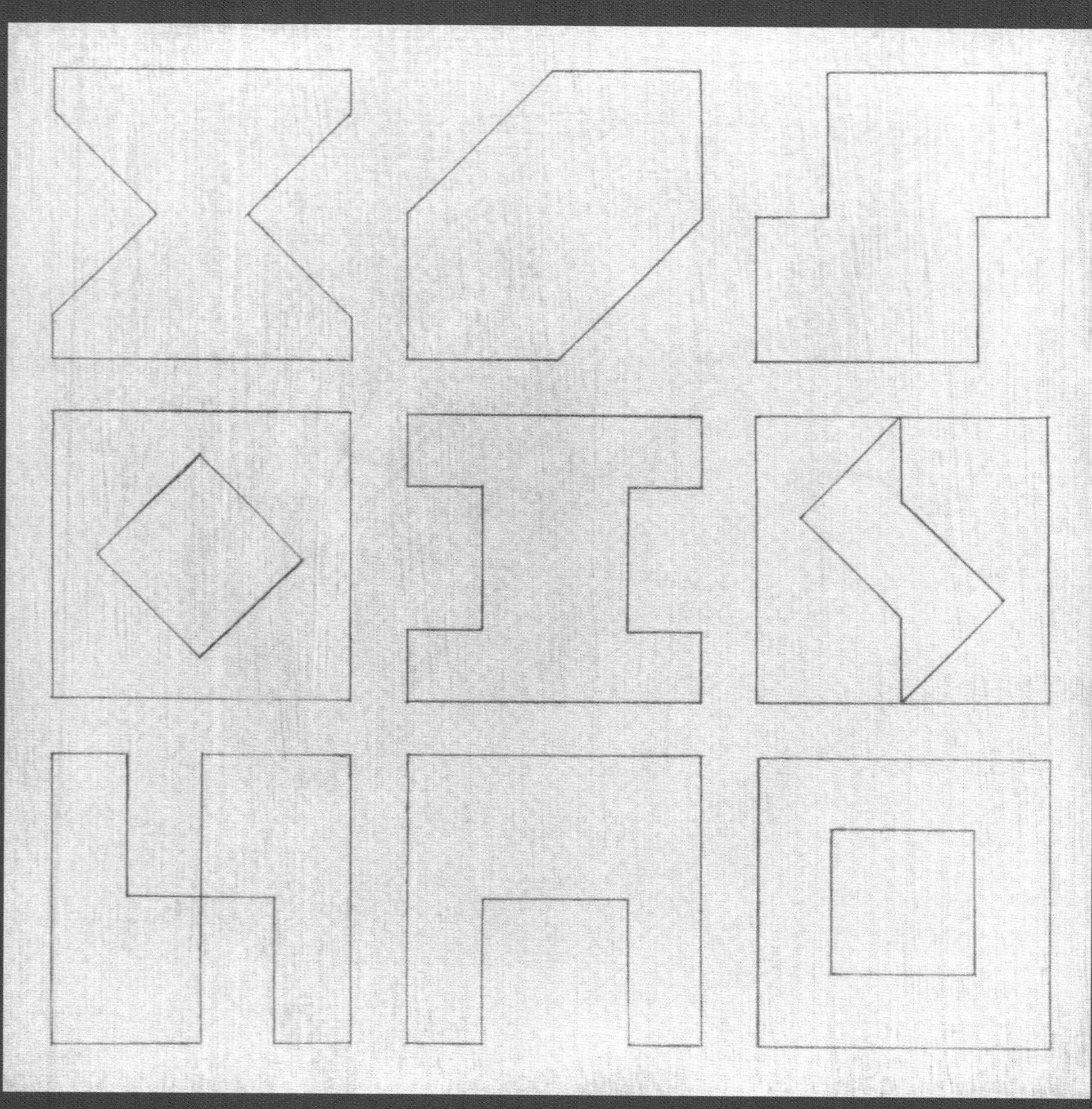

Michael Canney (1923-1999)

Three quarter square, late 60's

Acrylic on board, signed and titled to the reverse, signed, titled and dated - 29.5 x 29.5 cm.

'For a number of years now my work has been broadly related to the Constructivist tradition. However since 1979 it has relied upon a simple principle, in which the work constructs itself from itself [...] The majority of the paintings and reliefs pay homage to the square, a format selected initially in the interests of its non-associative properties, its mathematical simplicity, and its formal neutrality. Division of the square format is by fifths, quarters, thirds, halves and so on, all of them proportions that are easily appreciated by the eye [...] The imposition of these limits comes as a reaction against an earlier hedonistic period of improvisatory abstraction.' Michael Canney, Newlyn Art Gallery catalogue, 1983, pp. 4-7.

Michael Canney (1923-1999)

System with Circles no. 1, mid 1980's

Acrylic on board - signed and titled on the reverse - 35.6 x 35.6 cm.

Systems with circles and variations on squares, and occasionally stripes, were Canney's signature pieces of the 1980's: arguably his most productive decade. 'For a number of years now my work has been broadly related to the Constructivist tradition. However since 1979 it has relied upon a simple principle, in which the work constructs itself from itself [...] The majority of the paintings and reliefs pay homage to the square, a format selected initially in the interests of its non-associative properties, its mathematical simplicity, and its formal neutrality. Division of the square format is by fifths, quarters, thirds, halves and so on, all ofthem proportions that are easily appreciated by the eye [...] The imposition of these limits comes as a reaction against an earlier hedonistic period of improvisatory abstraction.' Michael Canney, Newlyn Art Gallery catalogue, 1983, pp. 4-7.

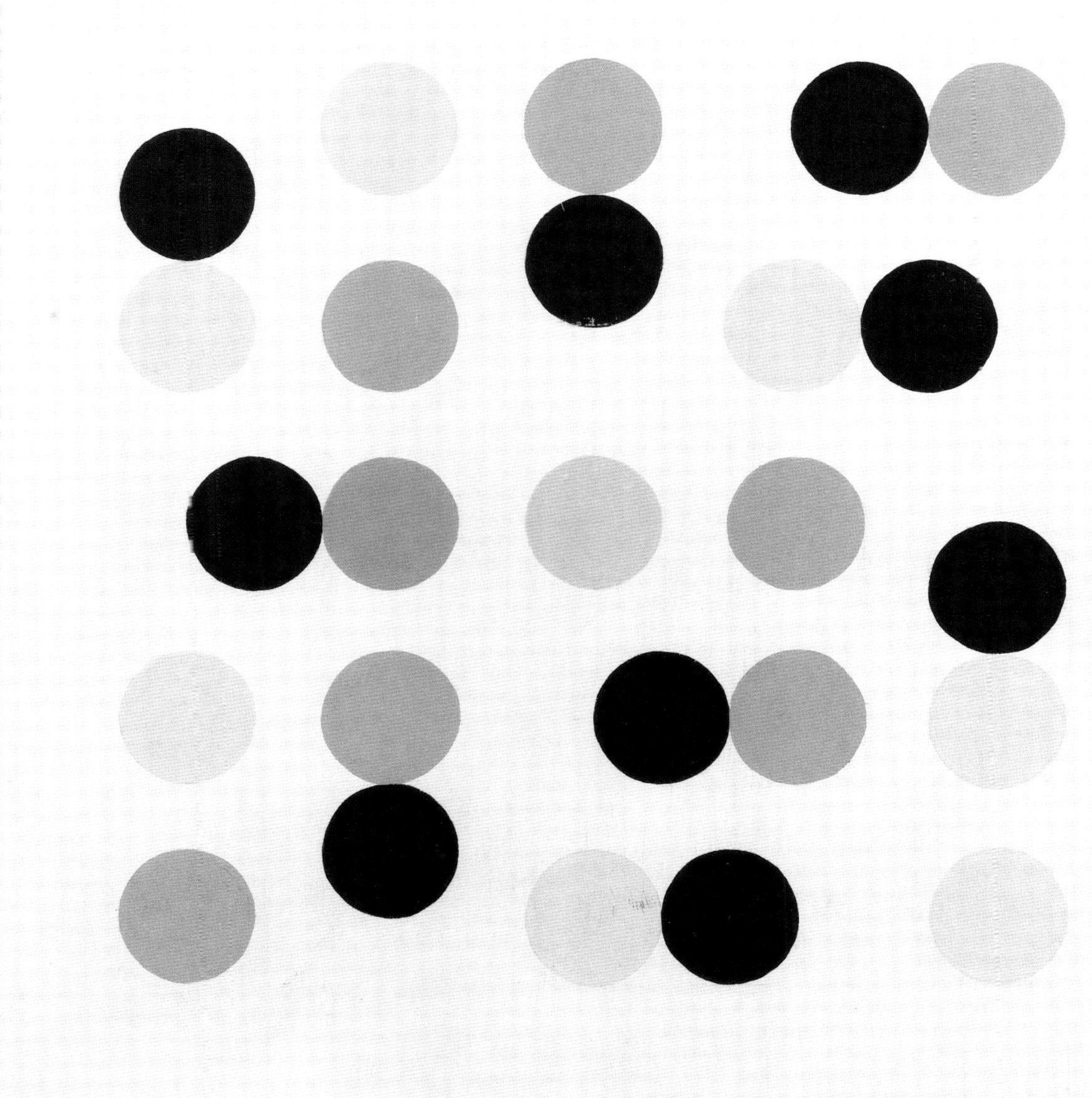

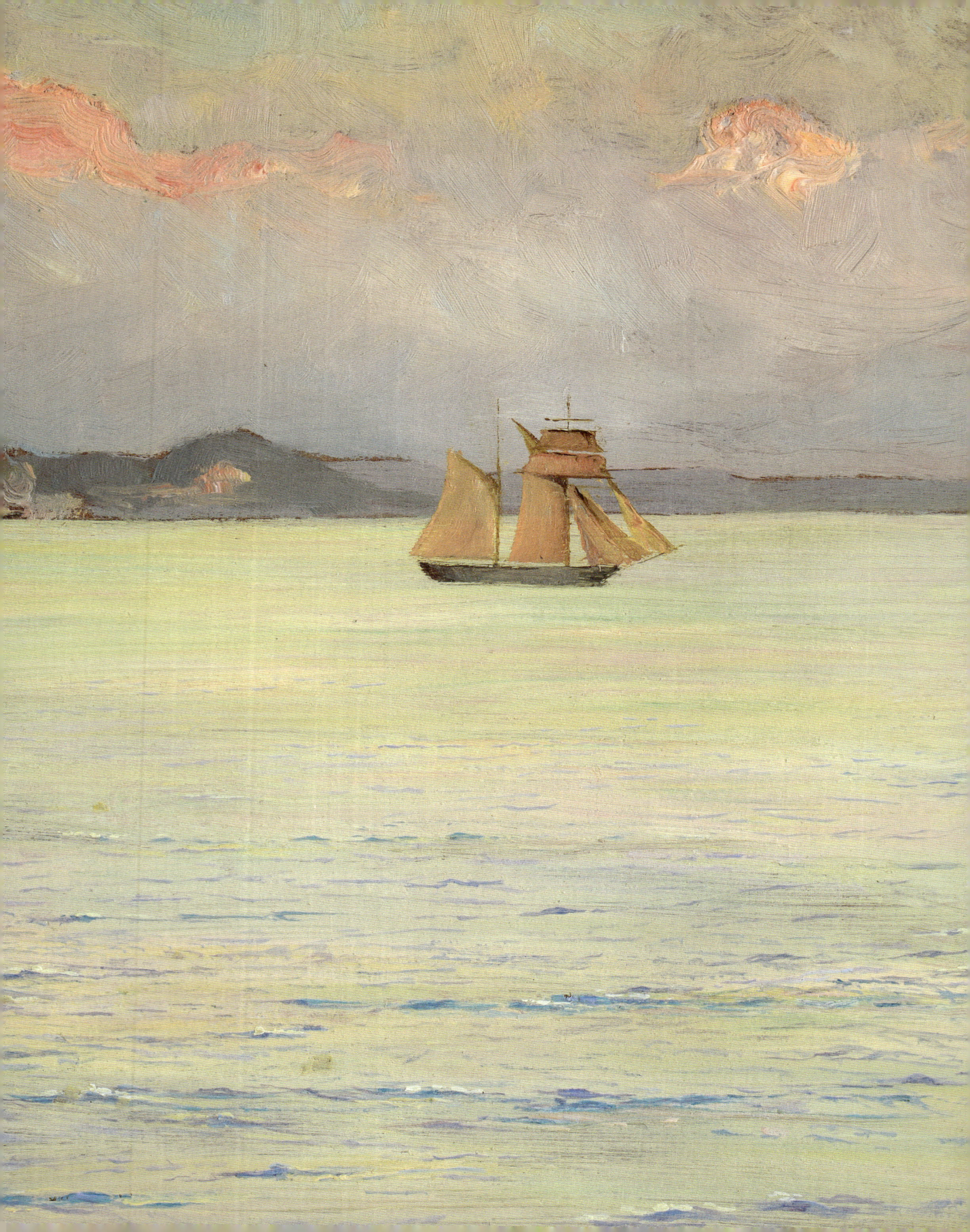

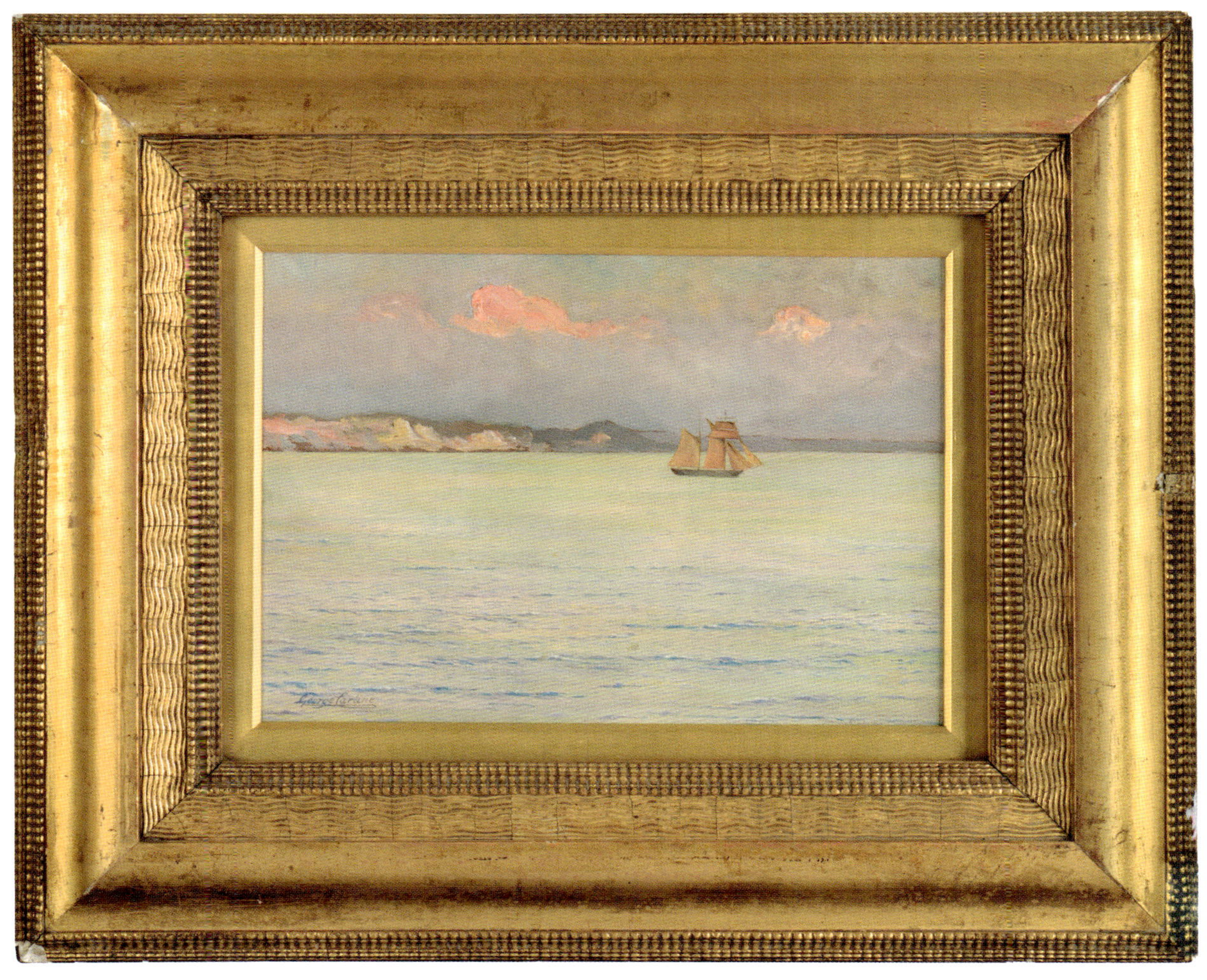

George Carline (1855-1920)

Seascape with sailing boat off the coast at sunset, c. 1890

Oil on canvas, signed- 20.3 x 28.5 cm.

George Francis Carline studied at Heatherley School of Fine Art, London, and then in Antwerp and the Académie Julian in Paris. He exhibited at the Royal Academy and the Royal Institute of Painters in Watercolours. He was a member of the Royal Society of British Artists and father of artists Sydney, Hilda, and Richard Carline. Both Richard and Hilda also married artists, Nancy Higgins and Stanley Spencer respectively.

Hilda Carline (1889-1950)

The Sitting Room at 3 Park Crescent, Oxford, c. 1910

Oil on canvas - 52.1 x 40.6 cm.

Hilda Carline studied at Percyval Tudor-Hart's School of Painting in Hampstead (1913) and served with the Women's Land Army (1916-18), before enrolling at the Slade School of Fine Art under Henry Tonks in 1918. Quickly gaining critical recognition, she exhibited at the LG (1921), the RA and the NEAC. This impressive start to her career faltered, particularly after she married, in 1925, the artist Stanley Spencer (1891-1959). Their turbulent union resulted in periods when Carline hardly painted at all, but after her divorce in 1937, Carline began working more frequently once again, producing numerous pastels which explored her religious beliefs. This early work is likely to show the sitting room at 3 Park Crescent, Oxford, where the Carlines lived from 1904 to early 1916.

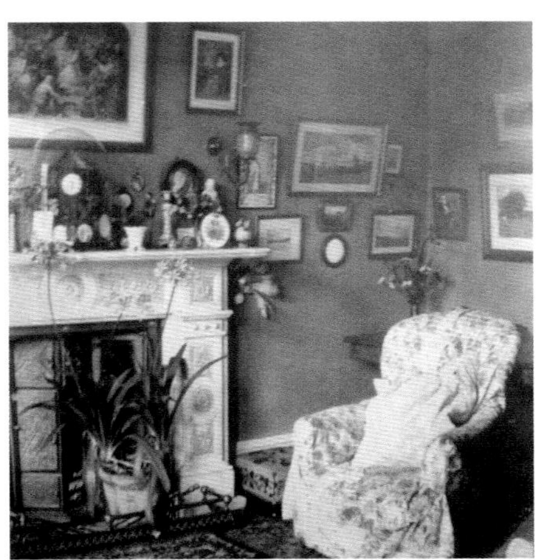

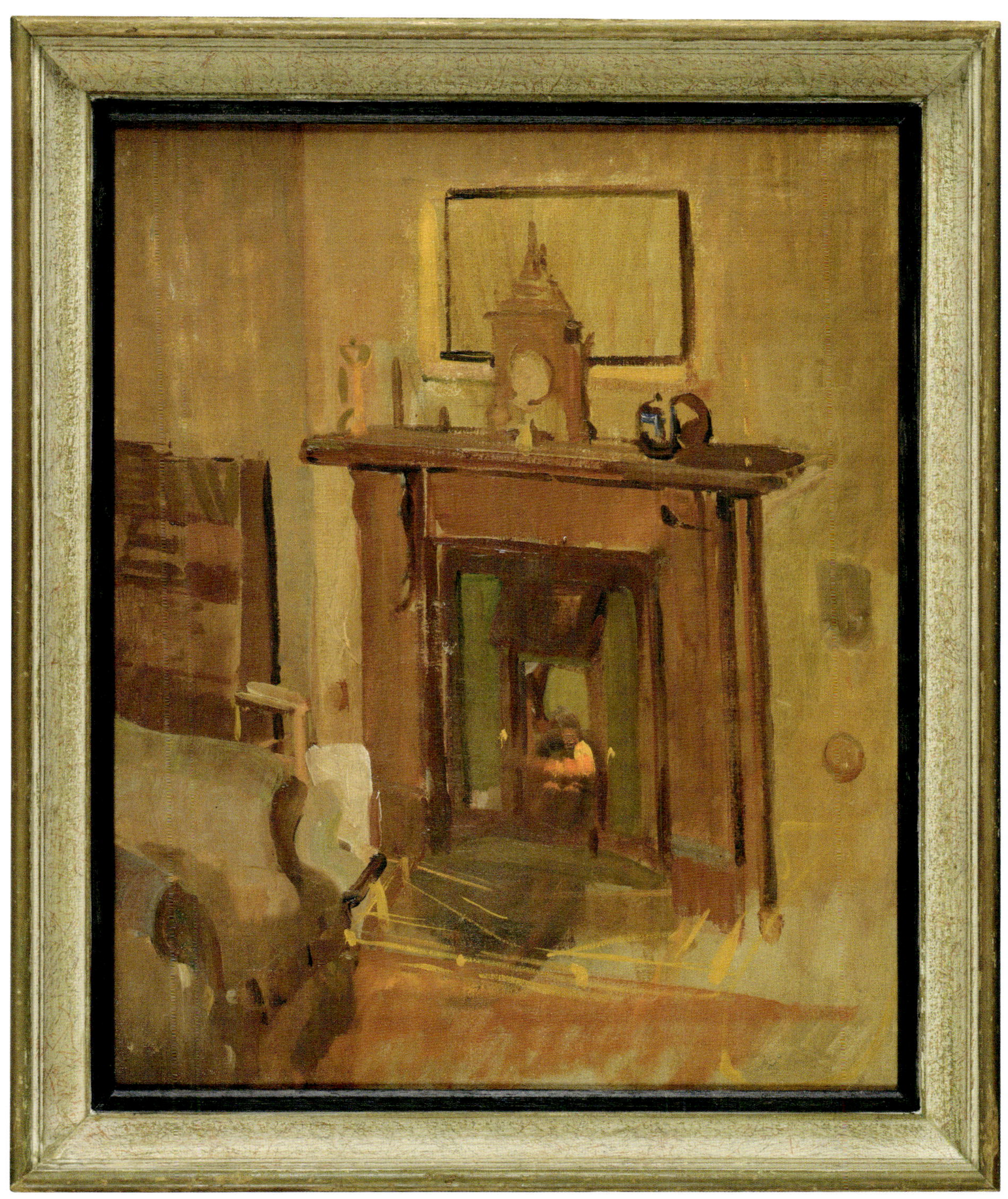

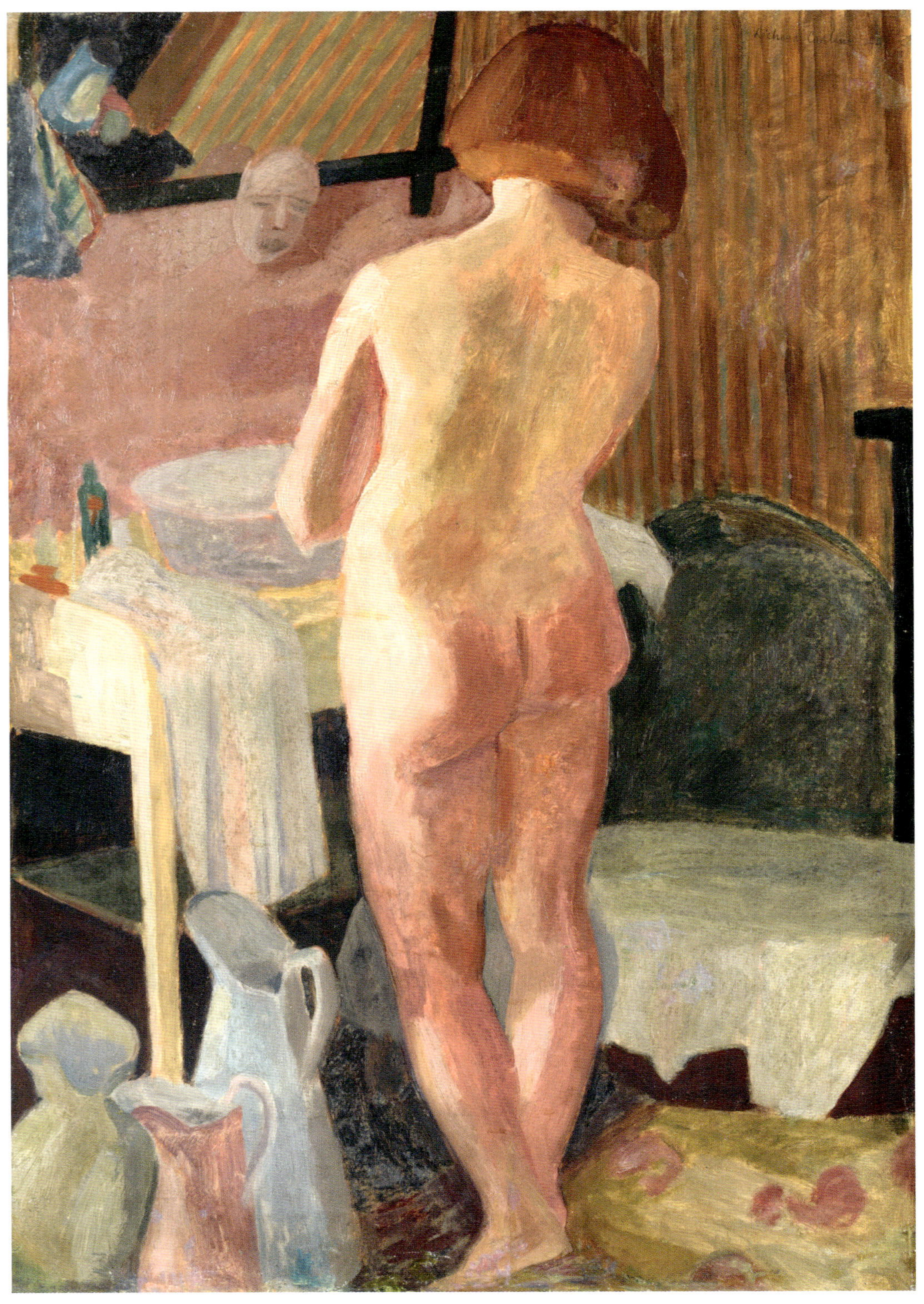

Richard Carline (1896-1980)

Nude

Oil on canvas - 73 x 50 cm.

The setting is likely to be 47 Downshire Hill, Hampstead, home of the Carline family and in the 1920s a popular meeting place for many artists living in Hampstead. Stanley Spencer lived with the Carlines and in 1925 married Hilda Carline; she possibly served as the model for this painting. Richard's bedroom also served as his studio and was crammed with decorative studio props.

Richard Carline (1896-1980)

From the Foremast in the Mid-Atlantic on the Grace Harwar, 1930

Oil on canvas - 108 x 70 cm.

From 1928 Richard Carline made an extensive trip to North America to lecture and travel. In 1930 he went further afield, sailing to Venezuela with his brother Sydney as well as fellow artist, John Duguid, in one of the last of the great square-rigged ships, the Grace Harwar.

Richard Carline was employed as an Official War Artist during the First World War, tasked with documenting aerial warfare or sketching battle grounds from the sky. This resulted in the use of daring compositional devices, with stooping lows and vertiginous highs, which in the decade following the war he transferred to maritime paintings.

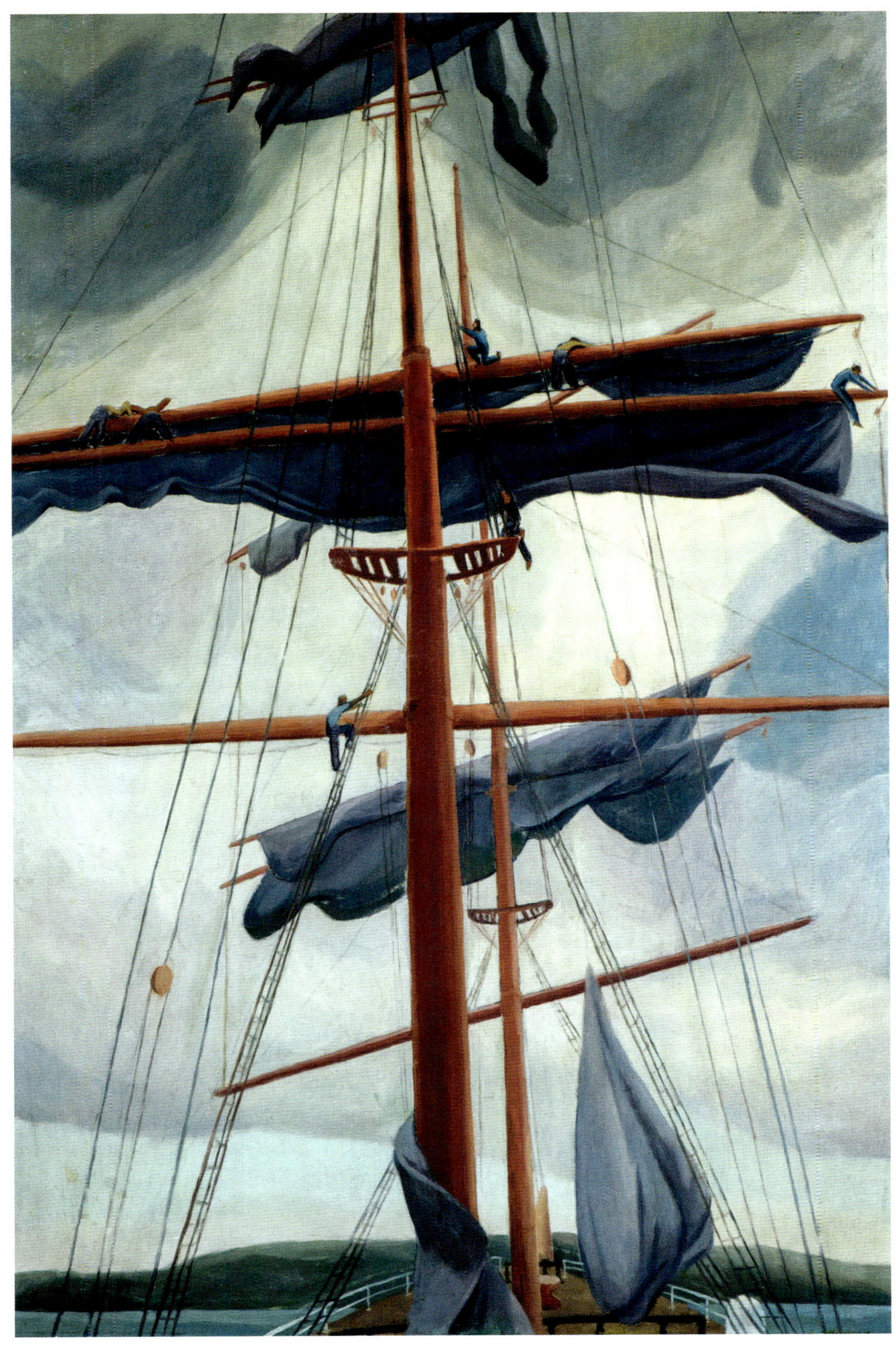

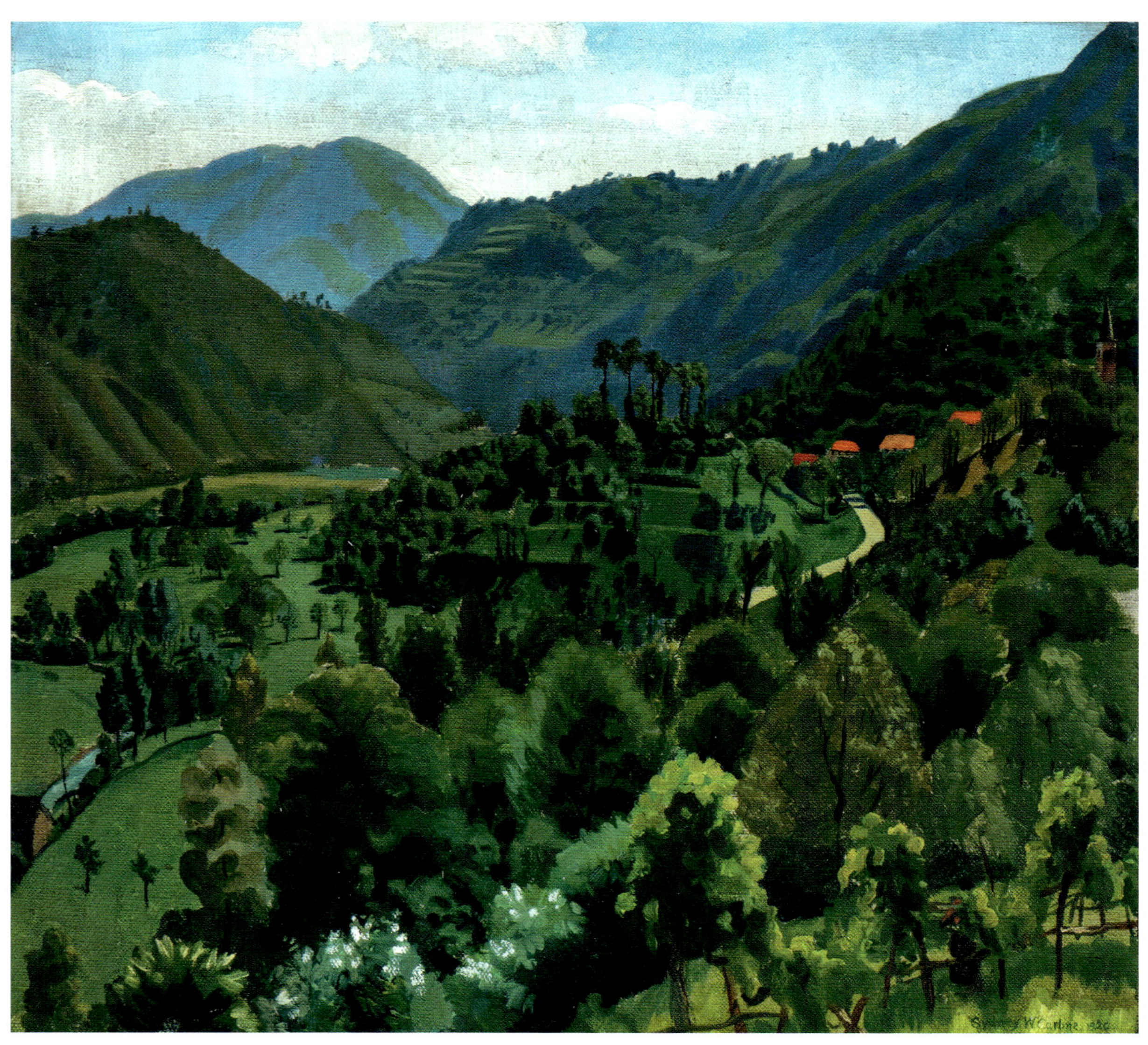

Sydney Carline (1888-1929)

Italian Valley, 1920

Oil on canvas, signed and dated - 55 x 60 cm.

Like his brother Richard, Sydney Carline was employed as an Official War Artist, tasked with documenting aerial warfare. Between 1918 and 1919, the Carlines produced dozens of works recording the Western and Italian Fronts in combat, returning to paint the same landscape in peacetime during 1920. This composition records the same valley as shown in British Scouts leaving their Aerodrome on Patrol over the Asiago Plateau, Italy, 1918 (Imperial War Museum Collection) .

The photographs, diaries and sketchbooks from the Carline brothers' travels in Italy are now owned by the Tate Gallery Archive.

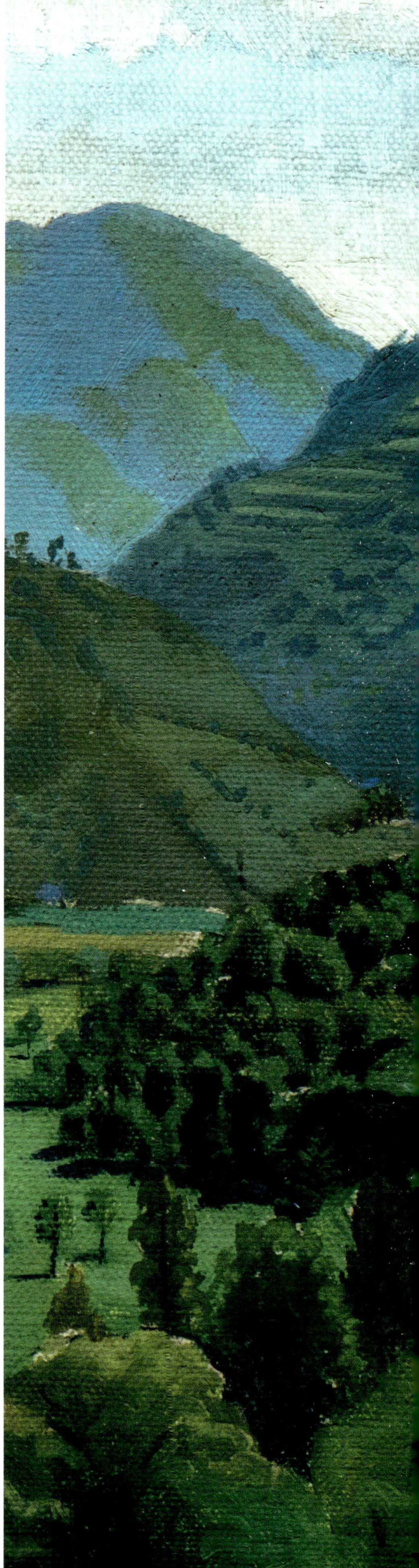

Leslie Carr (1885-1948)

Merchant Ships Tethered with Barrage Balloons, and a Dazzle Camouflage Destroyer, early 1940's

Oil on canvas, signed - 72.5 x 115.5 cm.

This dramatic World War II scene shows a dazzle-camouflaged Royal Navy destroyer (or frigate), with her white ensign visible at the stern, dashing forward to offer safe passage to various assembled merchant ships. The one on the right, with a tug or pilot boat nestling at its bow, has at least one lifeboat swung out - a precaution taken when travelling in perilous convoys in case of attack by submarines or aircraft. Alternatively, the lifeboat may have been swung out for another reason: these ships are clearly close to shore and only the Royal Navy ship is shown to be moving. The merchant ships have barrage balloons tethered to them to make air attack more difficult, and none has a bow wave. For this reason it is likely that this painting shows a convoy assembled in a British estuary such as the Mersey, getting ready for an outward voyage to North America, Africa, or the East. The fact that the ships are high out of the water suggests that they are sailing empty, to return with cargoes of grain, oil, or the numerous provisions required to feed Britain and fight the war.

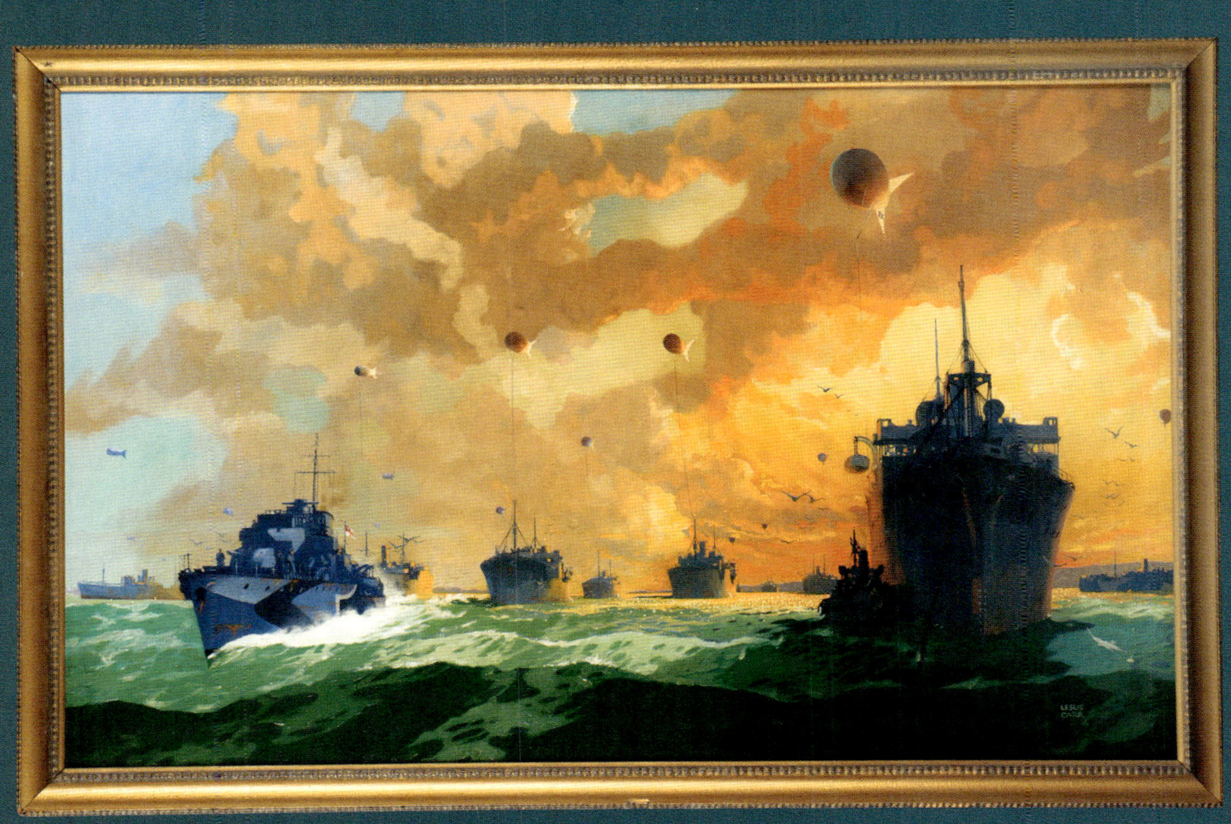

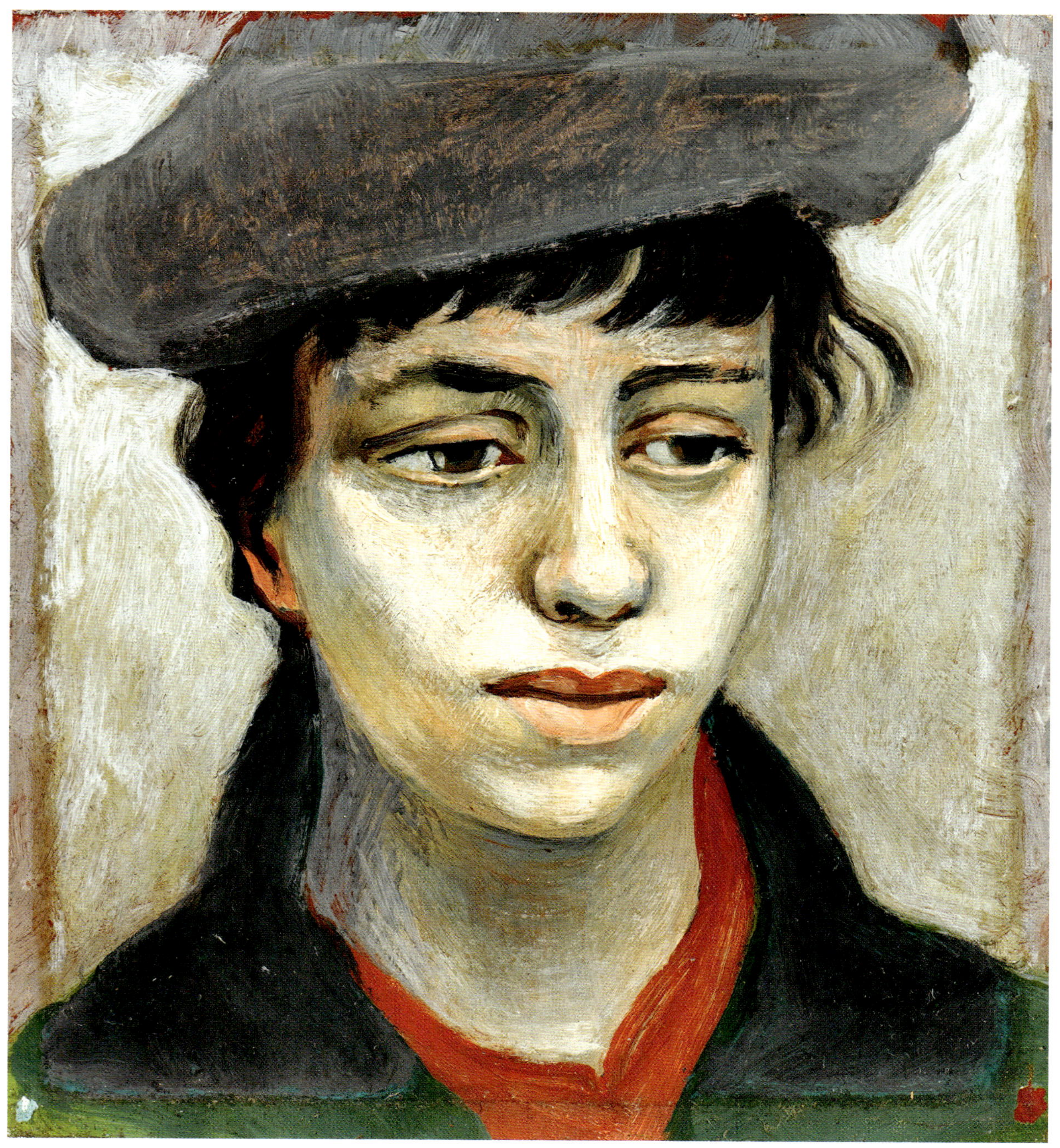

Fyffe Christie (1918-1979)

Portrait of the Artist's Wife Eleanor, 1950

Oil on panel - 16 x 14.5 cm.

Christie met his future wife Eleanor in 1950 when teaching evening classes at the Glasgow School of Art. With Eleanor, a sculptor, he moved to London in 1957 and again taught, while completing murals and much other work. Christie and his wife held a show at Woodlands Gallery in 1979, shortly before he died.

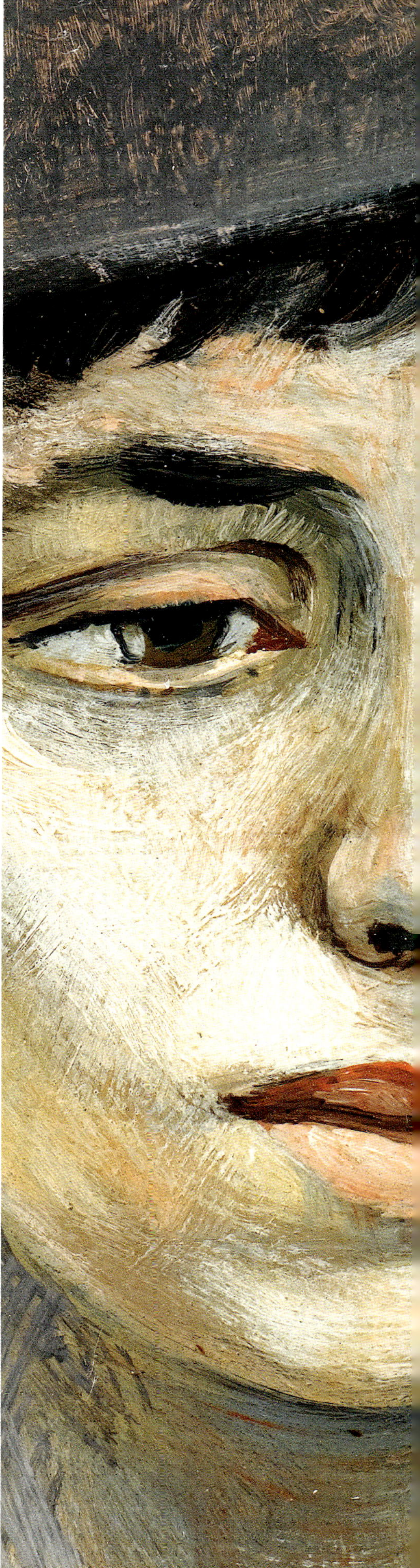

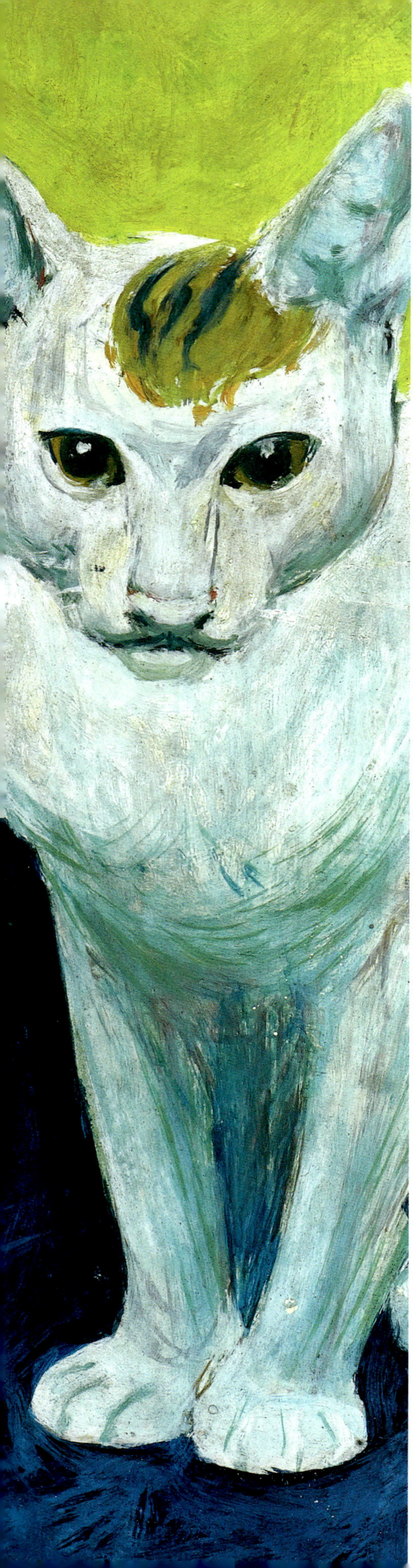

Fyffe Christie (1918-1979)

The Artists' Cat, Carmen, c.1955

Oil on board - 27 x 20.2 cm.

After their marriage in 1952 Fyffe and Eleanor Christie rented a flat overlooking the Botanic Gardens in Glasgow, with one large living /dining room/studio and one small bedroom adjoining. They shared a tiny kitchen and bathroom with the other tenants and their white Cat, called Carmen.

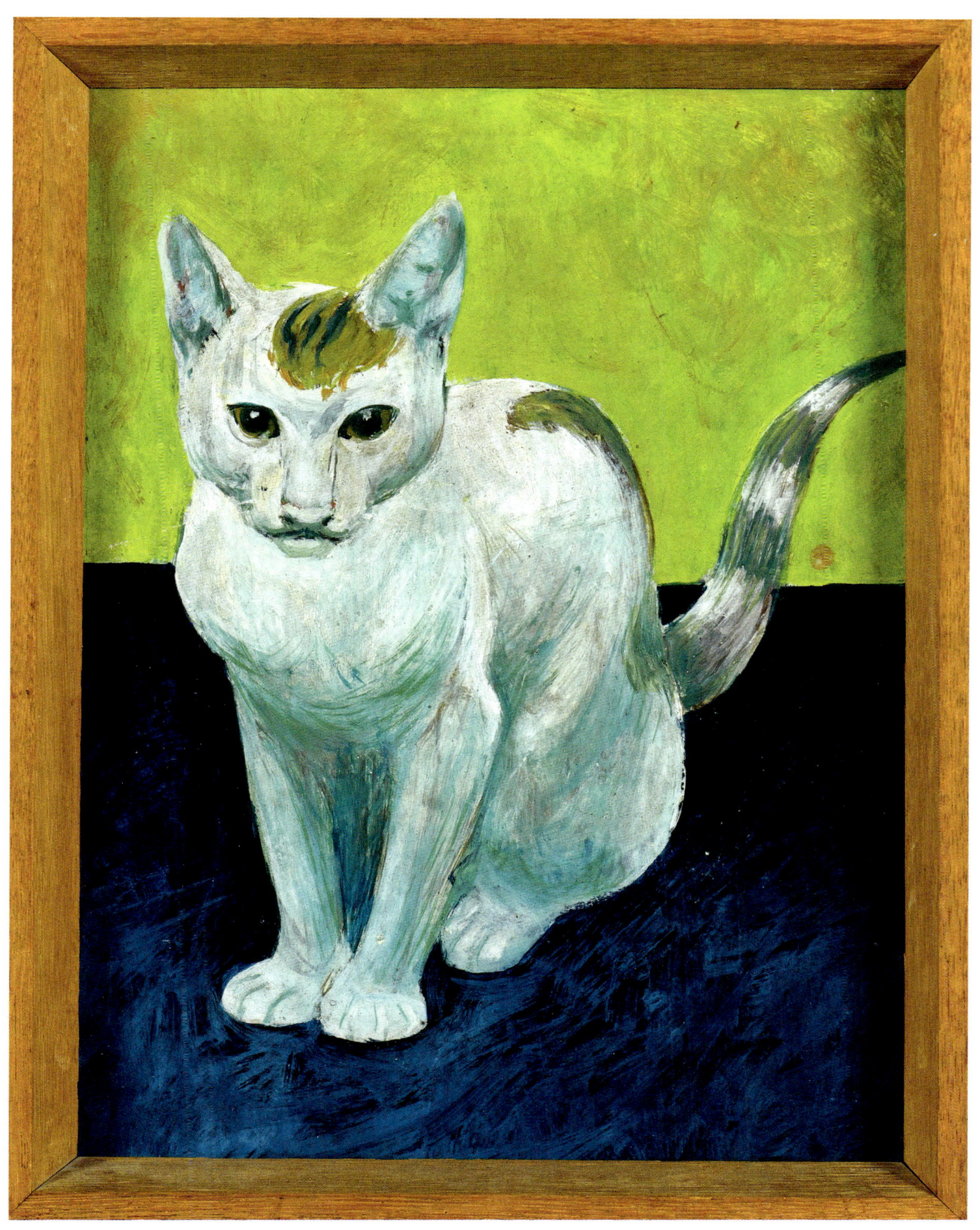

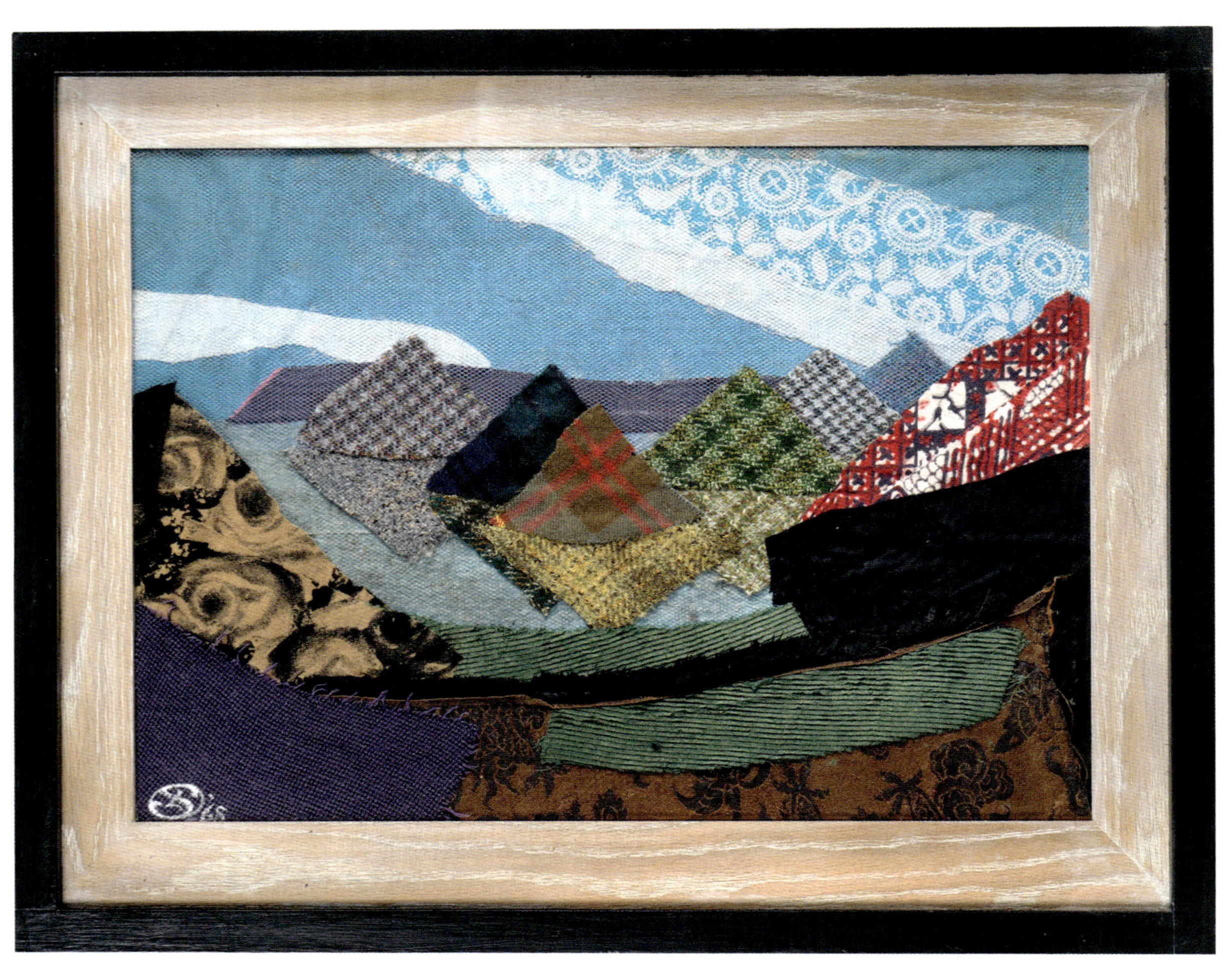

Ithell Colquhoun (1906-1988)

Highland Landscape, 1965

Fabric collage, signed with monogram, dated, signed and inscribed on the reverse - 40 x 50 cm.

Although collages, montages and constructions formed a large part of Colquhoun's output during the 1960's, today surprisingly few can be traced.

Her immediate inspiration for these works was Kurt Schwitters. In an article she wrote for The Times Educational Supplement, Rubbish Into Art, (1971), she explained 'In surrealism an alienation of sensation enables you to look at things simply as form and colour; ignoring their utilitarian aspect; then to see in them images apart from their first uses; and from this to find in many objects usually thrown away the raw material for new creations'.

Highland Landscape was exhibited in 1969 in Hamburg at the Gallerie für Zeitgenössische Kunst, Ithell Colquhoun: Constructions and Collages (No 21) and in 1970 at the Bristol Arts Centre, Ithell Colquhoun: Paintings, Constructions, Collages, (No 44)The Composition was possibly inpsired by Emeric Pressburger's iconic 1945 film, I know where I'm going, best-remembered for the sequence in which the landscape, traversed by a train travelling from London to Glasgow, transforms into a tartan Scottish dreamscape.

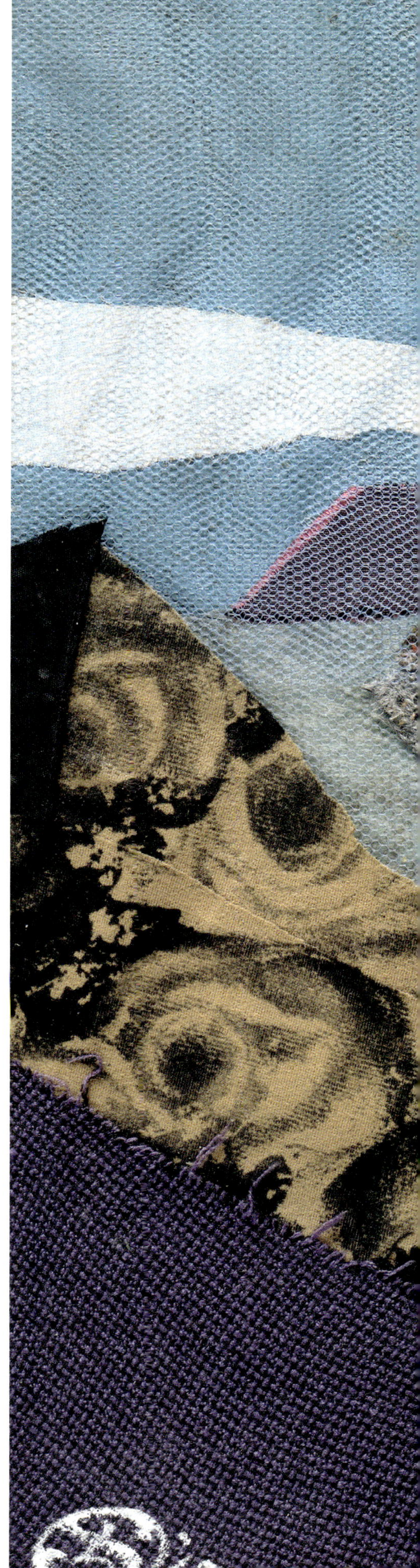

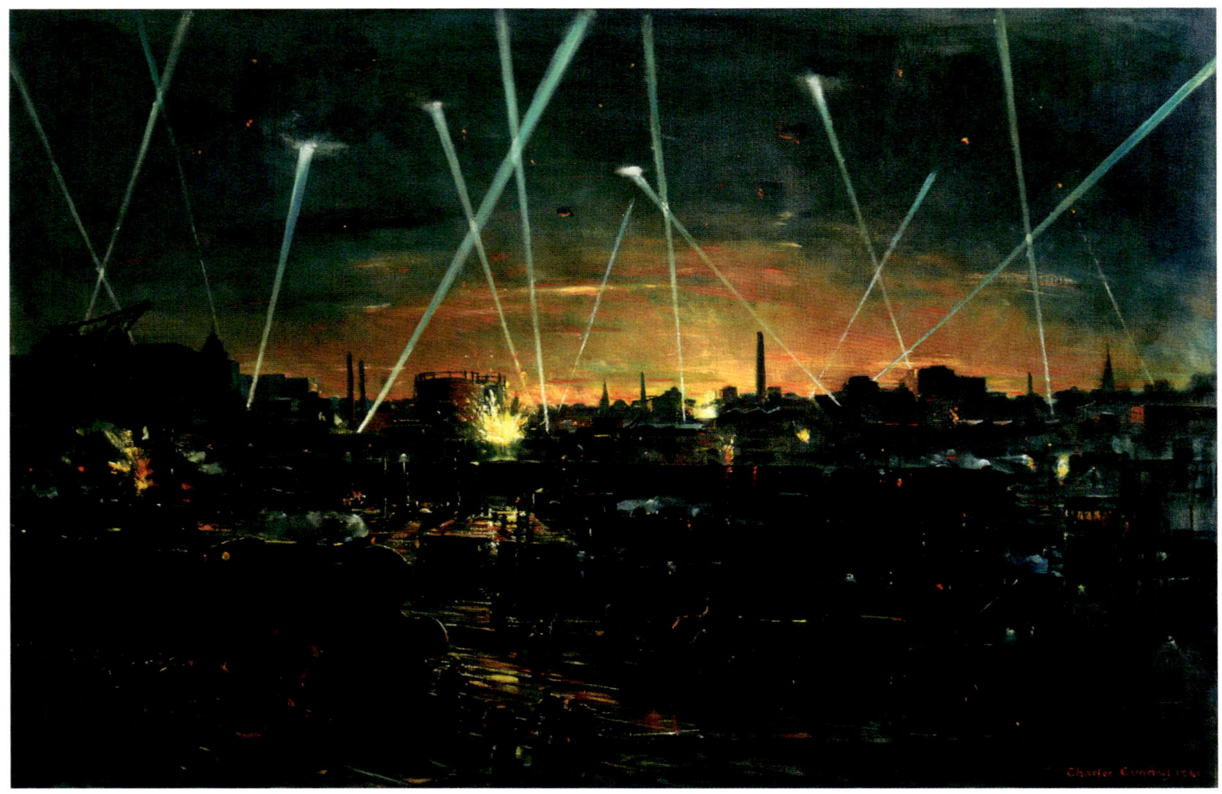

Charles Cundall (1890-1971)

The British Railways Carry On, 1941

Oil on canvas, signed and dated 'Charles Cundall 1941' - 80.5 x 122 cm.

Painted in 1941, the skyline is punctuated by searchlights, explosions and fires against which the silhouettes of barrage balloons and Luftwaffe bombers can be seen. In June 1941, 14,000,000 copies of a leaflet entitled 'Beating the Invader' were distributed to reinforce the UK government's 1939 exhortation 'Keep Calm and Carry On'.

Exhibited at The Royal Academy in the year of its execution, The British Railways Carry On may be viewed as a pictorial representation of that Great British sensibility, the maintaining of a 'stiff upper lip'.

According to the artist's daughter, Cundall 'really respected reality and didn't try and overload it with personal interpretation'. Cundall produced other works in this vein and on an epic scale, including his seminal The Withdrawal from Dunkirk (1940) now in the collection of The Imperial War Museum, London.

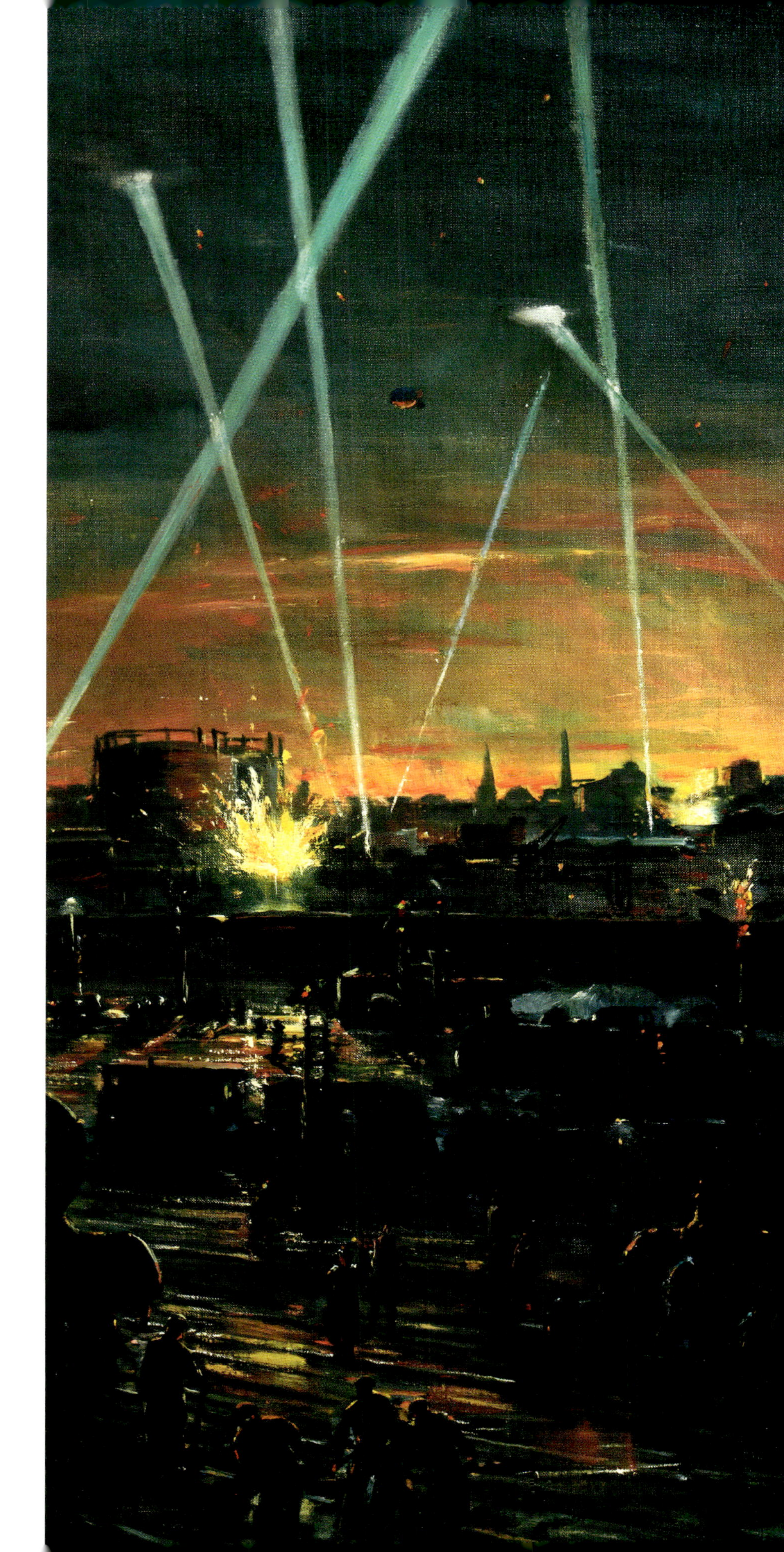

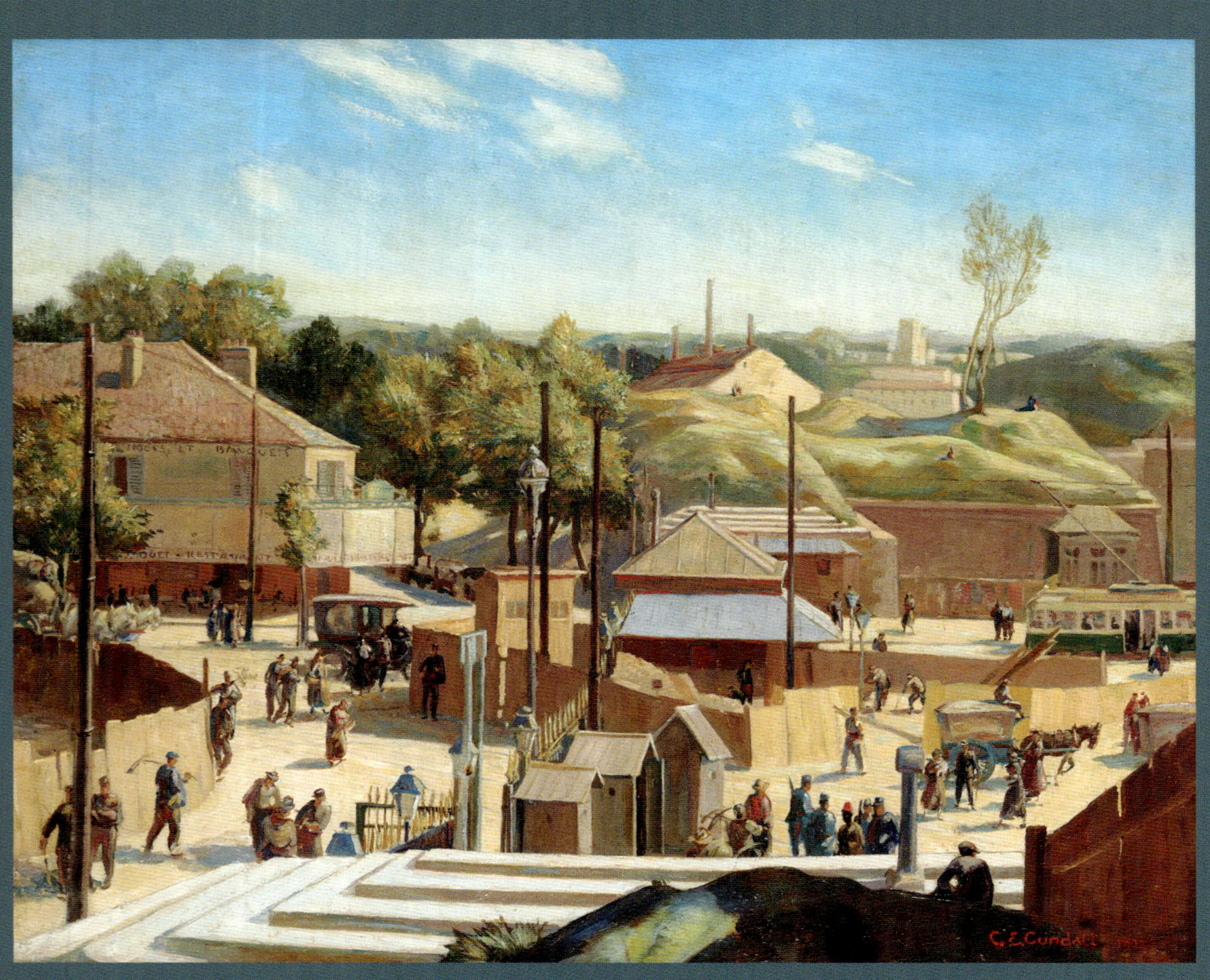
C.E.Cundall

Charles Cundall (1890-1971)

Porte St Cloud, Paris, 1922

Oil on panel, signed - 44.2 x 53.5 cm.

While Cundall made numerous sketching trips, travelling extensively in Europe, he was especially drawn to Paris. Painting en plein air, directly on to prepared panels, the best of his work retains a vitality which he sometimes lost when working up the finished, larger, paintings in his studio. Saint-Cloud is a wealthy commune in the western suburbs of Paris, which at the time of this painting was being transformed by the extension of the métro line from Boulevard Exelmans. This painting was exhibited at the Old Grosvenor Galleries in 1923 in an exhibition of works by Charles Cundall, Harold Knight, H.M.Livens and Fairlie Harmar (1876-1945). Out of thirty-two Cundalls included, four were of English views, with twelve French views (Paris and Normandy) and the remaining works of Italian topography.

Harold Dearden (1888-1962)

Model posed in a bathing suit, in the artist's studio, c. 1922

Oil on canvas, signed on the reverse - 81.3 x 106.7 cm.

Painted in the artist's Oakley Street studio in Chelsea, with draped studio props suggesting a backdrop of cliffs in silhouette, this work depicts a model posed as if on the beach. The painting can be dated by the model's hairstyle and the design of her swimming costume.

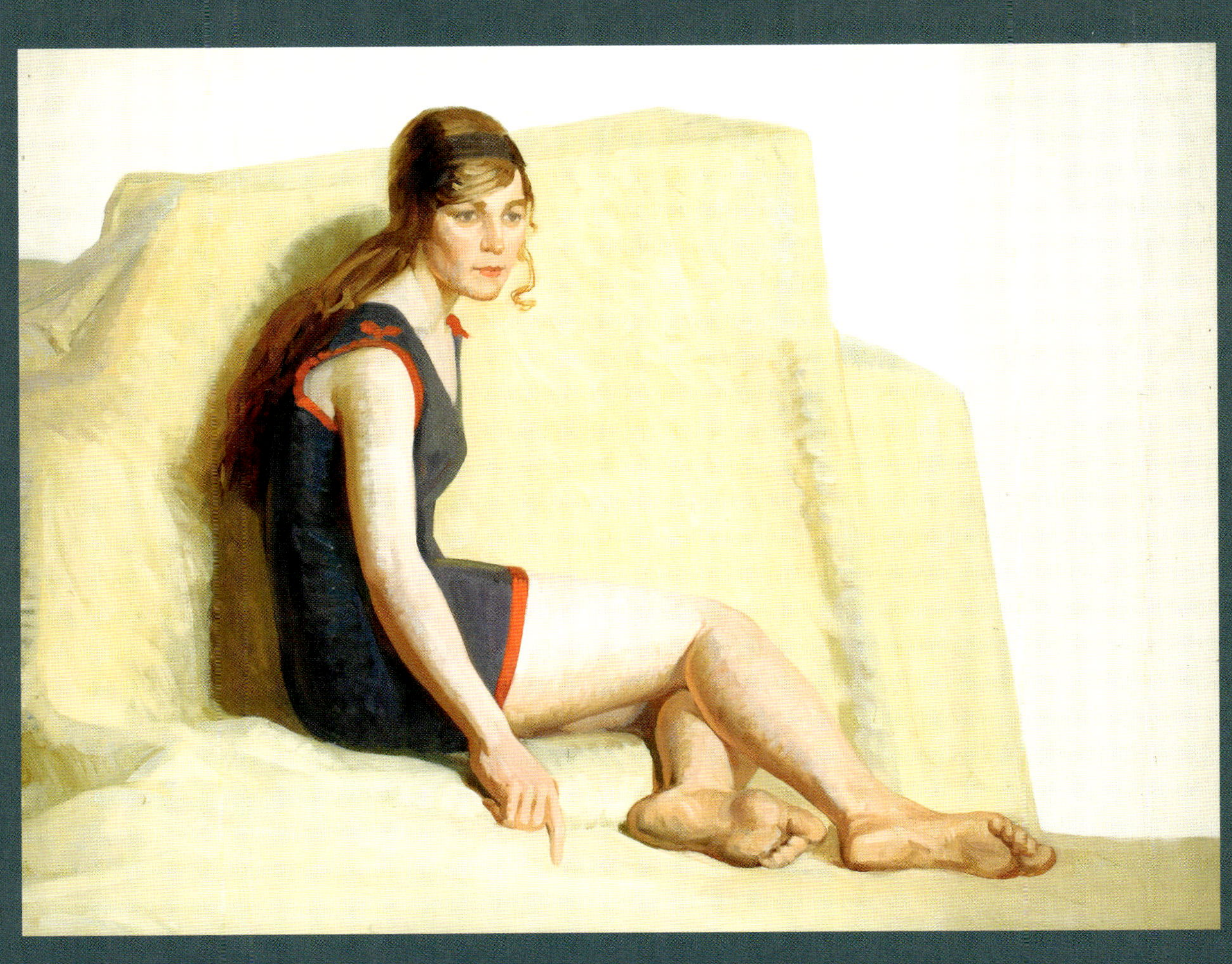

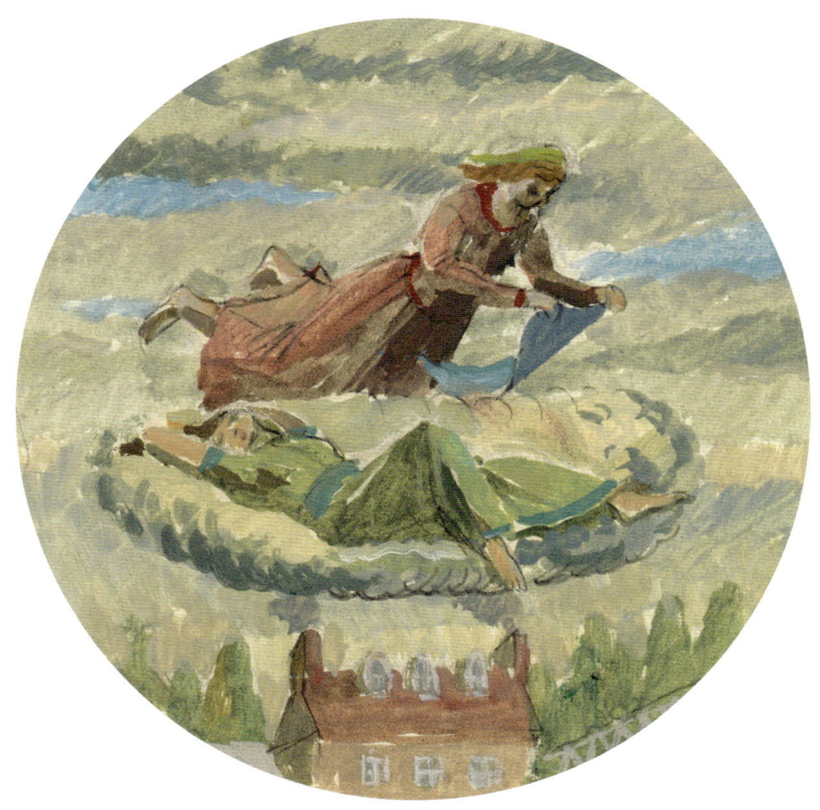

Evelyn Dunbar (1902-1960)

Industry and Sloth, c. 1935

Oil on paper - diameter 15.2 cm.

In late 1932 Evelyn Dunbar volunteered for an ambitious mural project at Brockley School for Boys, in south-east London.The project was to be led by Cyril 'Charles' Mahoney, Dunbar's mural tutor at the Royal College of Art.The central arcade ceiling was to feature 'the four winds of Hilly Fields' (Hilly Fields was - and is - the parkland on which the school stands). Dunbar abandoned the winds in favour of her own designs of goddesses (Juno and Minerva) rubbing shoulders with personifications of virtuous and not-so-virtuous qualities (Genius,Virtue and Reputation and, as in the designs above, Industry and Sloth.)The design evolved over time from the sketch to the finished version, but in both Sloth is asleep while Industry keeps busy.

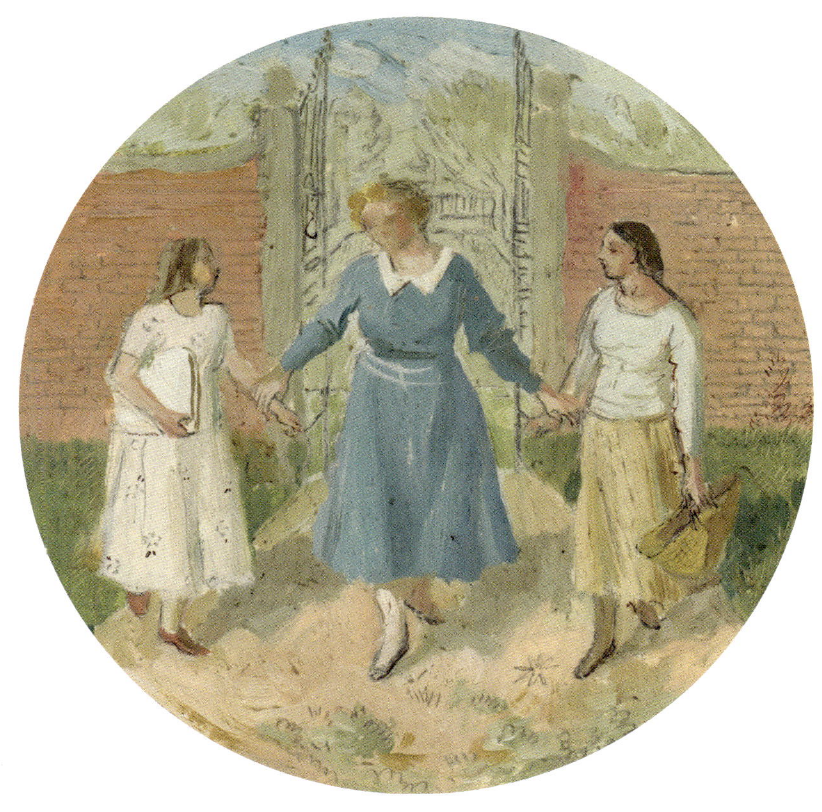

Evelyn Dunbar (1902-1960)

Allegory of Painting, c. 1935

Oil on paper - diameter 16 cm.

One of a pair of allegorical roundels in which two young women, one carrying a portfolio, the other a basket with a folding easel, are being guided by a modern-day Muse like central figure.

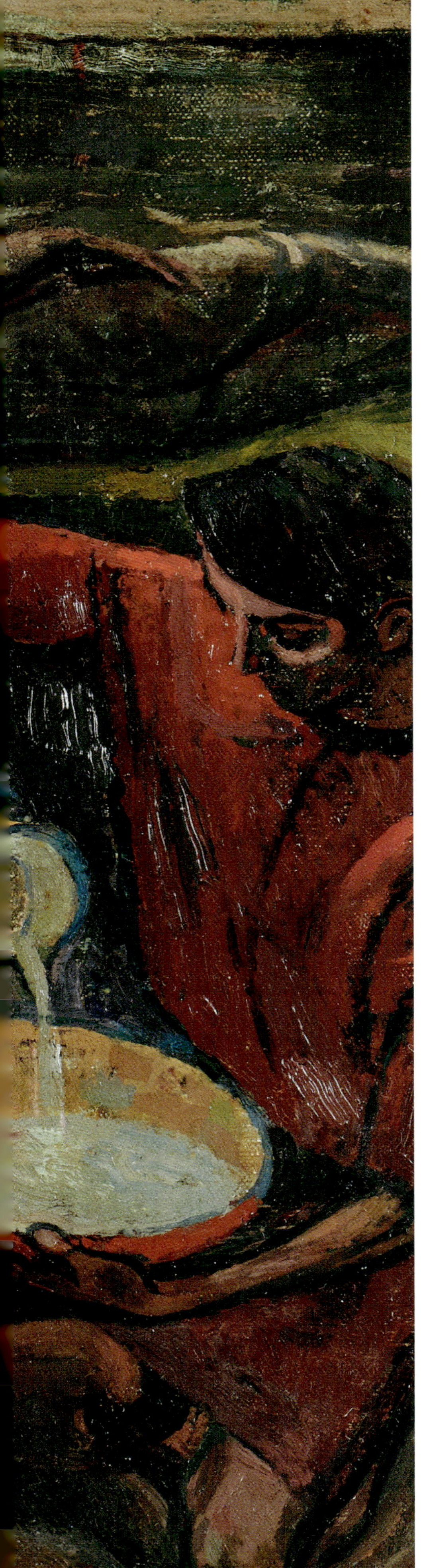

Evelyn Dunbar (1902-1960)

Joseph in Prison, 1949-50

Oil on canvas, signed with initials- 46 x 35.5 cm.

In 1938 Dunbar conceived the idea of painting the most significant moments in the Old Testament account of the life of Joseph (Genesis 37-41). She selected Joseph's Dream, Joseph in the Pit and Joseph in Prison. World War 2 and Dunbar's appointment as a war artist interrupted this project, but after the war she took it up again, completing Joseph in the Pit and Joseph in Prison in 1949-50, when she was living in Enstone, Oxfordshire.

Seen from above in quarter-profile, the figure of Joseph strongly resembles Dunbar's husband Roger Folley, a horticultural economist then working in Oxford University. A dawn sky can be viewed behind the bars of the prison window. Joseph pours milk for the sleeping fellow inmates - Pharaoh's butler and baker. According to the narrative in Genesis, Joseph's ability to interpret their dreams leads to his eventual release.

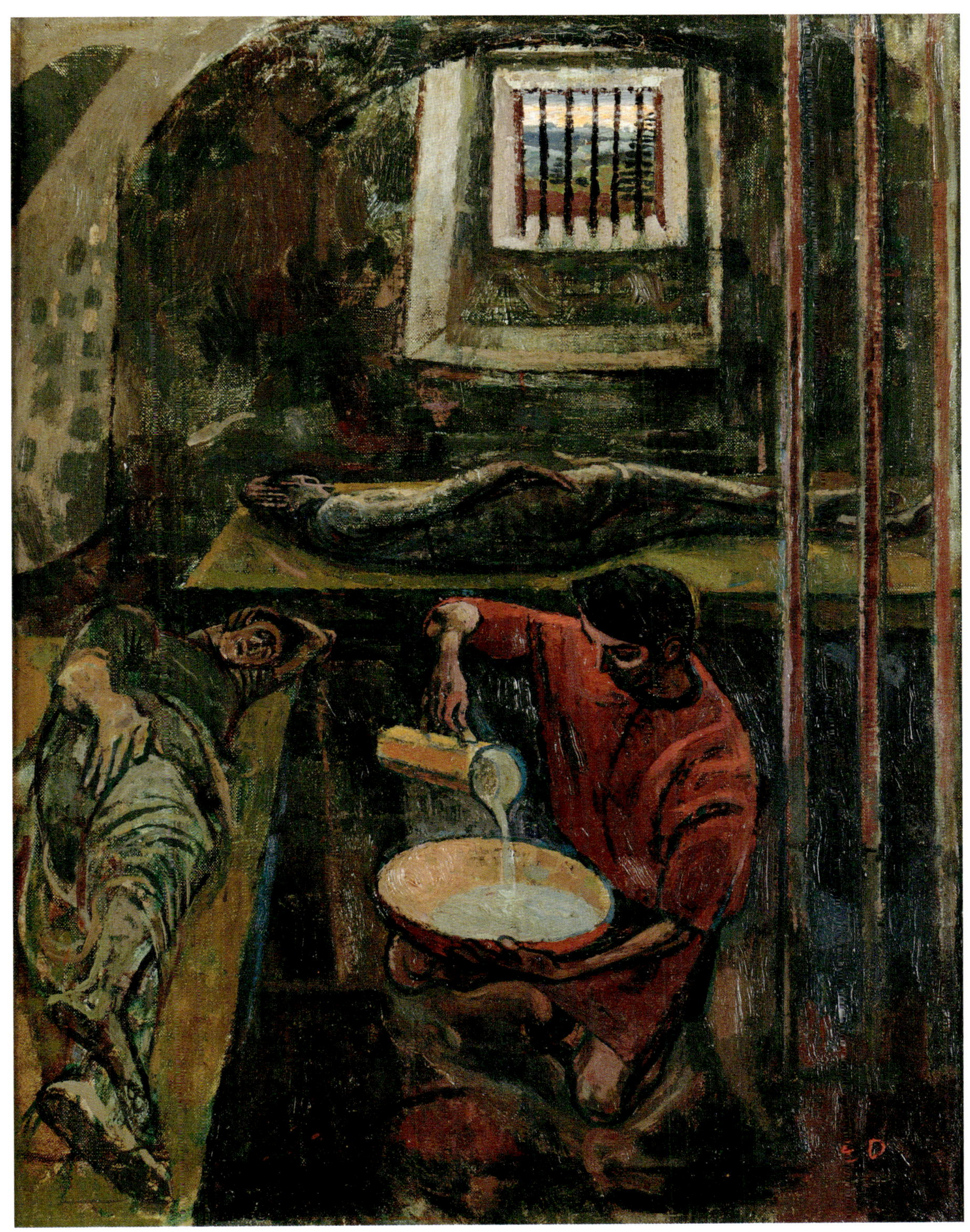

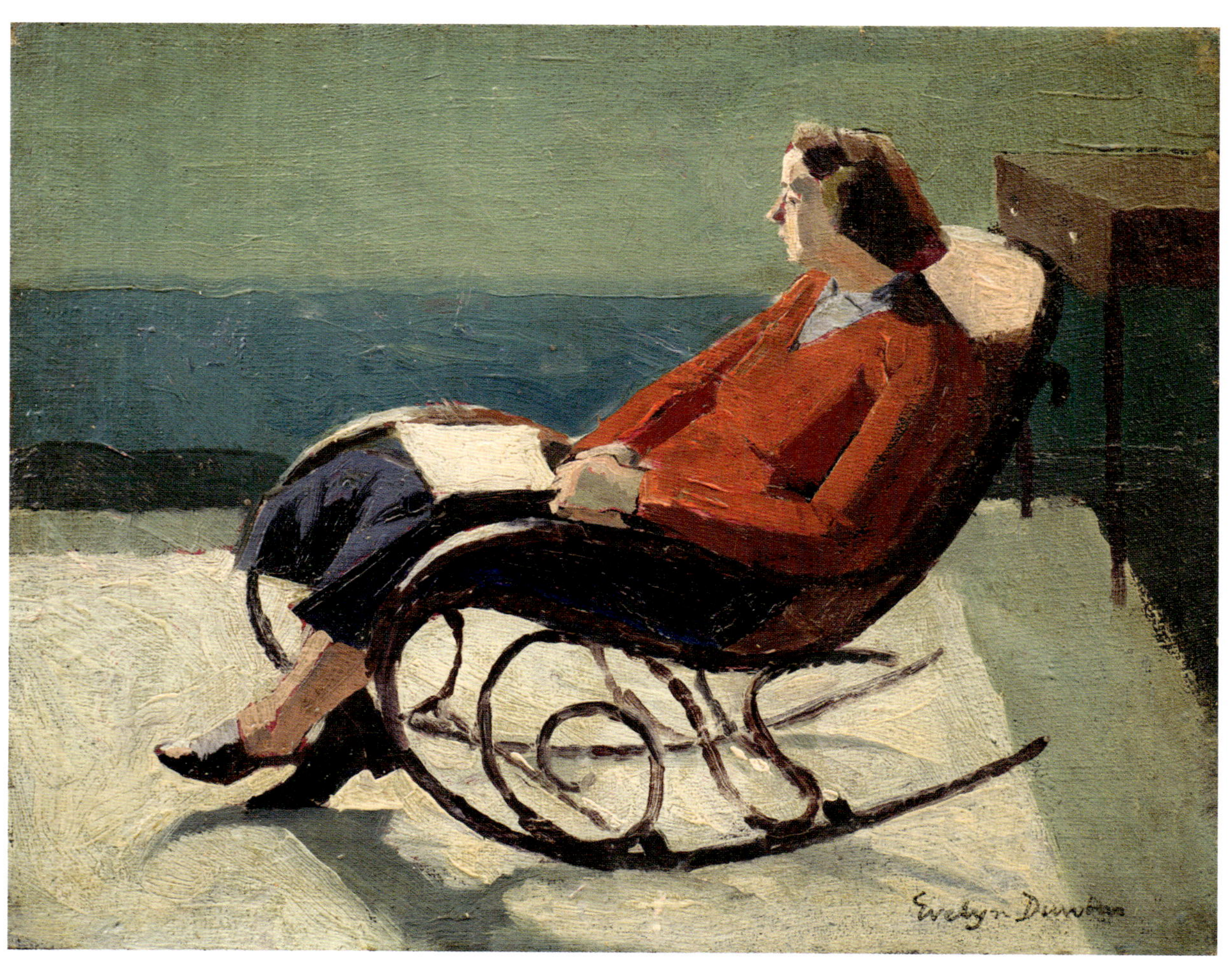
Evelyn Dunbar

Evelyn Dunbar (1902-1960)

Portrait of the Artist's mother, Florence, on a bentwood rocking chair, c.1930

Oil on canvas, signed with studio stamp - 20 x 25.4 cm.

Florence Dunbar, née Murgatroyd, was the daughter of a Bradford woolmaster. She met William Dunbar on one of his frequent visits to Bradford for textiles for his Reading bespoke tailoring and household linen business. They married in 1895. A tireless and green-fingered gardener, she also painted innumerable floral still lifes. Evelyn owed much to her unceasing encouragement. She died in 1944.

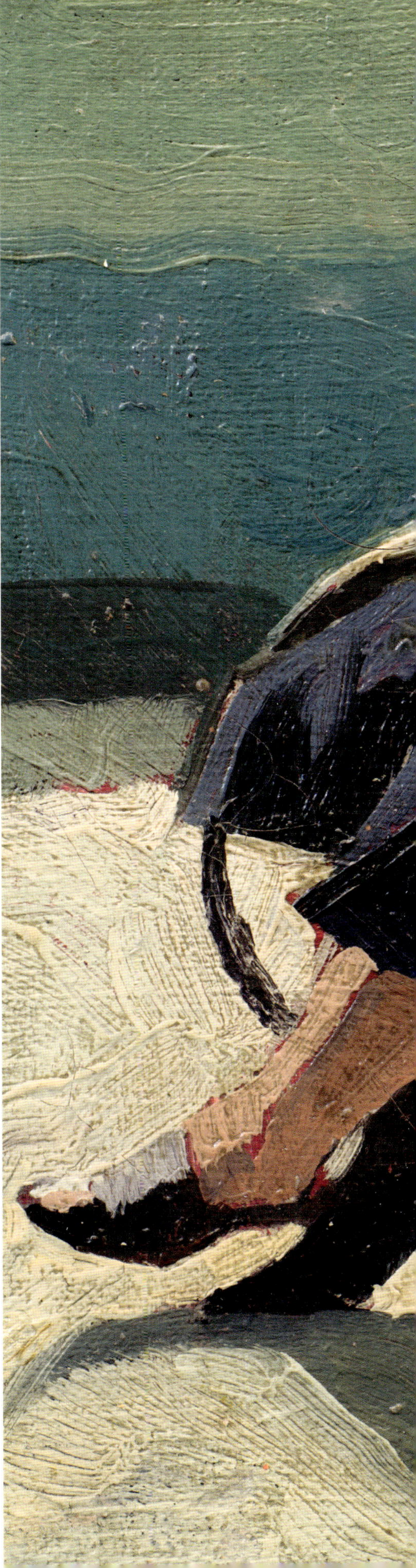

Hubert Arthur Finney (1905-1991)

Amy Ironing, c. 1953

Oil on canvas, signed - 76 x 63.5 cm.

Finney met his second wife, the artist Amy Dyer, whilst convalescing in 1945. He described her as ‘a lovely intelligent woman with gifts in the visual arts as a designer’ who had attended design and drawing class at Reading University, and knew Professor Betts who was the head of the fine art department. Through her connection with Betts she was able to secure Finney a part time teaching post at Reading which resulted in Finney being put in charge of life drawing, a position he held until his retirement in 1970.

As an artist Finney was ambitious. He strove throughout his career to create a vision that would be enduring. Amy Ironing combines all his strengths: his admiration for Old Masters (especially Vermeer), his love of the night, and his ability to replicate a sense of the aching loneliness of the artists that he admired, such as Edward Hopper.

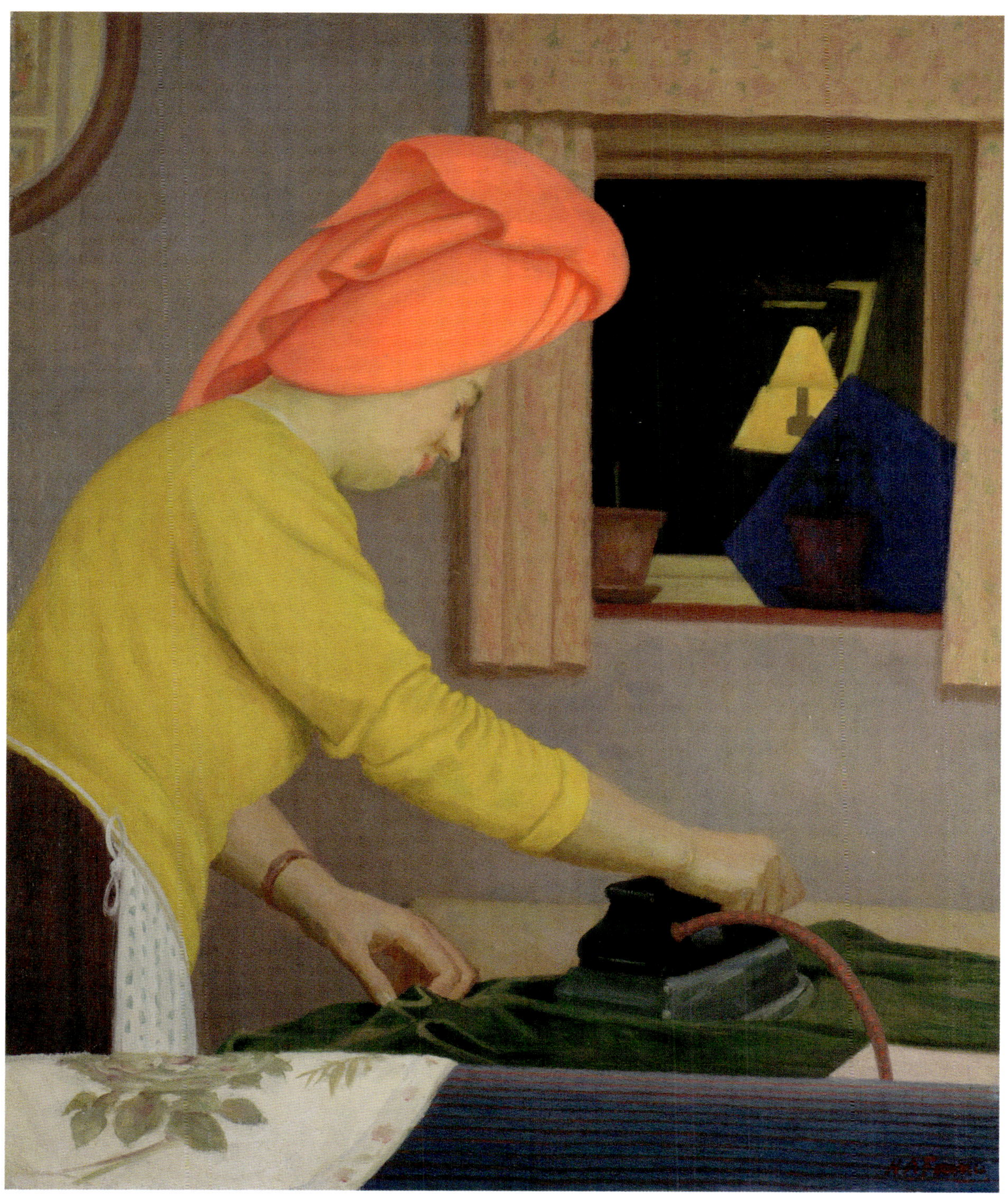

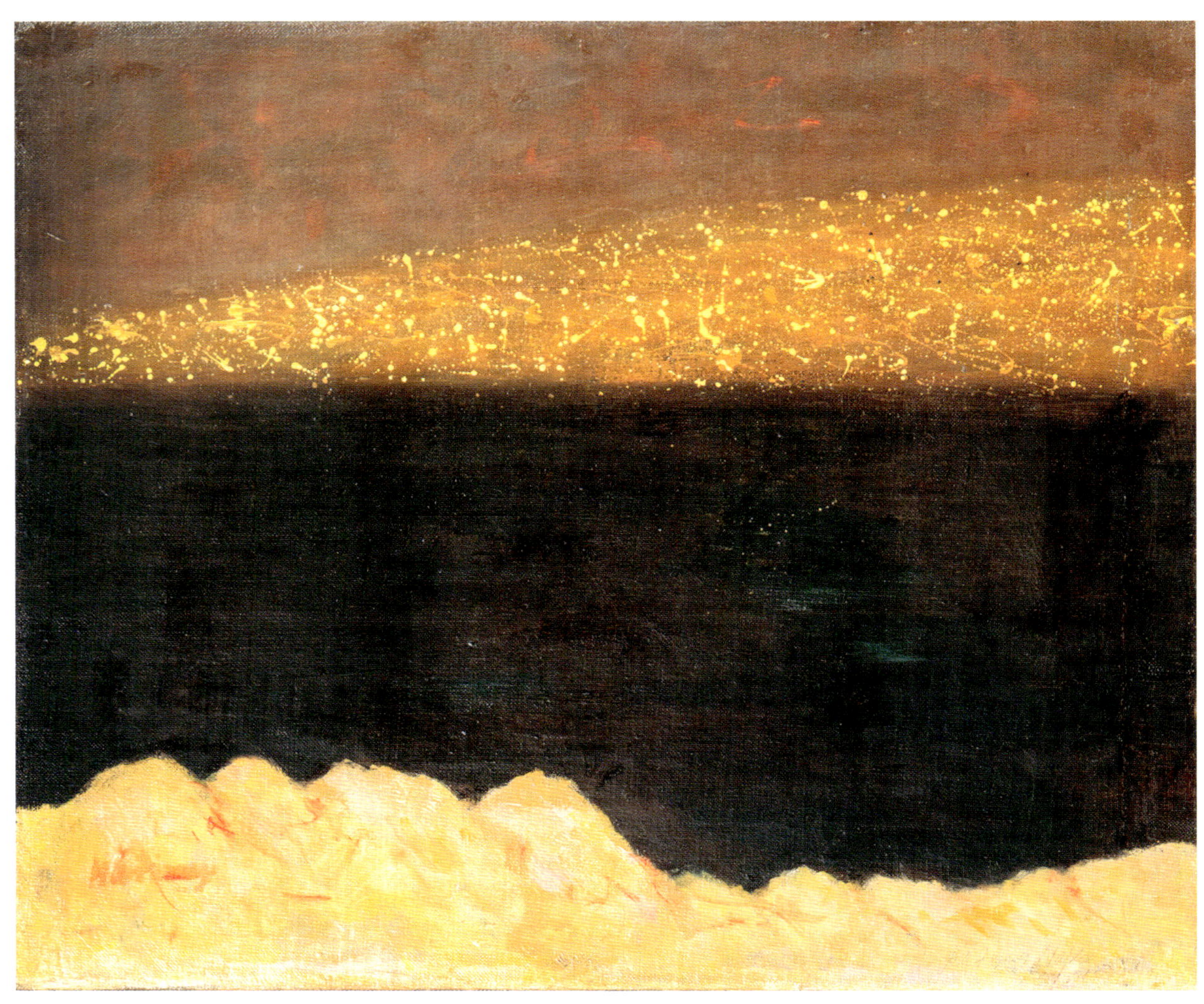

Hubert Arthur Finney (1905-1991)

Naples Bay at night, en route to Athens, 1960

Oil on canvas, signed - 51 x 60.5 cm.

In 1960 Finney and his wife Amy flew to Athens. The aerial views from the journey made a great impression on Finney and became the inspiration for a series of paintings.

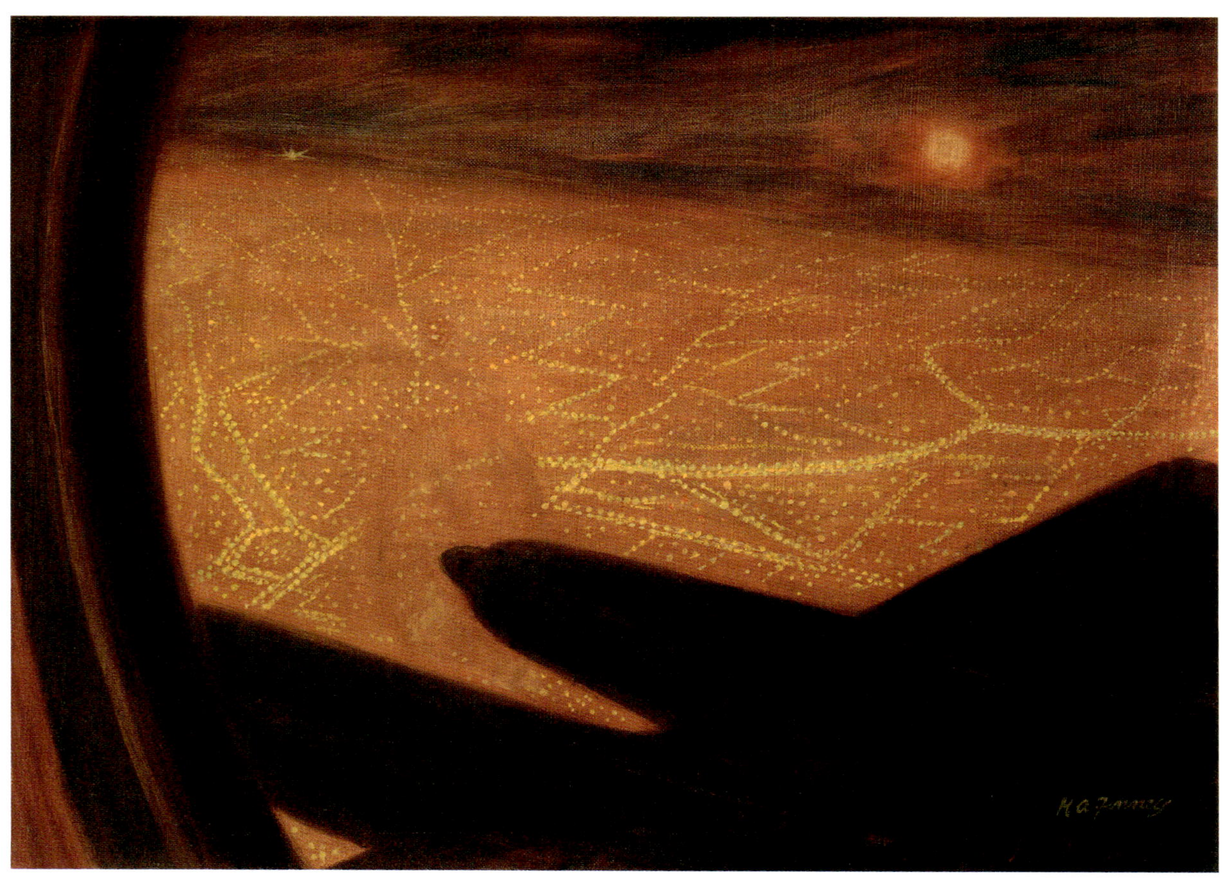

Hubert Arthur Finney (1905-1991)

Dusk, 1966

Oil on canvas, signed - 42.5 x 58.3 cm.

In 1966 Finney spent a year in America on an exchange programme at the University of Wisconsin, living in Milwaukee. During this time he produced a vibrant body of new work inspired by friendships with American artists such as Joe Freibert and Danny Pierce. This composition encapsulates Finney's excitement on taking this transatlantic flight and the new lease of life it gave to him in terms of artistic creativity.

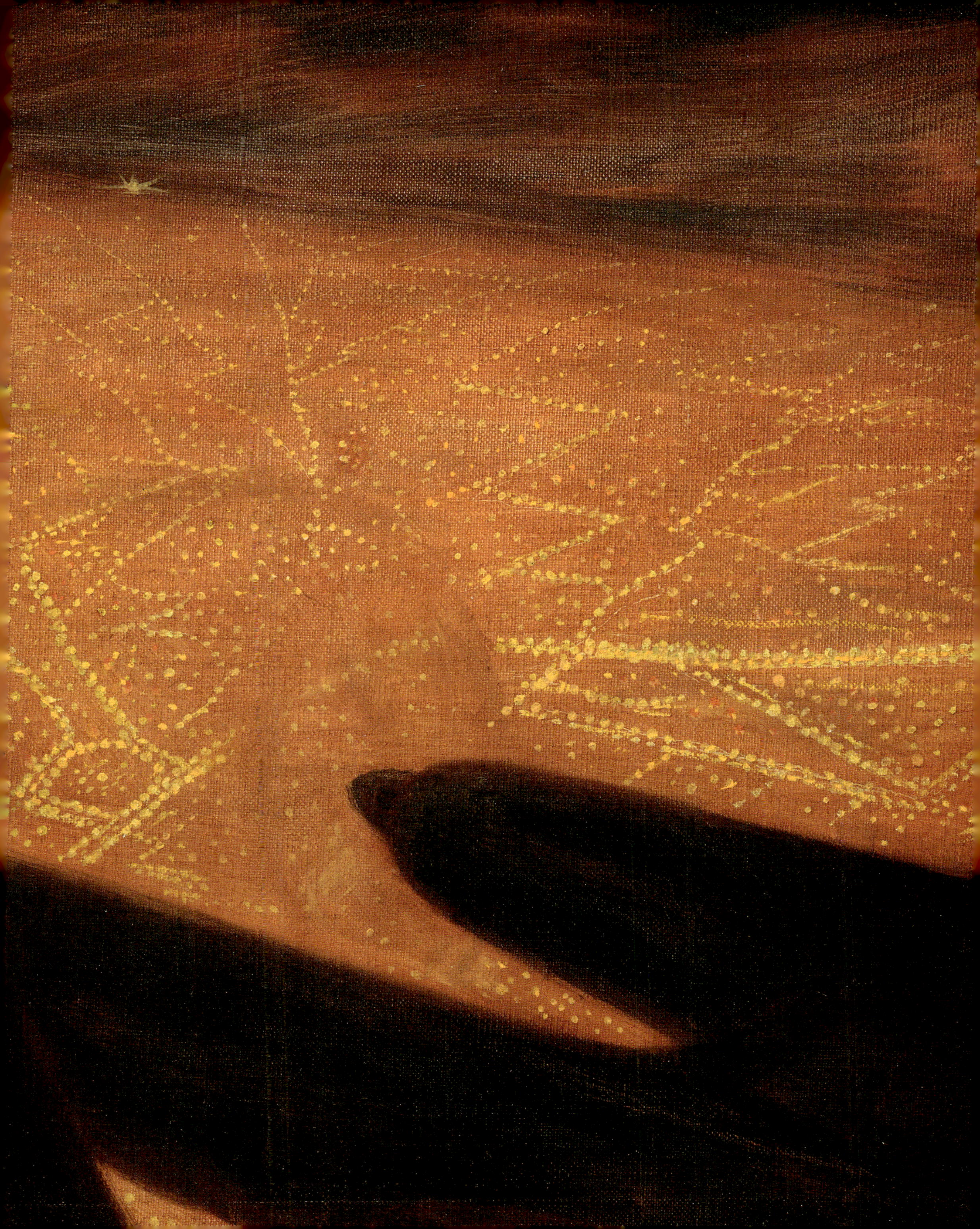

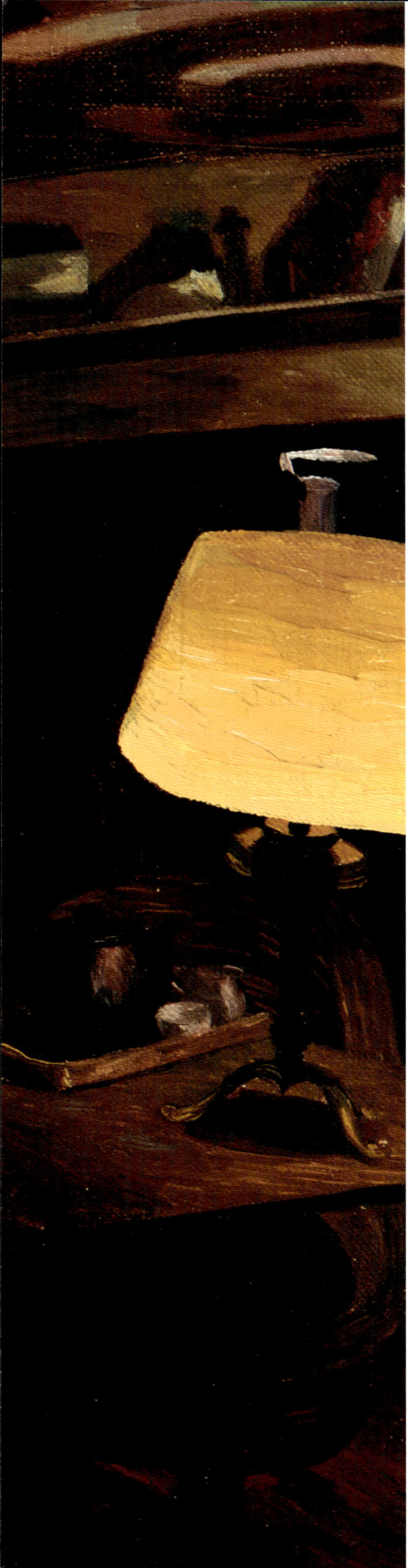

Barnett Freedman (1901-1958)

Claudia Writing by Lamplight, c. 1940

Oil on canvas - 30 x 40 cm.

Claudia Guercio was of Anglo-Sicilian parentage. She studied at Liverpool School of Art and the Royal College of Art. Working initially under her maiden name, she took the name Claudia Freedman on her marriage to Barnett Freedman in 1926. Compared to her husband, Claudia Freedman's output was relatively small, but works such as the autolithographed book My Toy Cupboard (undated but published in the 1940s by Noel Carrington's Transatlantic Arts) show that she had considerable talent. This intimate night-time scene shows Claudia at work in the country cottage which the Freedmans rented at Princes Risborough during World War Two.

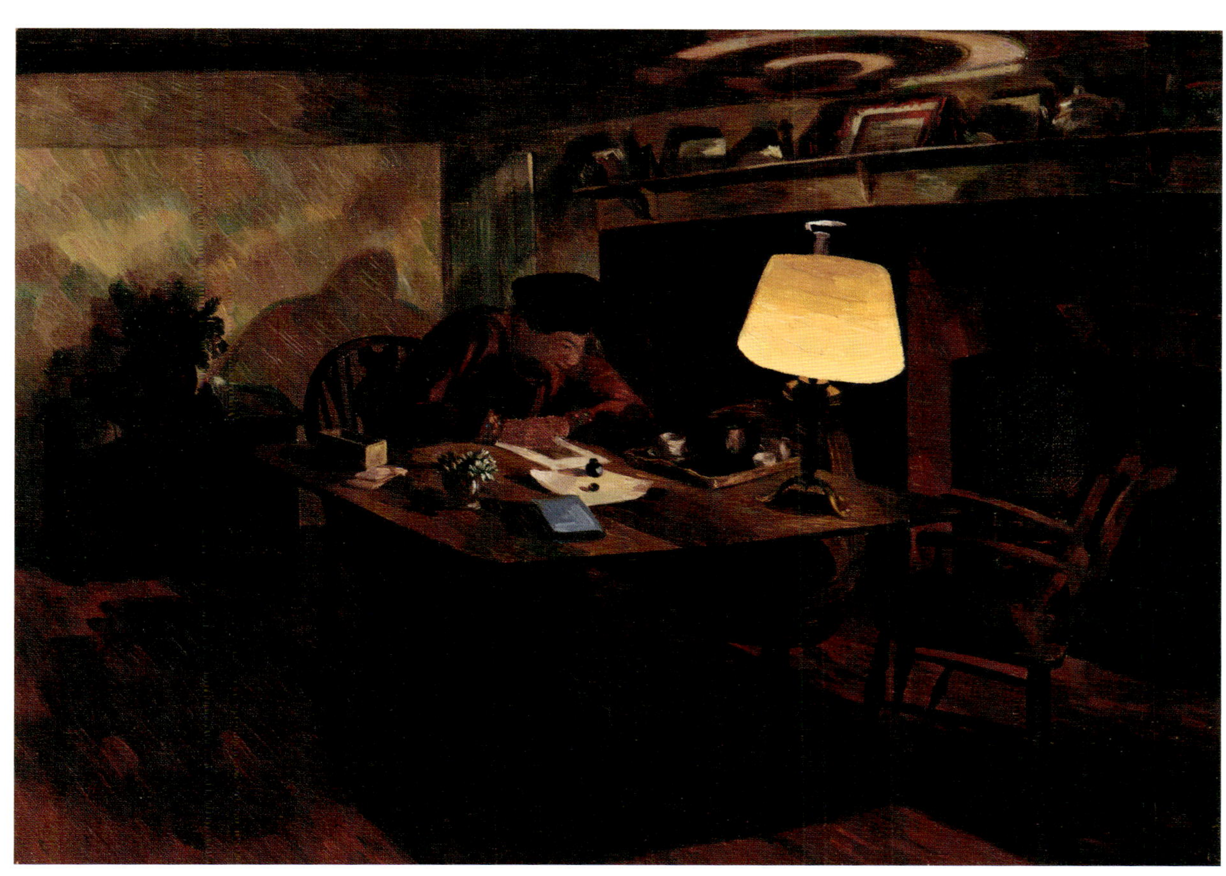

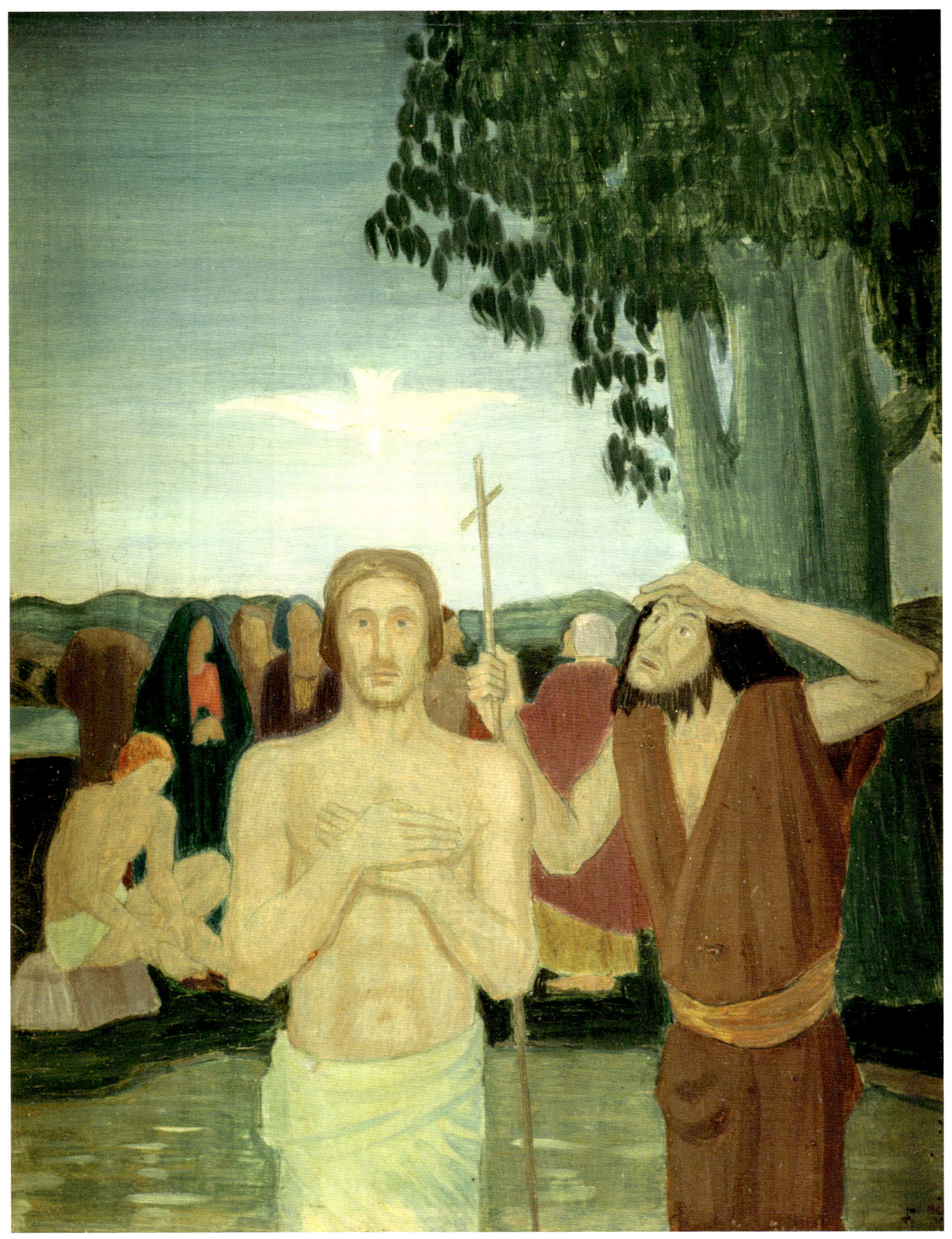

Margaret Gere (1878-1965)

The Baptism, 1924

Tempera on panel - 23.8 x 18.5 cm.

Margaret Gere, one of the leading lights in the Tempera Revival, was a self-confessed Piero acolyte, having been to Italy and studied Piero's Triumph of Battista Sforza in the Uffizi, Florence, in 1905, the year that she enrolled at the Slade. By the 1920s, when this work was created, passion for Piero had become main stream – indeed the engraver Claire Leighton recalled: 'Living, with my fellow students, in the world of early Italian painters, even to the point of dressing like figures from the world of Piero della Francesca, we did not need to search for other stimulation'.
Gere's panel is a conscientious homage rather than a pastiche. Charles Eastlake, appointed first Director of The National Gallery in 1855, purchased Piero's Baptism of Christ in 1861.
The Baptism was included in The Barbican Art Gallery's groundbreaking The Last Romantics exhibition, (catalogue No. 101)

Duncan Grant (1885-1978)

Landscape near Settignano, Florence, 1907

Oil on panel, signed with initials, title inscribed on reverse- 32.5 x 23 cm.

This painting likely dates from Duncan Grant's second visit to Florence in 1907, where he spent much of his time at I Tatti, the home of the connoisseur Bernard Berenson, in the nearby village of Settignano. Grant's introduction to Berenson is thought to have come through his cousin, Elinor Rendel (née Strachey), who was staying there. The artist arrived at I Tatti most afternoons; he took part in mixed bathing parties in a lake surrounded by trees and was smitten by the beauty of the local scenery, the fountains, the marble balustrades, cypresses and vistas of blue hills.

Grant's letters from this period speak of his frequent trips to the quarries of Settignano, a place inevitably linked in his mind to Michelangelo. Settignano was the site of the Buonarroti family's ancestral home, and where, according to his biographer Vasari, he imbibed his skills as a sculptor in the milk of his wet nurse, the wife of a stonecutter in the nearby quarries. Frances Spalding writes that while here, Grant 'slept under the trees, suffering terribly from mosquitoes and eating black bread and drinking black wine. Despite these hardy conditions, it was a romantic experience, especially when the moon rose over the vast, deserted caves held up by monolithic pillars'.

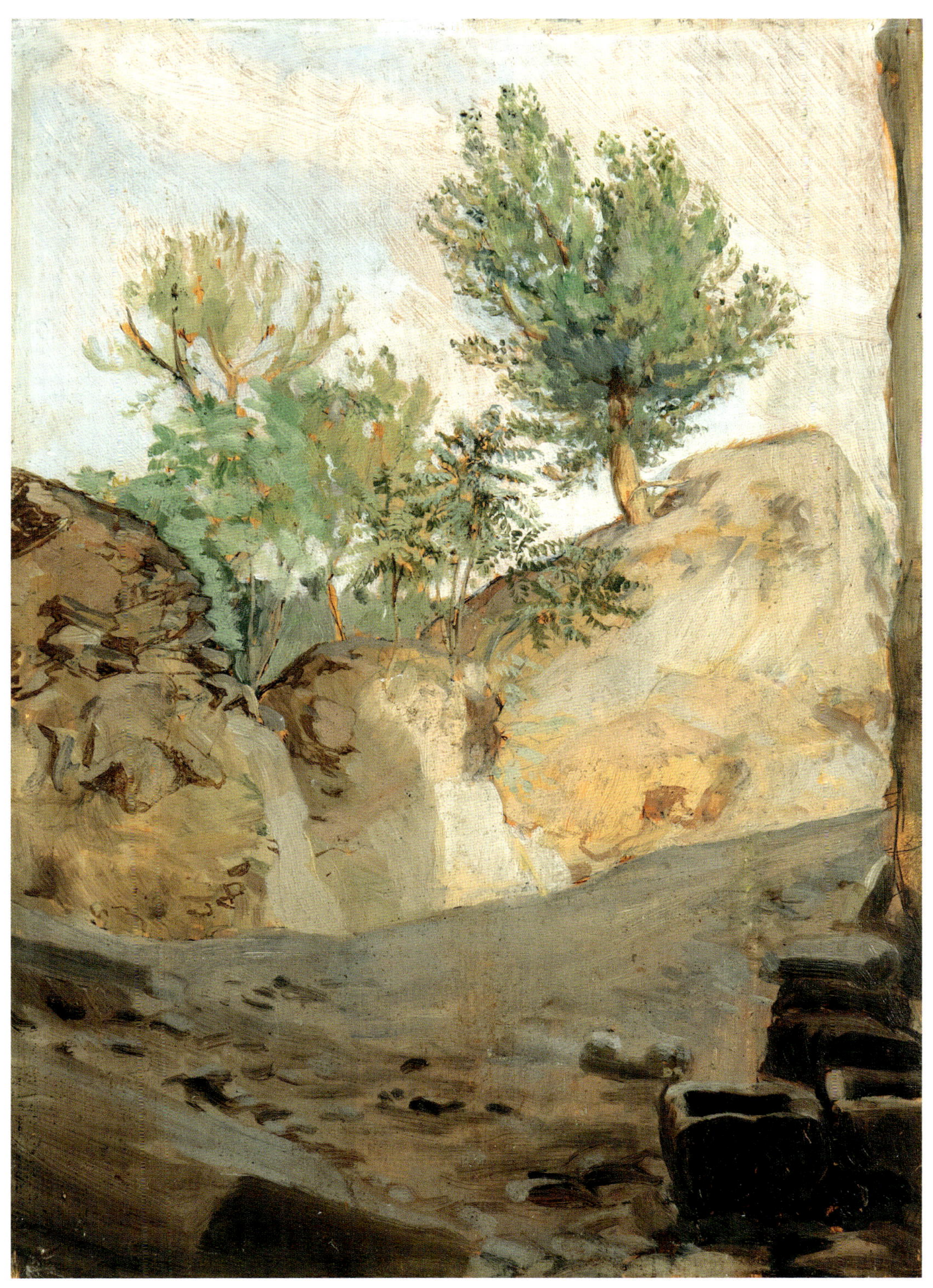

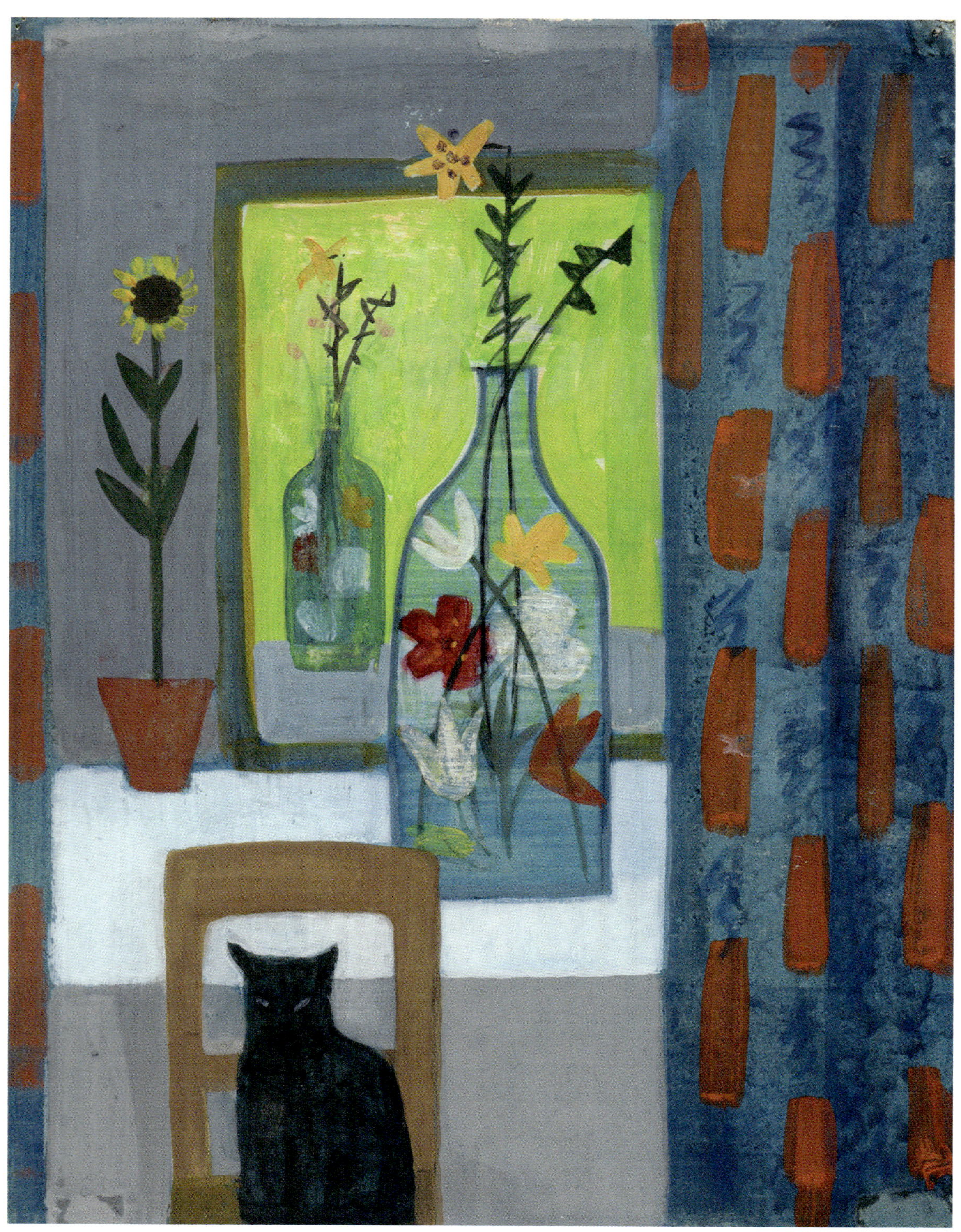

Kathleen Guthrie (1905-1981)

Cat and Flowers, late 1950's

Mixed media - 44.5 x 34.5 cm.

In the post-war years Guthrie moved towards abstraction, a process accelerated by her introduction (by Linnet Guthrie, the daughter of her first husband Robin) to the technique of silk screen printing. Increasingly her compositions evolved around the characterisitics of silkscreen printing whereby layers of pure colour could be laid over one and another without bleeding or distortion.

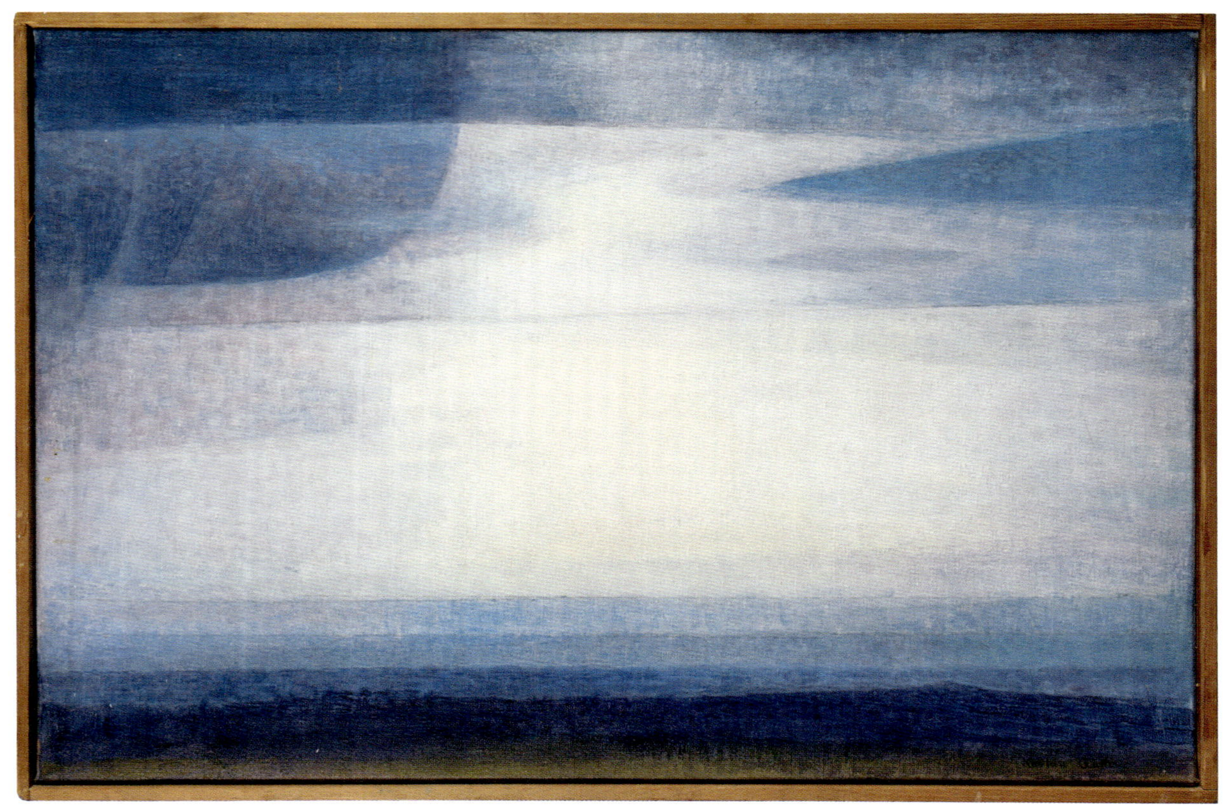

Kathleen Guthrie (1905-1981)

Wales III, c. 1960

Acrylic, signed 'Kathleen Guthrie - 56 x 76 cm.

In the 1960s Guthrie made a series of landscape painting in Wales that explored the limits between nature and abstraction.

Trained at the Slade School of Art, and married to fellow painter Robin Guthrie, Kathleen Guthrie's pre-war work was firmly figurative. Her abstract painting dates to the post-war period, after she married the Cecil Stephenson in 1941. Although clearly influenced by Stephenson, she retained a distinctive luminous, soft palette, and her brushwork remained very consistent, avoiding the hard edges and sometimes vigorous impasto of his paintings.

A solo exhibition of her work was held at the Drian Gallery in London in 1966.

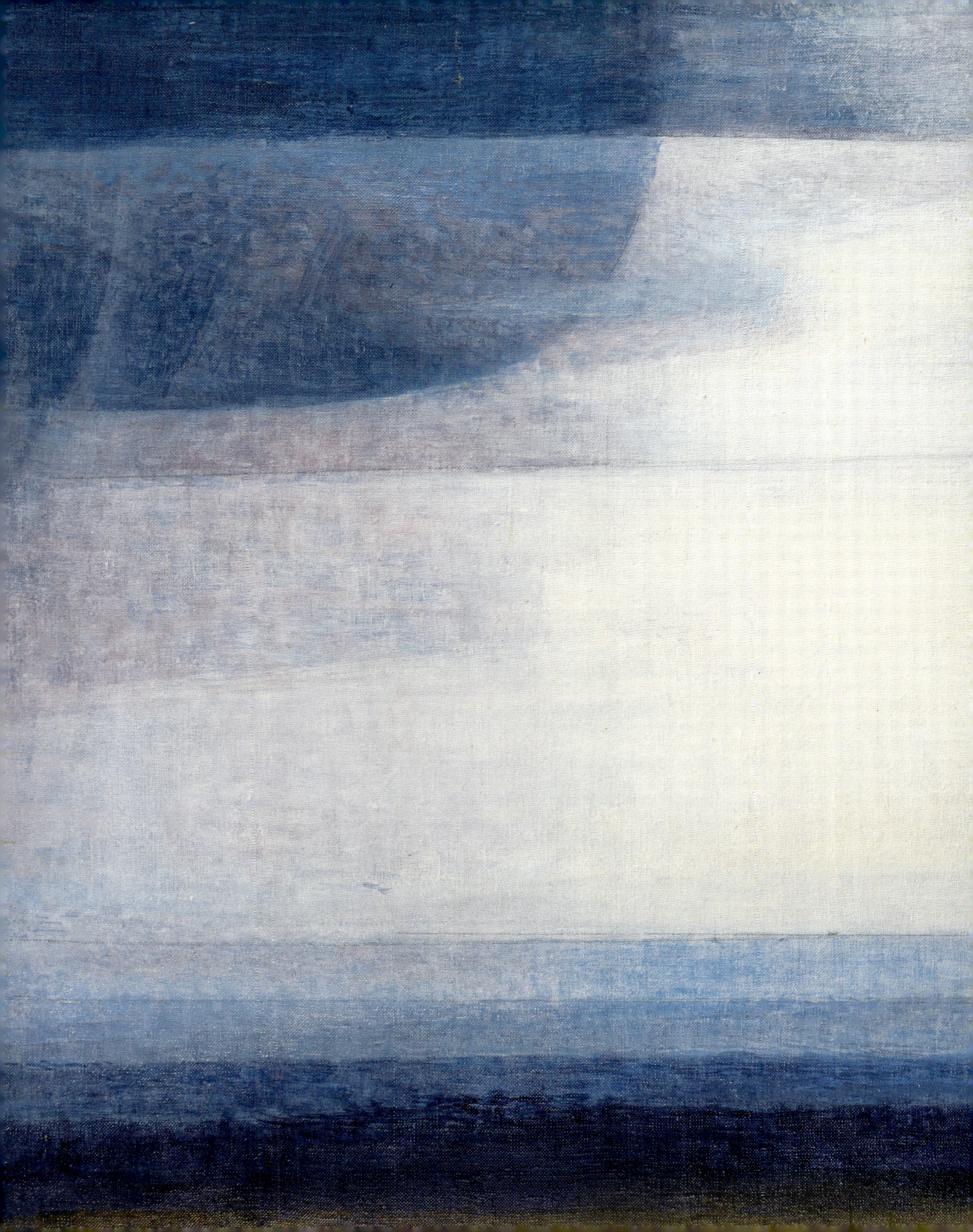

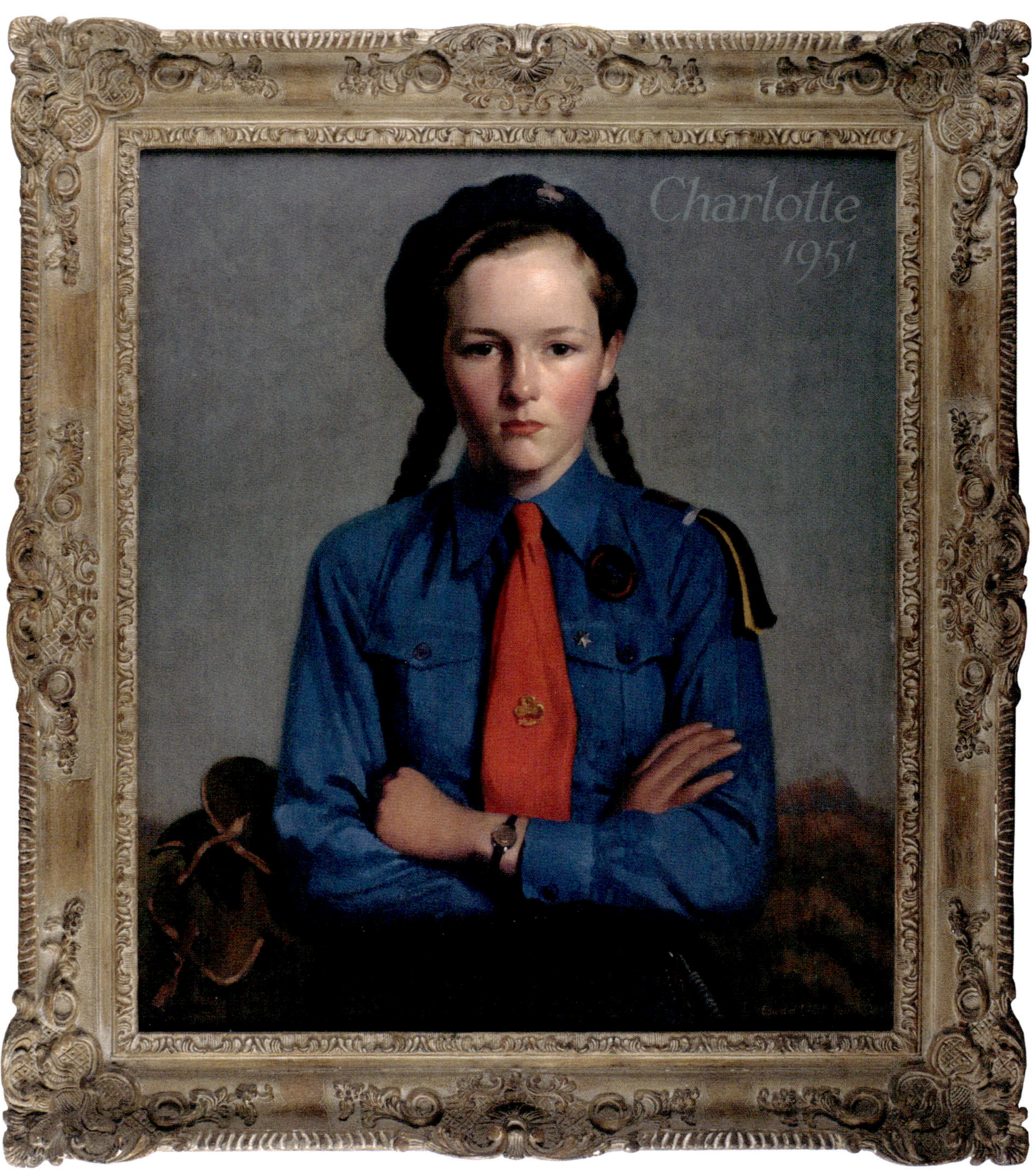
Charlotte
1951

Edward Halliday (1902-1984)

Charlotte, The Artist's Daughter, 1951

Oil on canvas, signed, titled and dated - 76.5 x 63.5 cm.

The Girl Guides formed when a group of girls stormed into a Scout rally at Crystal Palace in 1909, demanding of Robert Baden-Powell to start a sister organisation to the Scouts. The junior Guiding section, known originally as the Rosebuds and later the Brownies, was founded in 1914.

Girlguiding quickly grew into a vast and vibrant network of members, who became particularly active during wartime. Between 1914 and 1918, Guides acted as messengers for confidential information for The Marconi Wireless Telegraph. In 1940 their members raised over £50,000 to help the war effort. They even set up a committee to select and train Leaders for relief work after the war, called the Guide International Service.

Halliday's portrait of Charlotte was captured shortly after this period and before the Coronation of Elizabeth II in 1953, who was herself a former guide, and opened an international festival dedicated to the movement. The dress of the sitter reflects uniform common to the group in the 1950s. Charlotte wears a tunic shirt in 'headquarters blue', with a trefoil promise pin affixed to her tie. She wears the traditional beret and shoulder knots, whilst the badge on her chest indicates the patrol group that Charlotte belonged to.

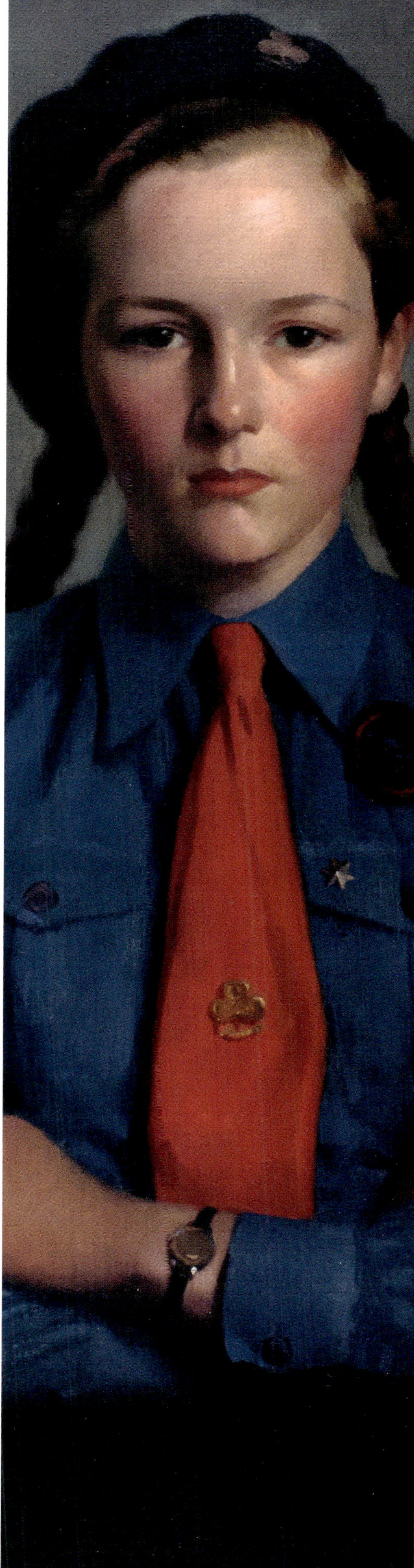

Edward Halliday (1902-1984)

Roof-terrace of the British School at Rome, 1926

Oil and tempera on panel, signed and dated lower right - 36.8 x 44.4 cm.

This evocative informal study shows Edward Halliday's fiancée, Dorothy Hatswell, and fellow student Russell Meiggs (holder of the 1925 Pelham Studentship) relaxing in deck chairs on the roof terrace of the British School at Rome. A panoramic view of the Borghese Gardens - suggesting, in its painstaking technique, the influence of fellow Rome Scholar Winifred Knights - can be seen behind.

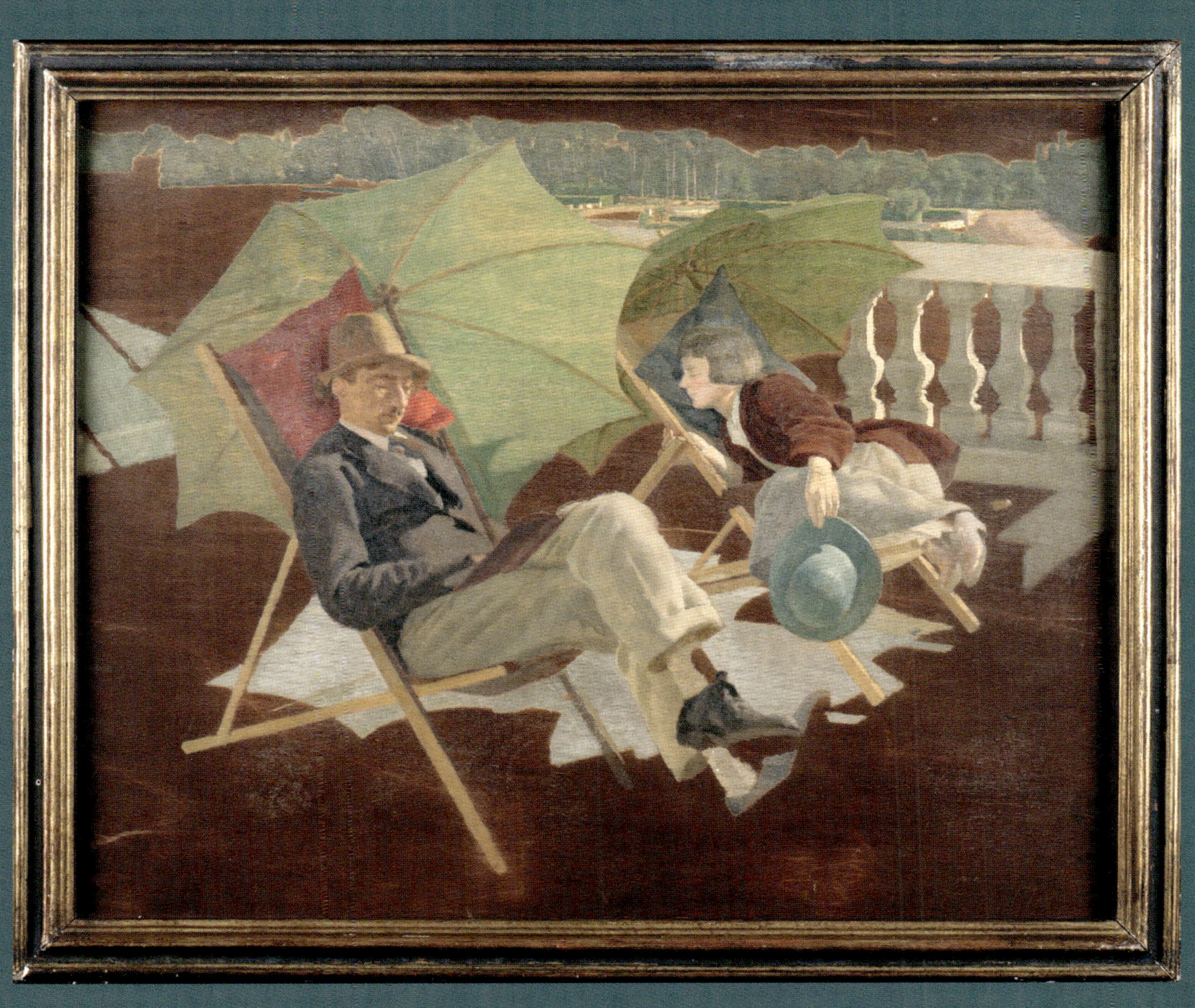

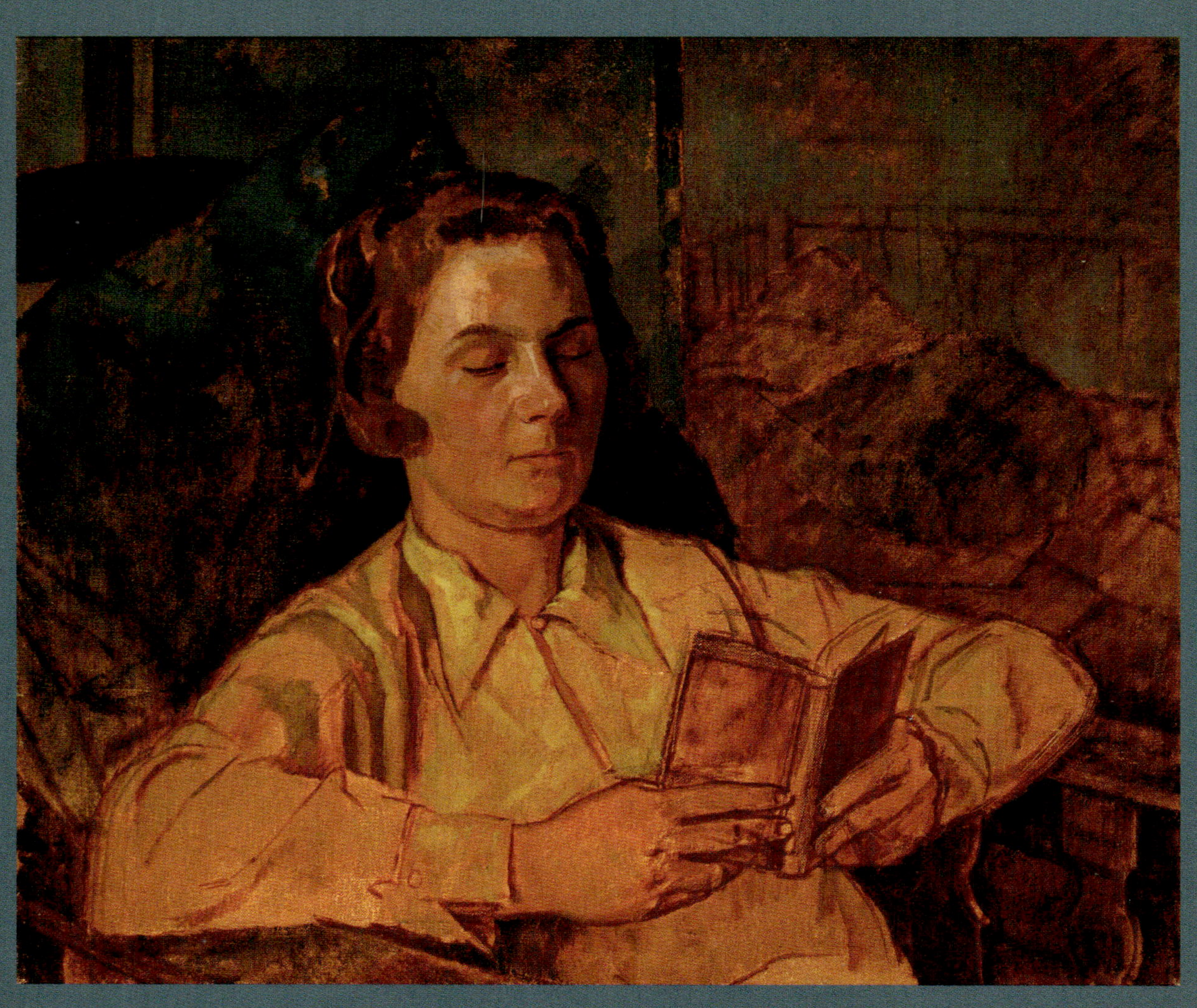

Percy Horton (1897-1970)

Joan Jenner reading, c. 1925

Oil on canvas, signed with studio stamp on reverse (2/26) - 51 x 61 cm.

Born in Brighton, Percy Horton attended the School of Art there from 1912-1916. During the First World War he became a conscientious objector and was sentenced to two years' hard labour in Calton Prison, Edinburgh, from 1916-18. After the war, he took up his studies again at the Central School of Art 1918-20 and the Royal College of Art 1922-24. Joan Jenner had a distinguished career as secretary to the Ruskin School of Drawing and Fine Art, University of Oxford, where Percy Horton was Ruskin Master. It was through the introduction of Percy Horton that Jenner met her future husband, the artist Geoffrey Rhoades, at a Royal College Ball, in the mid 1930s.

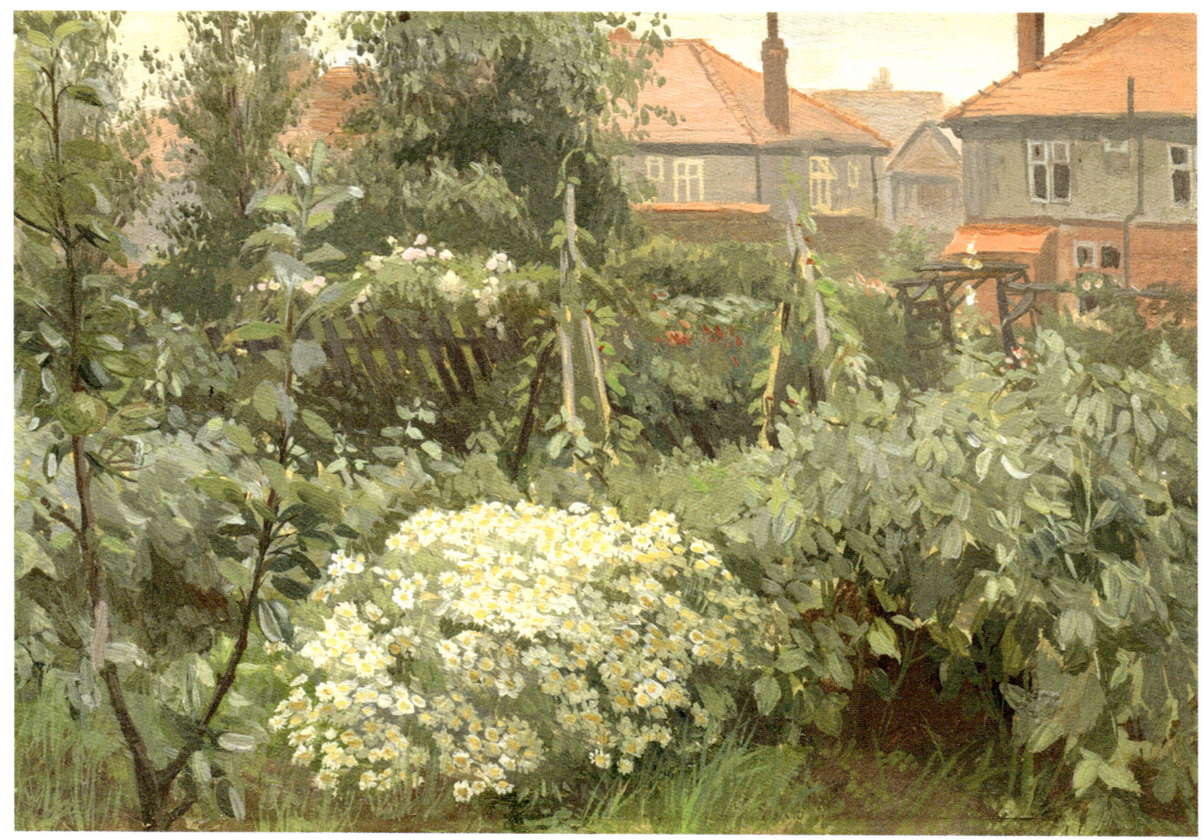

Percy Horton (1897-1970)

Suburban Garden, 1921

Oil on board, titled on a label to the reverse, with studio stamp, reference number 1/43 - 18 x 25.5 cm.

This composition probably shows back gardens in Dulwich. Percy and Lydia Horton lived at 11 Pond Cottages in Dulwich from the early 1920s to the late 1930s. Their neighbours were fellow artists James and Margaret Fitton.

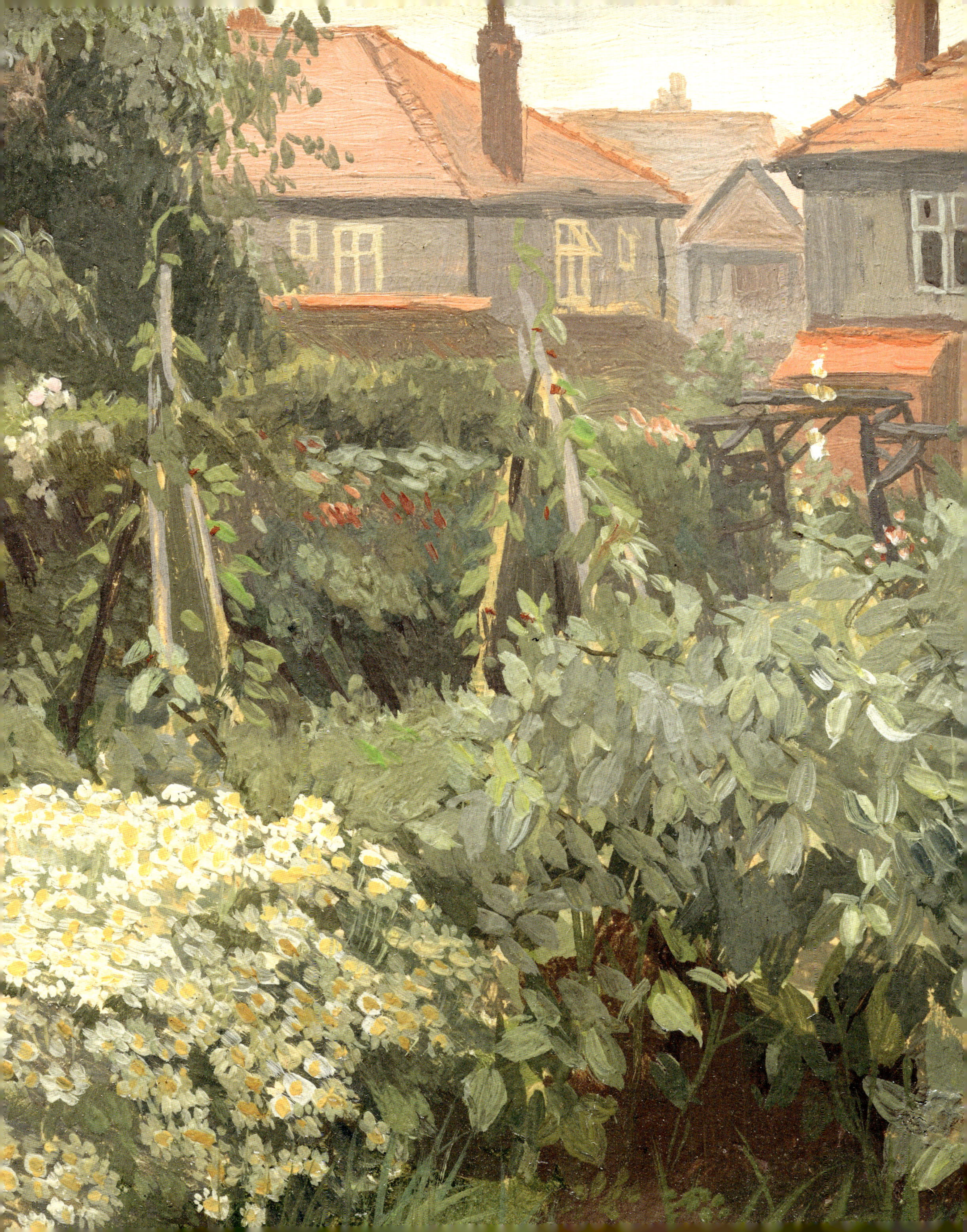

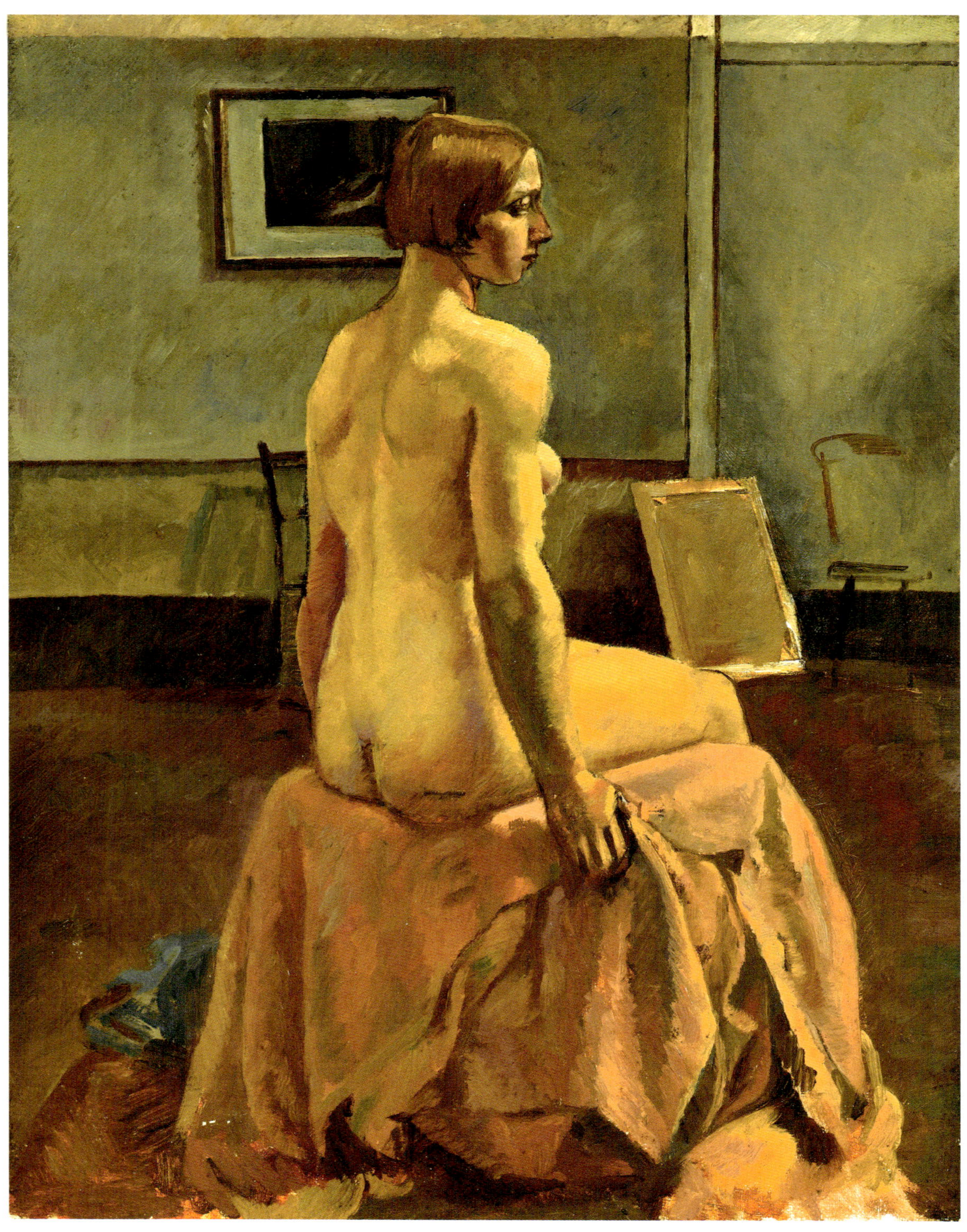

Percy Horton (1897-1970)

A Seated Model in the Studio, Three Quarter Rear View, c. 1925

Oil on canvas, signed with studio stamp on reverse (3/6) - 56 x 40.5 cm.

In 1925 he was appointed art master at Bishop's Stortford College and also began giving classes at the Working Men's College in London. As a member of the AIA (Allied International Artists) during the 1930s he believed that artists should be socially committed. He painted a series of portraits of the unemployed during the Depression.

Horton taught at the RCA between 1930 and 1949. During the Second World War the college was evacuated to Ambleside, where he produced a series of paintings of the Lake District and its people. At the request of the War Artists' Advisory Committee he drew portraits and painted scenes in war factories; this collection is now in the Imperial War Museum. In 1949 Horton was elected Ruskin Master of Drawing at Oxford University. He remained in this post until his retirement in 1964.

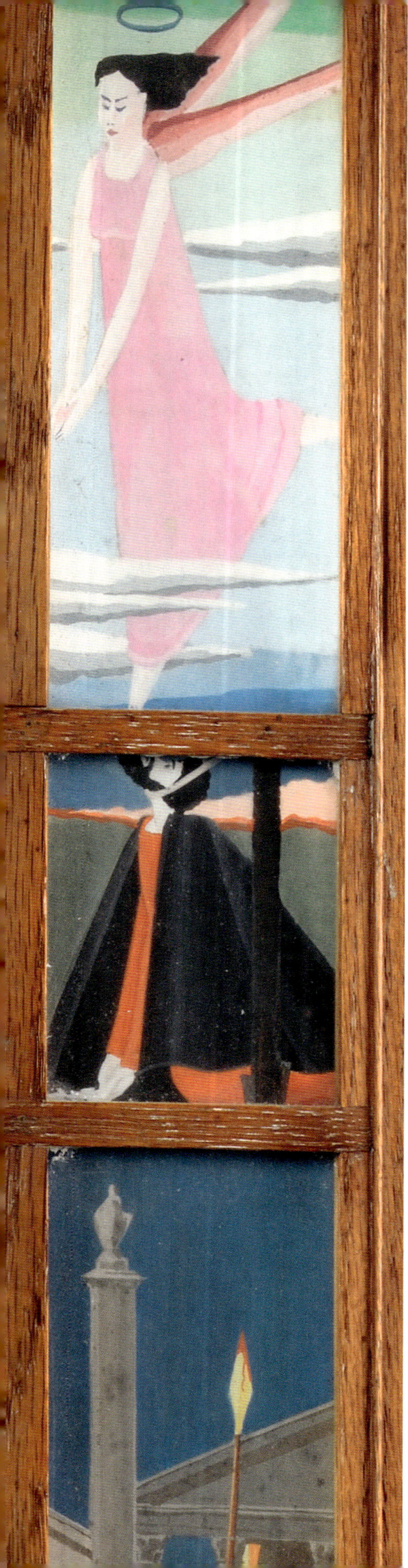

Laura A. Jewis (1896-)

Scenes from the Life of Christ, 1937

Tempera on panels, signed and dated - 89 x 50 cm.

The polyptych form of this altarpiece, with its specially designed plain wooden frame, is highly original. This central section depicts a combined crucifixion and deposition; the figure in the foreground on the right is possibly a Dominican or a Benedictine saint. Little is known about Jewis - though this work has similarities to that of David Jones, the striking colour combinations and composition suggest that she had a highly distinctive style of her own. The artist was evidently fully aware of the work of David Jones.

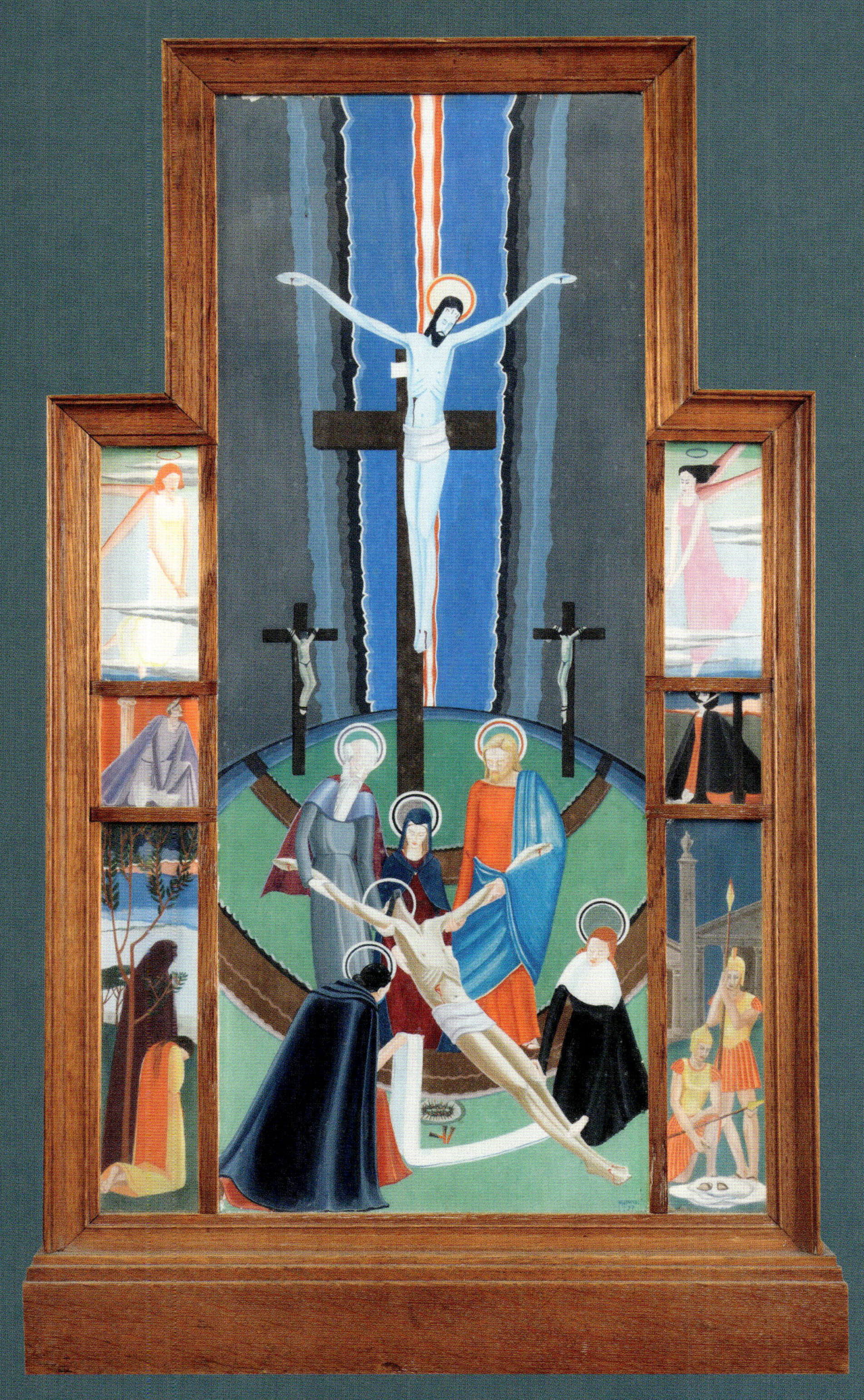

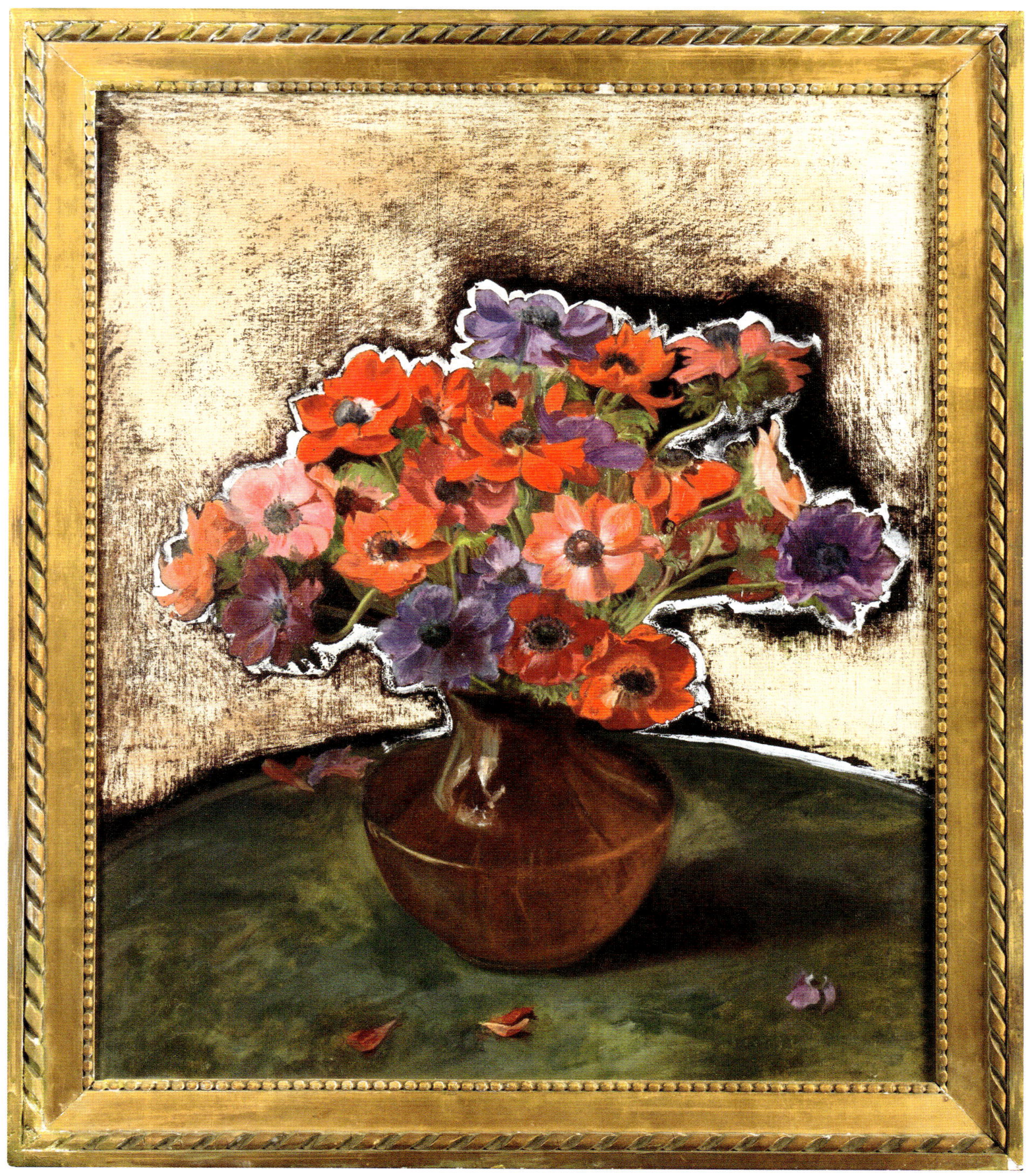

Sir Gerald Kelly (1879-1972)

Still Life with Anemones, c. 1930

Oil on canvas - 70 x 52 cm.

Kelly painted still lifes only rarely and mostly for his own pleasure. He was brilliantly adept at this: in this virtuoso performance Kelly has built the composition from the bottom up, first painting the green foreground, which acts as a foil for three weightless fallen petals. The background, in this case unfinished, to dramatic effect, would have been painted in last.

John Napper, Kelly's studio assistant, recalled: 'His slow painstaking methods made sure that there was always work in hand in the studio: portraits, landscapes, Burmese dancers, still-lives, started sometimes many years previously, would be got out, washed down, worked on, put away, and so on.'

Napper also bemoaned the fact that Kelly was obsessive about never using the same brush twice without it being cleaned, so that his colours remained jewel-like. This resulted in Napper having to clean as many as 200 brushes a day.

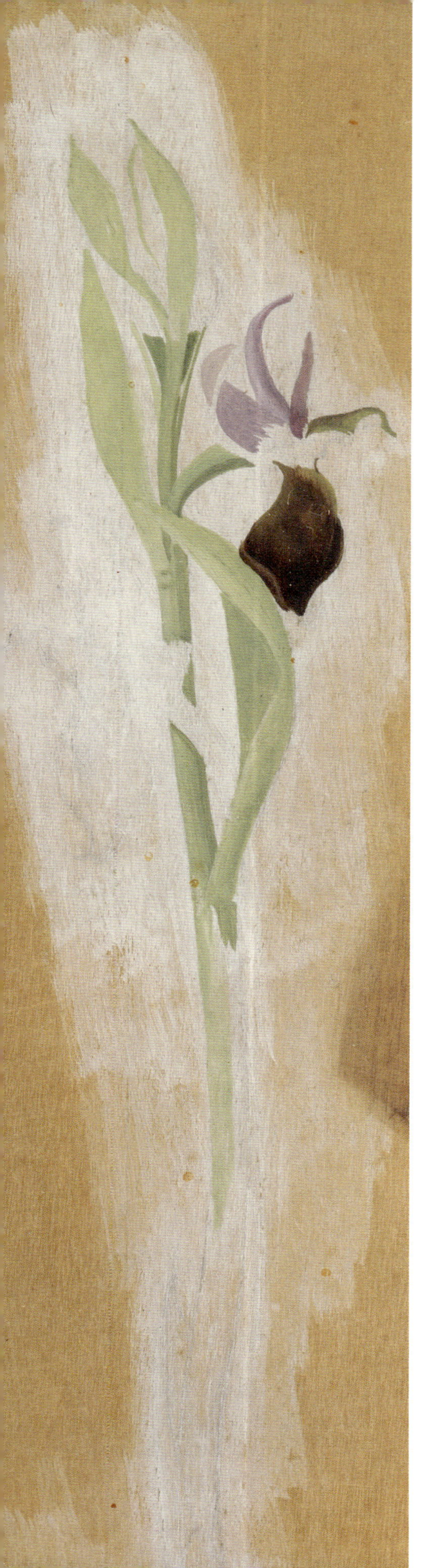

Winifred Knights (1899-1947)

Study of *Ophrys Bertolonii*, commonly known as Bertoloni's Bee Orchid, c. 1925

Tempera on panel, inscribed to reverse - 16 x 15 cm.

'Two nights ago, I stood and listened to a nightingale singing in a garden nearby it was delicious, quite near me in a tree overhead. I could have stayed for hours. Oh this is a wonderful place, I went to Lake Nomi again the fields are one mass of purple orchids and white Narcissi & pink cyclamen, & blue anemones. I never saw such wild flowers.' (Letter from Winifred Knights to her mother, The British School, Valle Giulia, Sunday 17th April 1921.)

This study, painted en plein air whilst Knights was in Italy, shows a bee orchid, possibly Ophrys Bertolonii, commonly known as Bertoloni's Bee Orchid.

Knights drew flowers throughout her life. Her last last major painting, which was never completed, The Flight into Egypt, was set along a bank of bluebells and narcissi.

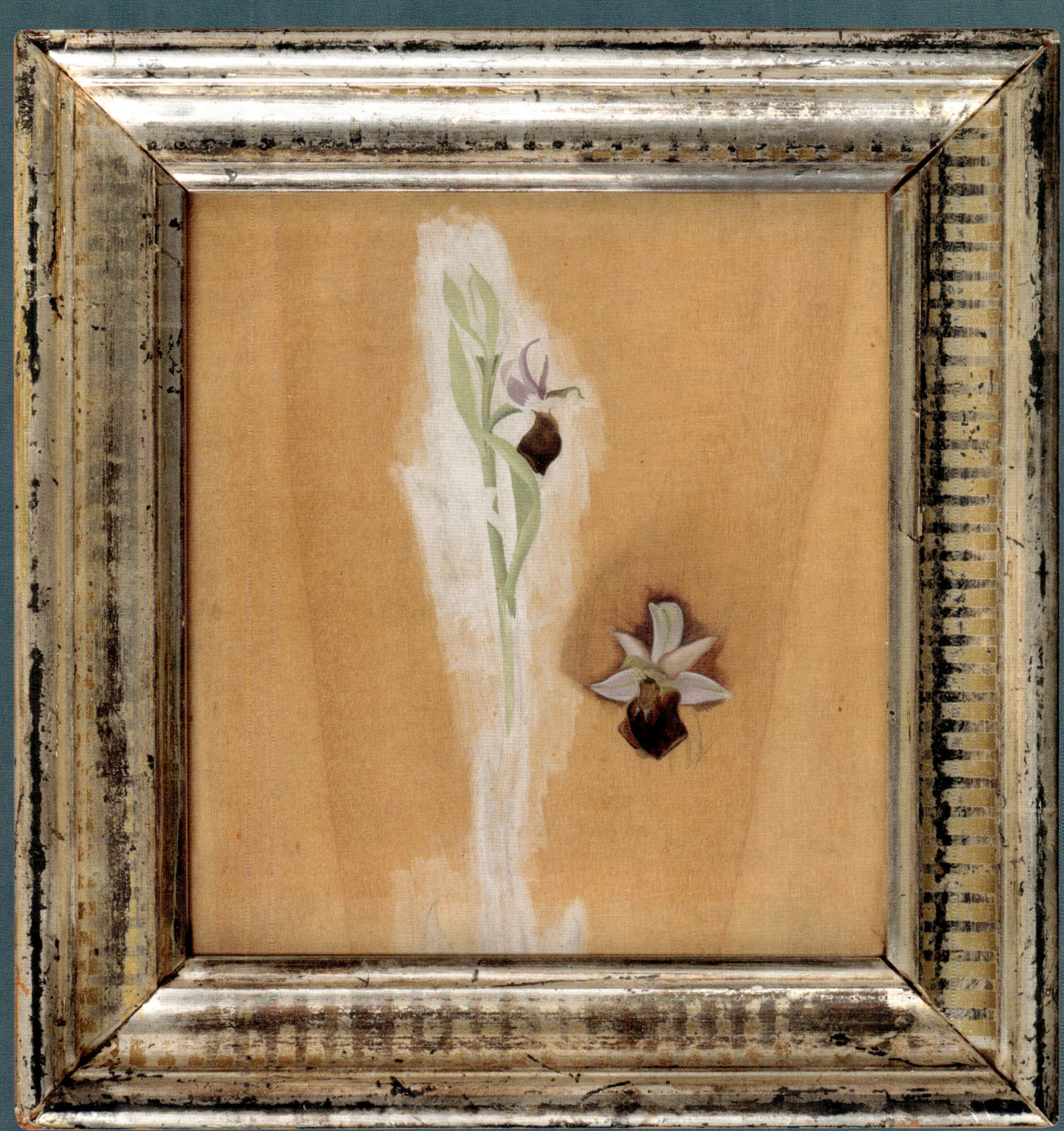

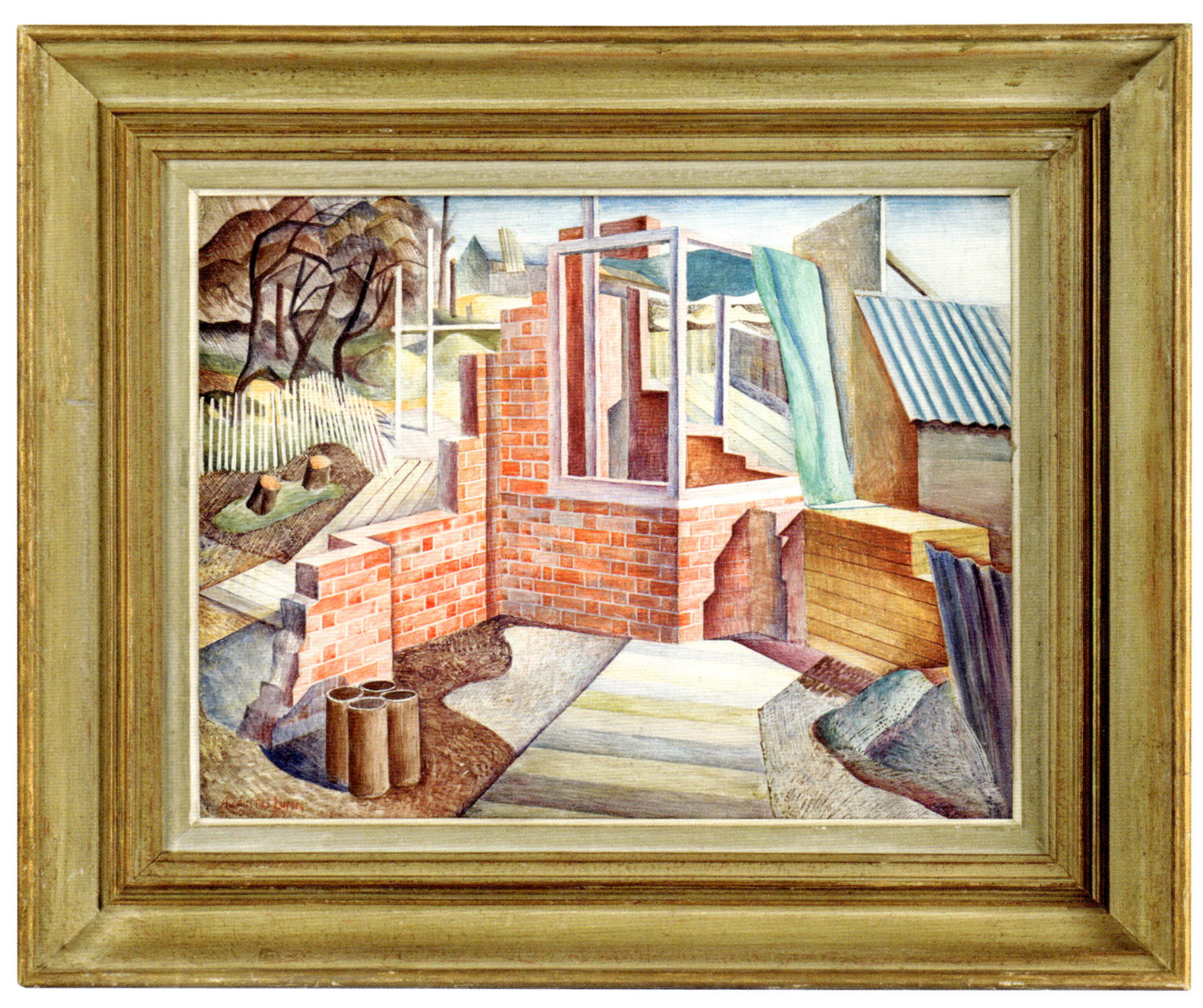

Augustus Lunn (1905-1986)

Building Site, 1937

Tempera on panel, signed and dated - 29.5 x 37.5 cm.

Augustus Lunn was a key figure in the revival of tempera painting in Britain. He trained at the Royal College of Art, to which he won a scholarship, during the principalship of William Rothenstein. Lunn admired the work of Giorgio de Chirico and Fernand Léger, and a strongly Surrealist element is present in much of his output, as well as a tendency towards abstraction. Of his own compositions he explained, 'I am never interested in recording a scene. I want to reconstruct.'

Charles Mahoney (1903-1968)

Children sleeping – illustration to a fable, mid 1920s

Oil on board - 25.5 x 30.5 cm.

From his earliest days as an art student Mahoney showed a vivid imagination in the form of illustrated letters (see Tate Archive, especially his correspondence with Bawden) and a keen interest in Mural and Theatre design, especially after meeting Geoffrey Rhoades in 1924. His daughter Elizabeth (born in 1944) recalls that her father loved to recount children's stories: Beauty and the Beast, Hansel and Gretel, Jack and the Beanstalk, the Tale of the Very Fat Man, the Very Tall Thin Man, and the Very Short Man.' The fables of the Brothers Grimm were amongst his favourite stories. A study related to this picture is in the collection of the V&A Museum of Childhood.

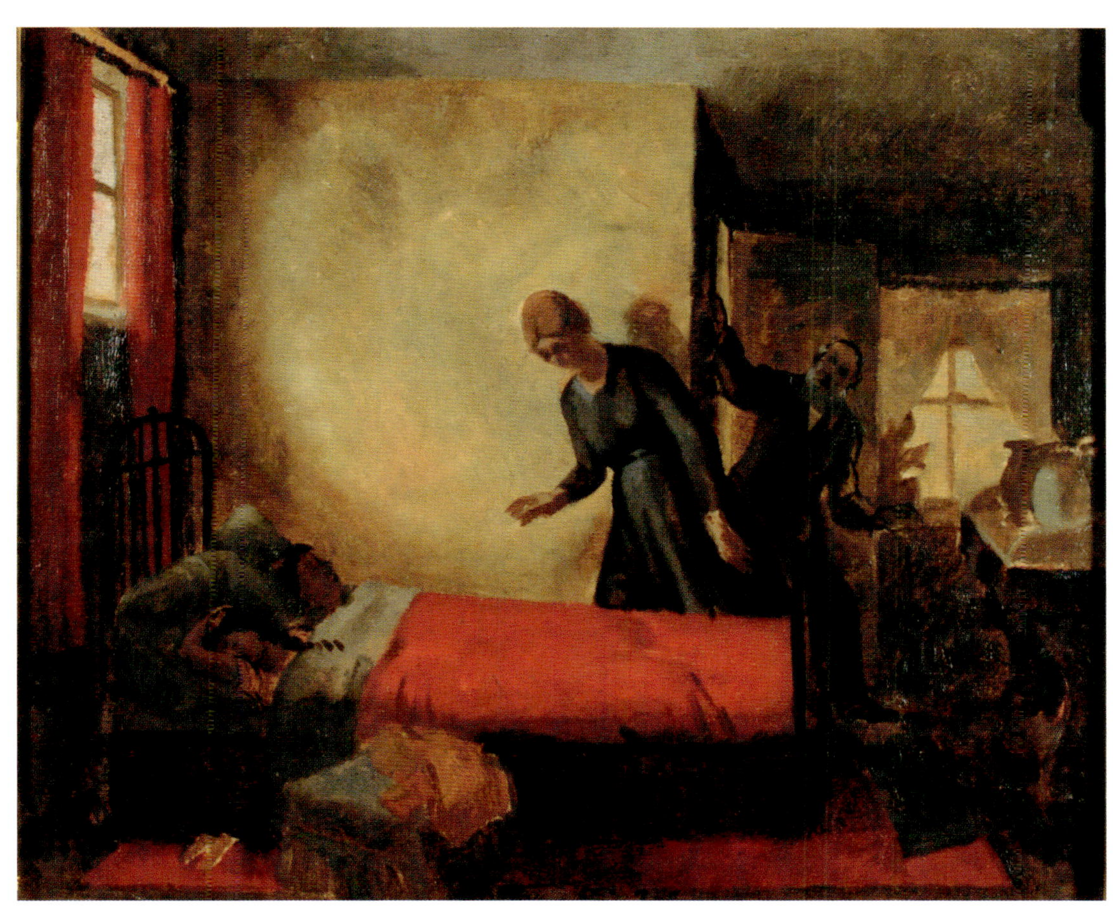

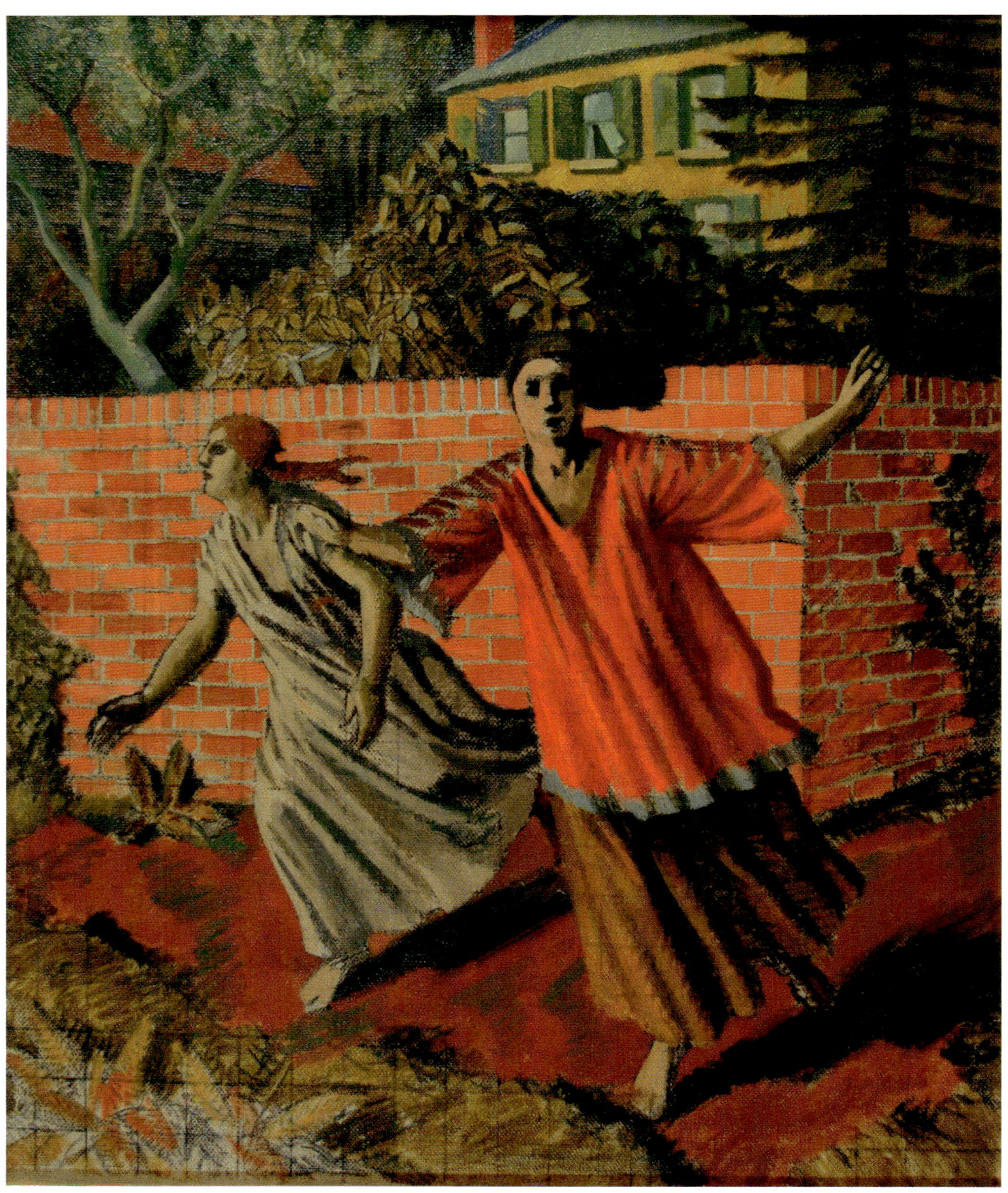

Charles Mahoney (1903-1968)

Fleeing figures, mid 1920s

Oil on canvas - 71 x 61 cm.

Elements of this painting – the palette, the application of the paint and the squaring-up for transfer – suggest that it might relate to one of Mahoney's mural schemes of the period. The device of the brick wall dividing the middle ground recalls the work of Stanley Spencer. Mahoney, in turn, might have influenced Carel Weight (five years his junior) for whom tilted, fleeing figures became his favourite leitmotif. Dreams, sometimes nightmares, were a recurrent theme in Mahoney's oeuvre. He was very intrigued, and in part influenced, from the mid 30s onwards by the advent of surrealism.

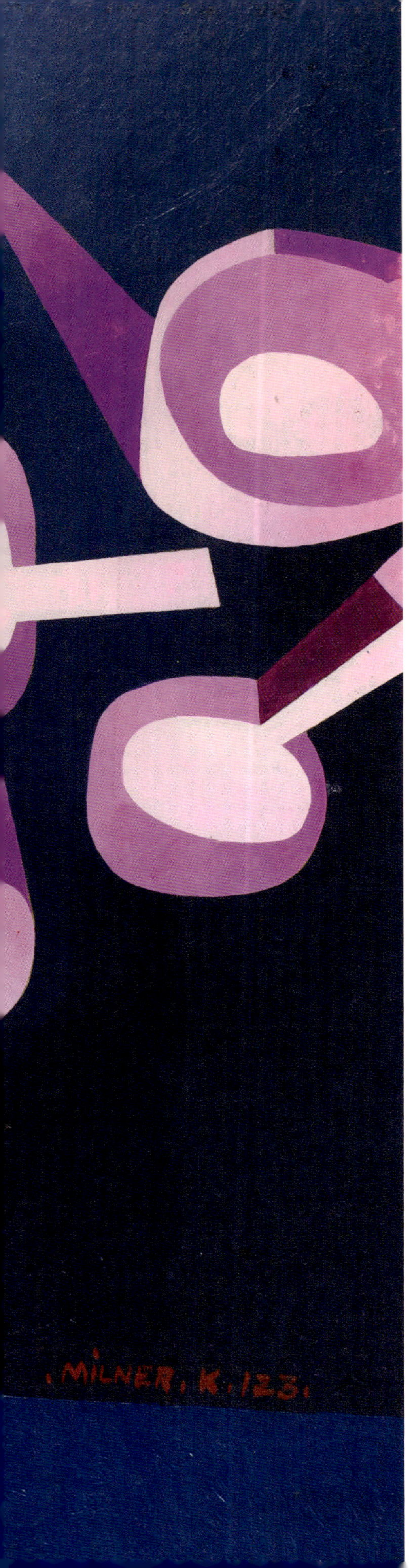

Allan Milner (1910-1984)

The match (K123), 1960

Oil on board, signed and inscribed - 50.5 x 62 cm.

The numbers that appear alongside Milner's signature are actually the titles of his pictures, which were classified by a series of figures, often prefixed by a letter. His abstract compositions show him to have been a technically brilliant artist with a highly developed sense of form and colour. Milner exhibited in mixed exhibitions at the Mayor Gallery, Redfern Gallery and Gimpel Fils and had solo shows at E.L.T. Mesens London Gallery (1949) and Woodstock Gallery (1967).

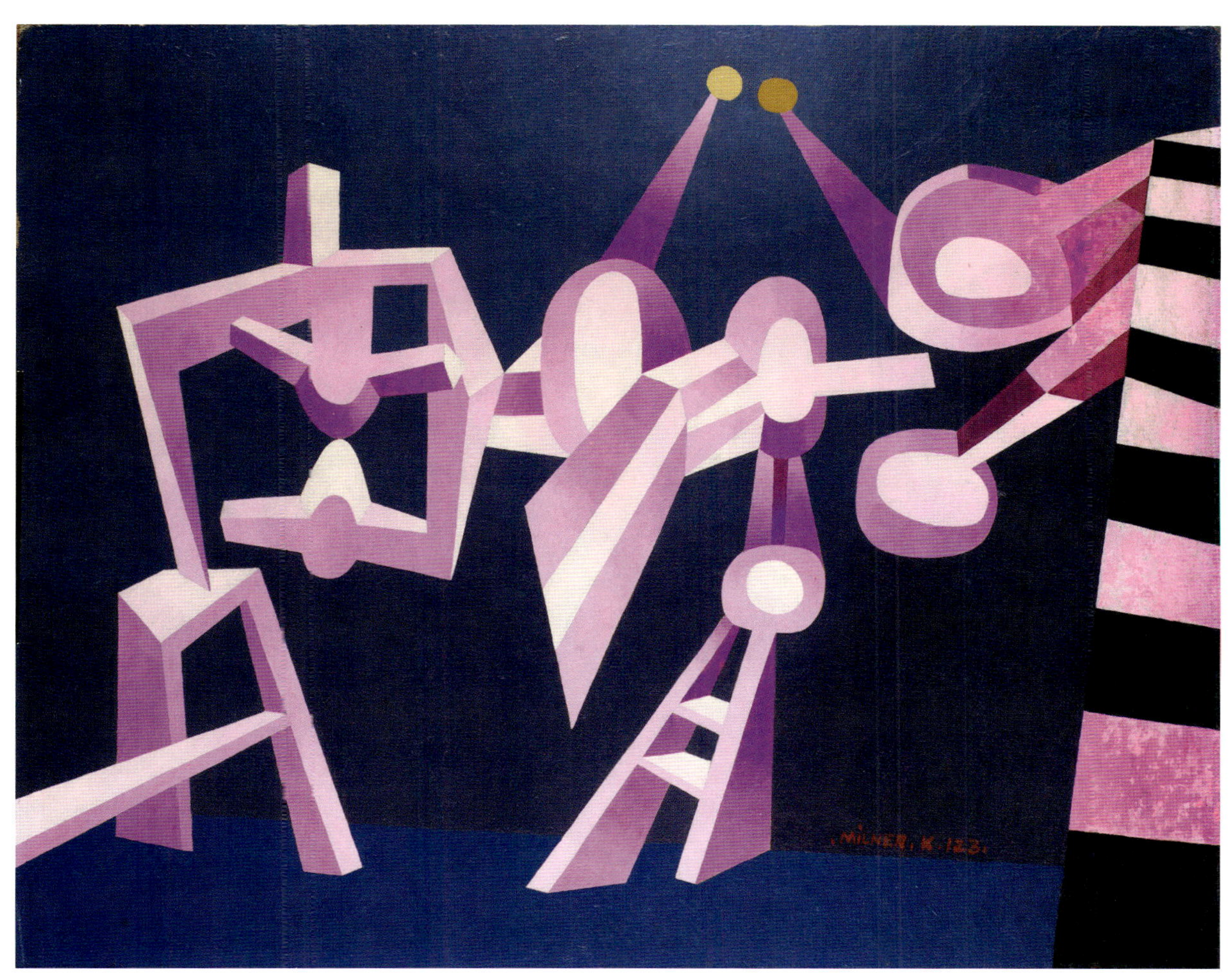
.MILNER. K.'23.

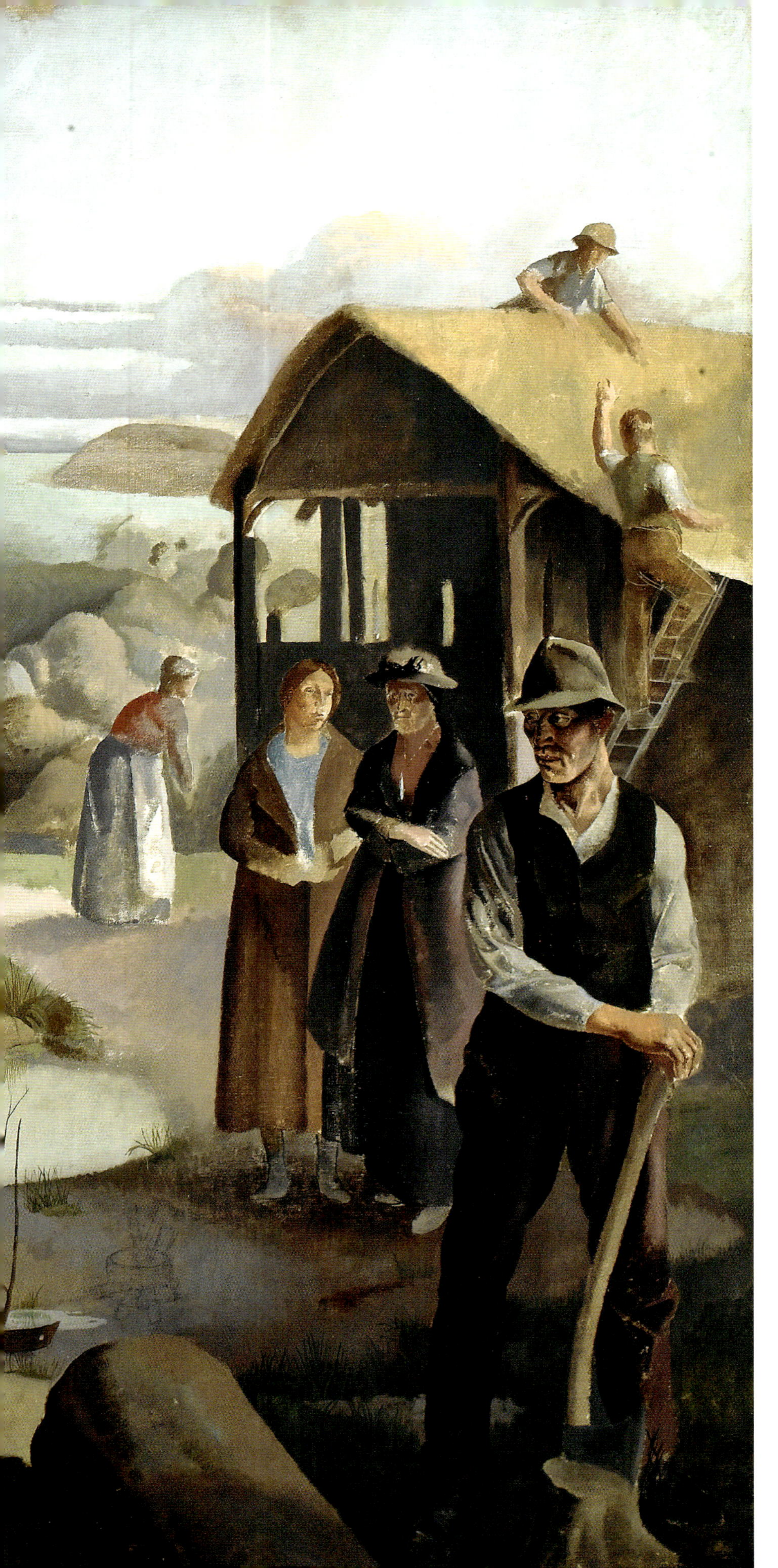

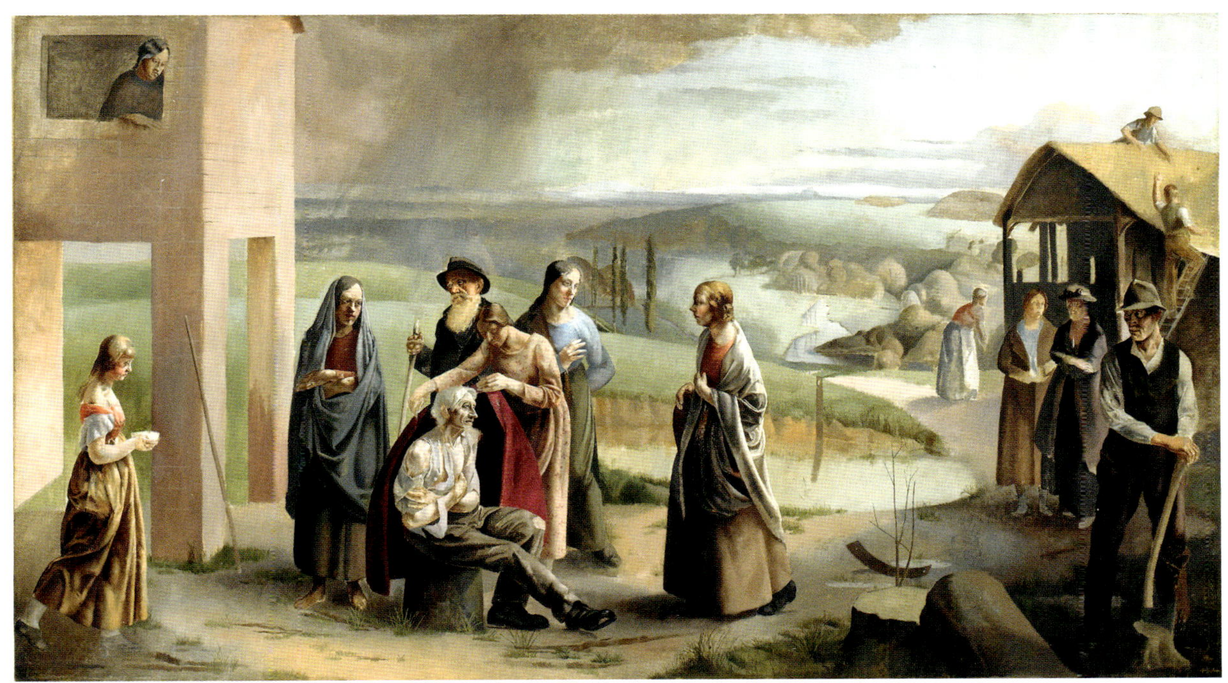

Sir Thomas Monnington (1902-1976)

Winter, 1922

Oil on canvas - 122 x 216 cm.

Winter was Monnington's winning submission for the 1922 British School at Rome Scholarship in Decorative Painting. The landscape is based on studies looking towards Clerebury Rings, near Salisbury, undertaken during visits in 1921 to the artist's cousin Dr R. C. Monnington. In a review in The Observer (22 February 1923), P. C. Konody praised Monnington's painting for being steeped in the best traditions of the Italian Renaissance : 'His colour is dull, but there is a marked sense of style in his design'.

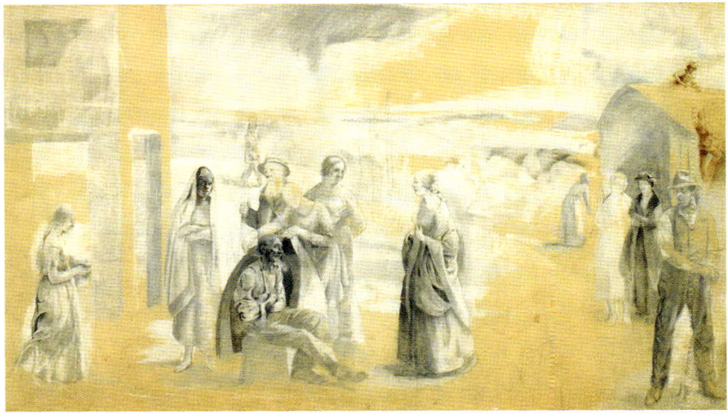

Cartoon for Winter

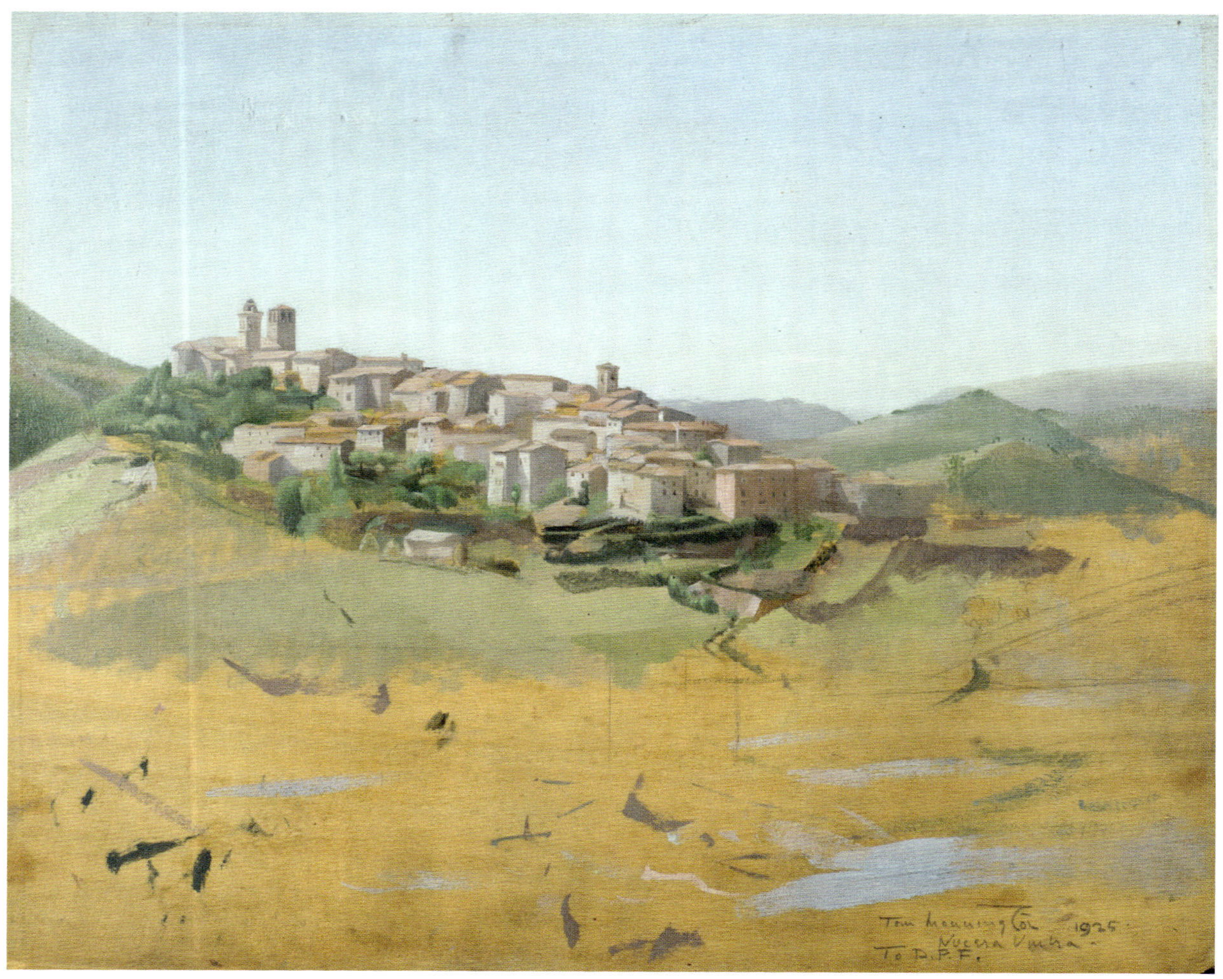

Sir Thomas Monnington (1902-1976)

Nocera Umbra, 1925

Tempera on panel, signed, dated, titled and dedicated 'to DPF' in pencil - 25.5 x 30.5 cm.

In 1925, Monnington was completing his final year as the 1922 Scholar in Decorative Painting at The British School in Rome. Having married Winifred Knights in 1924 the newly-weds made several painting trips outside Rome visiting their favourite haunts, especially in the province of Perugia. This panel, painted en plein air, was produced in the same year that Monnington was completing his epic Allegory, now in the Tate.

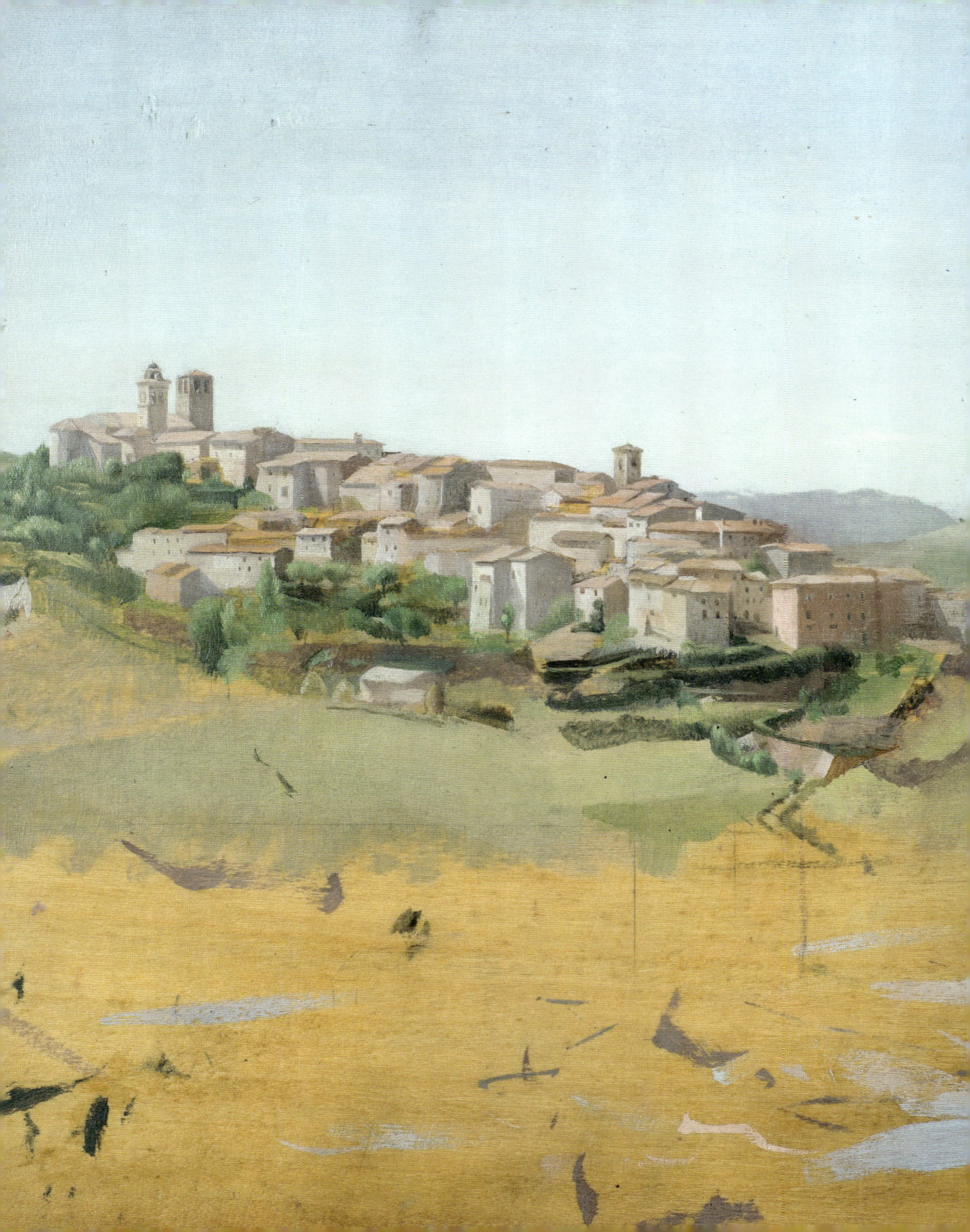

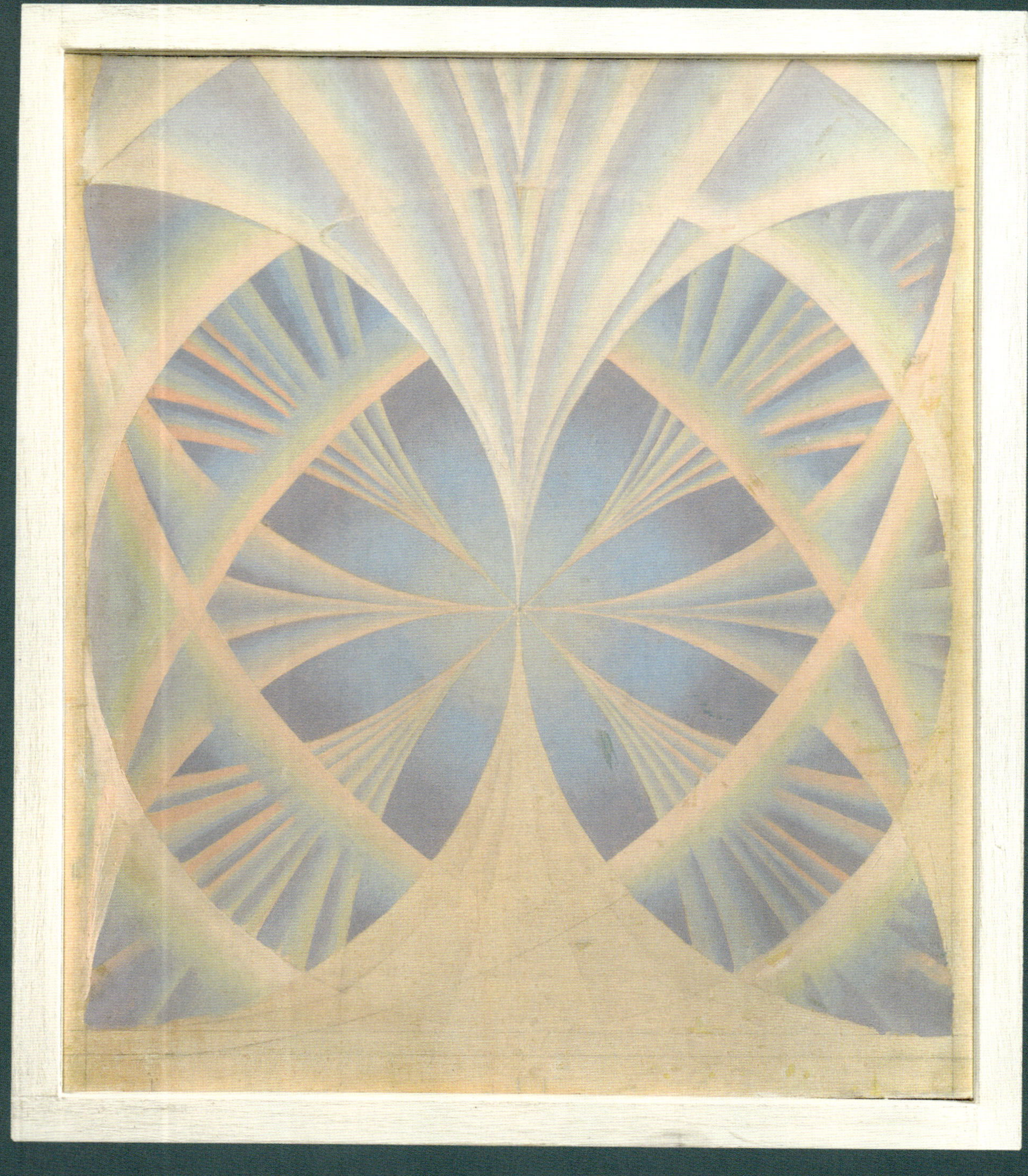

Sir Thomas Monnington (1902-1976)

Study for Bristol Ceiling, 1953

Tempera on panel, signed - 60 x 52 cm.

Monnington was commissioned to paint the ceiling of The New Bristol Council House, designed by Vincent Harris, in 1953. The ceiling, measuring 95 x 45 feet (over 4000 square feet), is amongst the largest post-war decorative schemes in Europe. Monnington insisted on painting in the Renaissance manner, directly on to wet plaster. The colours were ground and mixed with an emulsion of eggs, chalk and water. Bristol's Clerk of the Works delivered baskets of eggs daily.

According to Judy Egerton, 'A suggestion by the Bristol city fathers that the subject should be 'something connected with the Merchant Adventurers' fell on deaf ears. Monnington determined that his design should instead commemorate those scientific achievements which future Bristolians would associate with the mid-twentieth century, and which he himself had become excited by over the last twenty years: modern nuclear physics; electronics, which had enthralled him first in the shape of radio masts and later in radar equipment; aeronautics, whose laws he had begun to comprehend during the war; and biochemistry, where enlarged photographs of recent research revealed amazing quasi-abstract patterns.'

Monnington's design bears similarities to the paintings of the Italian futurist Balla but is underwritten by his deep admiration for Piero della Francesca, constructed as it is along the lines of the Golden Section. A number of studies for the ceiling are in the collection of the Victoria and Albert Museum, The Science Museum and Bristol City Art Gallery. Monnington's assistant W.B. (Peter) Lowe recalls: 'Tom maintained that it was difficult to draw angels in the twentieth-century and was comforted by the enduring qualities of geometry and light.'

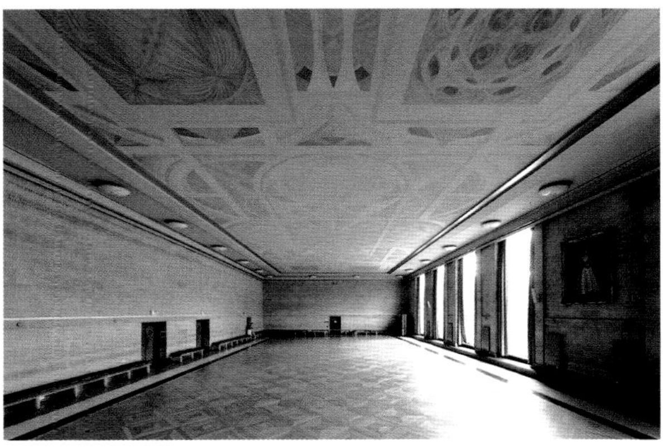

Sir Thomas Monnington (1902-1976)

Design for Students Union, University of London, 1969

Tempera on panel - 43.2 x 33 cm.

'It has been a failing all my life that I take a long time to resolve a painting problem. I take a year to do one painting because I make innumerable studies preparing the way. I am now preparing something for the summer exhibition, I expect that I will use that as a basis for the mural' (interview in The Sunday Express, 1969).

The mural to which Monnington refers, and for which this painting is the study, was commissioned by the Edwin Austin Abbey Trust for Mural Painting in Great Britain and completed and installed in the early 1970s. It was later removed from the Students' Union and is assumed to have been destroyed.

Monnington was the first President of the Royal Academy to encourage the exhibition of abstract works at the Academy, including his own. Although in 1967 the Chantrey Bequest acquired Square Design 1966 for the Tate Gallery, his significant contribution to post-war art in Britain has since been largely ignored.

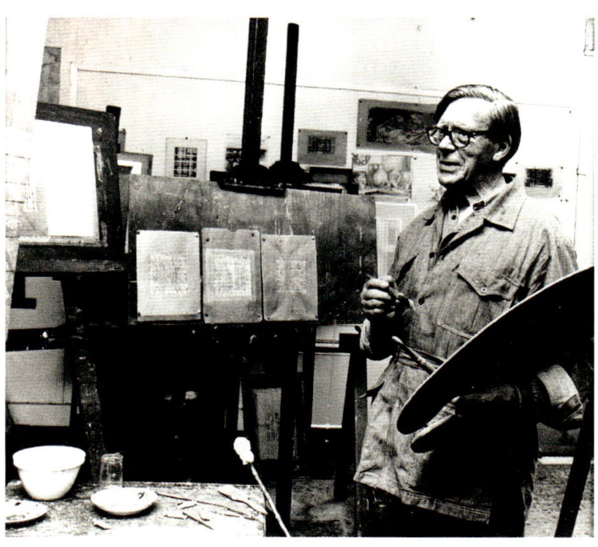

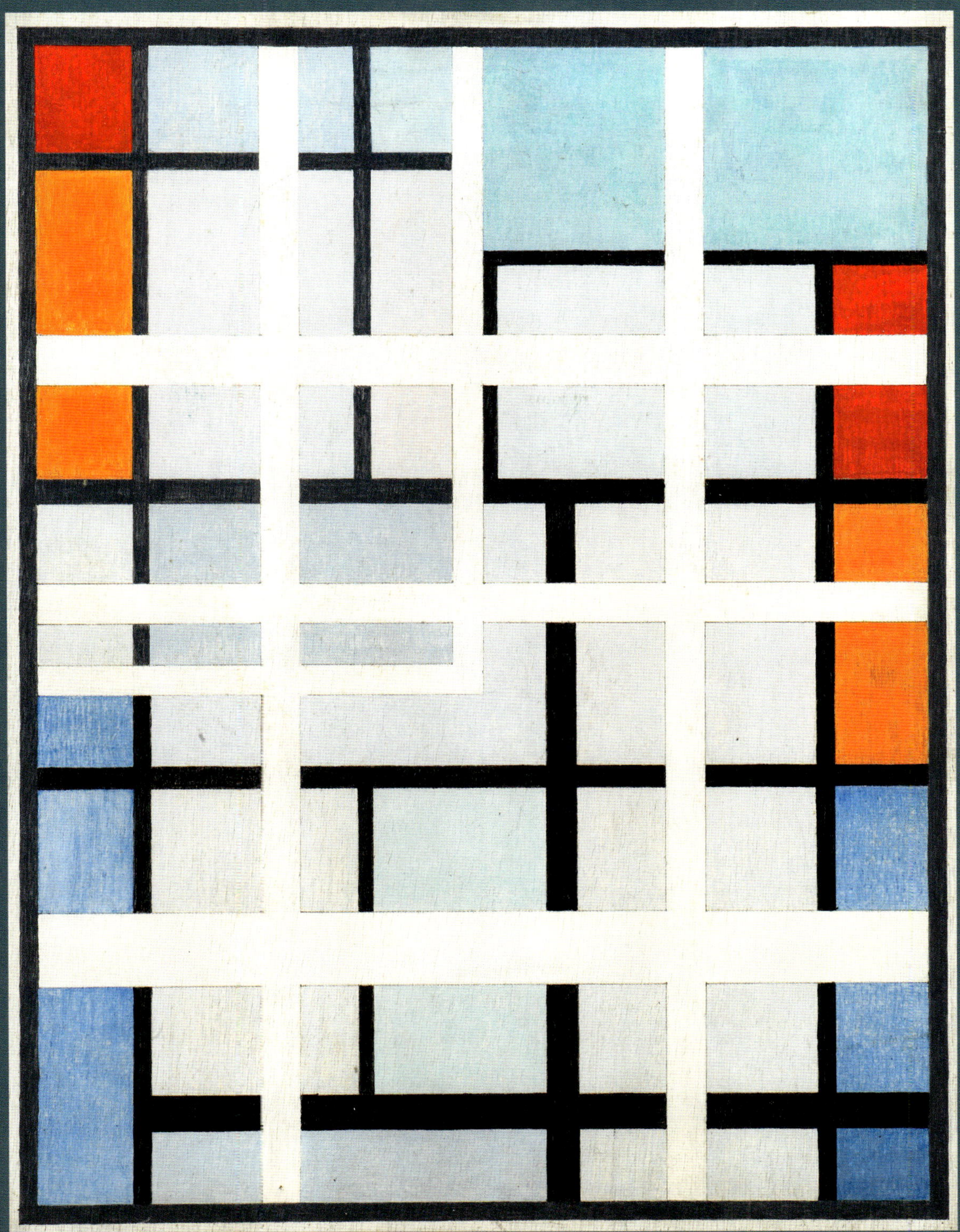

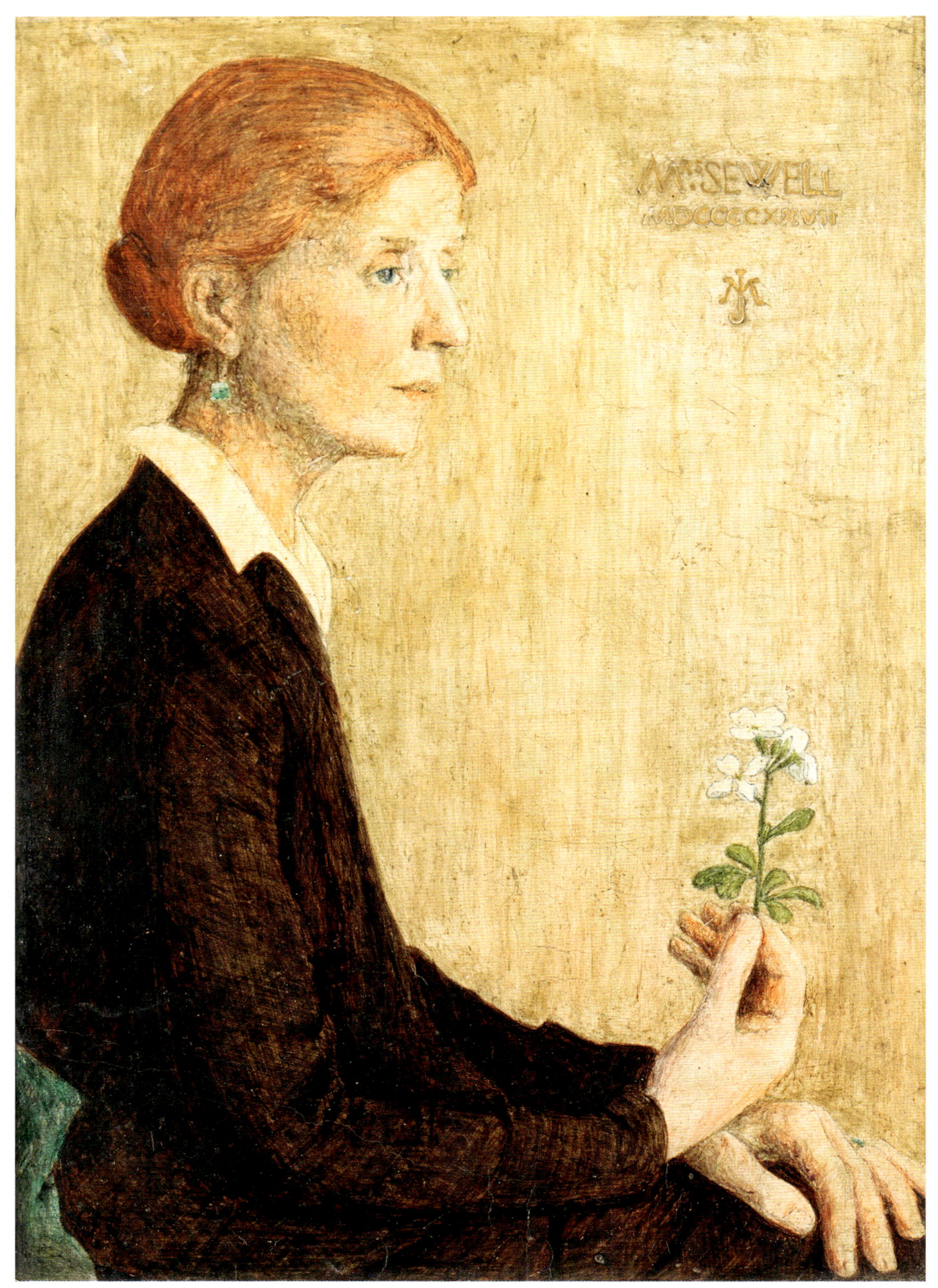
Mrs SEWELL
MDCCCCXXVII

John Moody (1906-1993)

Margaret Sewell, 1927

Egg tempera on board - 20.9 x 15.2 cm.

Margaret Ley, a talented miniaturist, and William Sewell, a gifted artist and book illustrator, first met when they were students at Herkomer's Art School. In this poignant portrait of 1927, John Moody expresses the grief felt by Margaret on the tenth anniversary of her husband William's death: he died in 1917, aged 41, at the battle of Arras. Still in mourning, she holds in her hand a specimen of the Cardamine plant, known for its healing properties for heart ailments.

Born in 1906 Moody had been too young to participate in the war, but he suffered its consequences. His poignant woodcut, War, produced in 1928, sums up his sense of the futility of war and his antagonism towards the 'old order' which had condemned so many to a needless death.

As such he was expressing the mood of his generation.

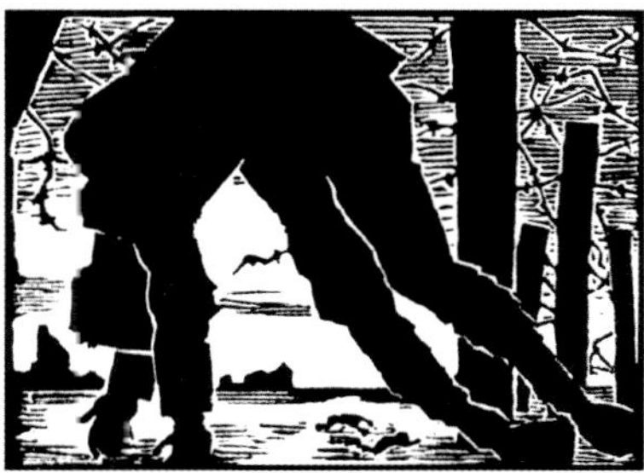

John Moody, War 1928,, Woodcut - 19 x 16.5 cm.

Rachel Reckitt (1908-1995)

Matador, c. 1955

Oil on panel, signed - 99.1 x 73.7 cm.

Reckitt studied wood engraving at the Grosvenor School of Modern Art in London from 1933 to 1937, where she was taught by the School's founder, Iain Macnab. Although painted in oil, this work has all the geometric stylisation of a print and stays true to the mission of the School in its rendering of ordinary subject matter with great movement and vitality.

Reckitt travelled extensively in Europe, on painting trips from which studies would form the inspiration for larger studio compositions painted on her return. In the mid 1950s she travelled through Spain, resulting in an impressive series of paintings of matadors and bullfighting.

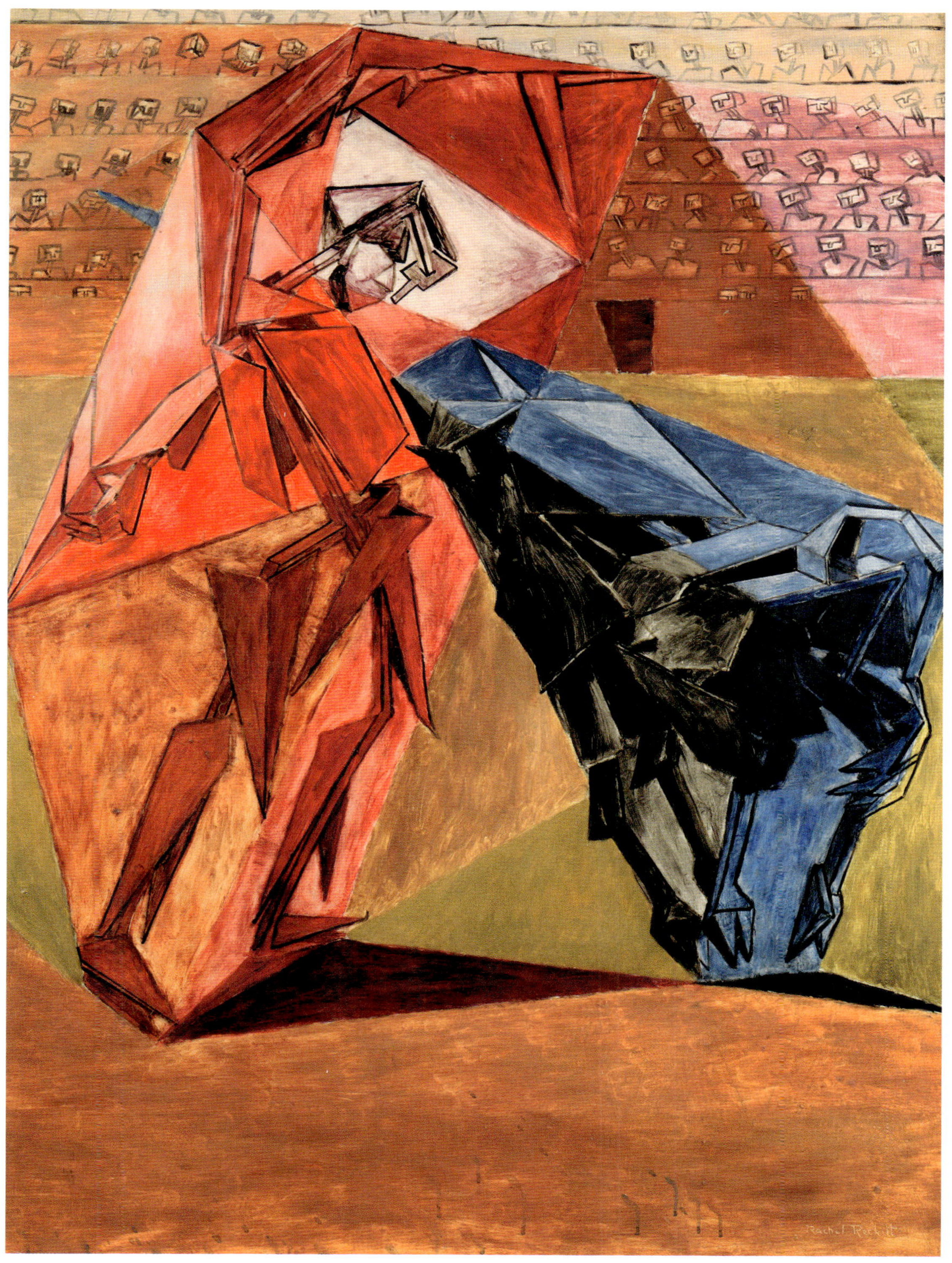

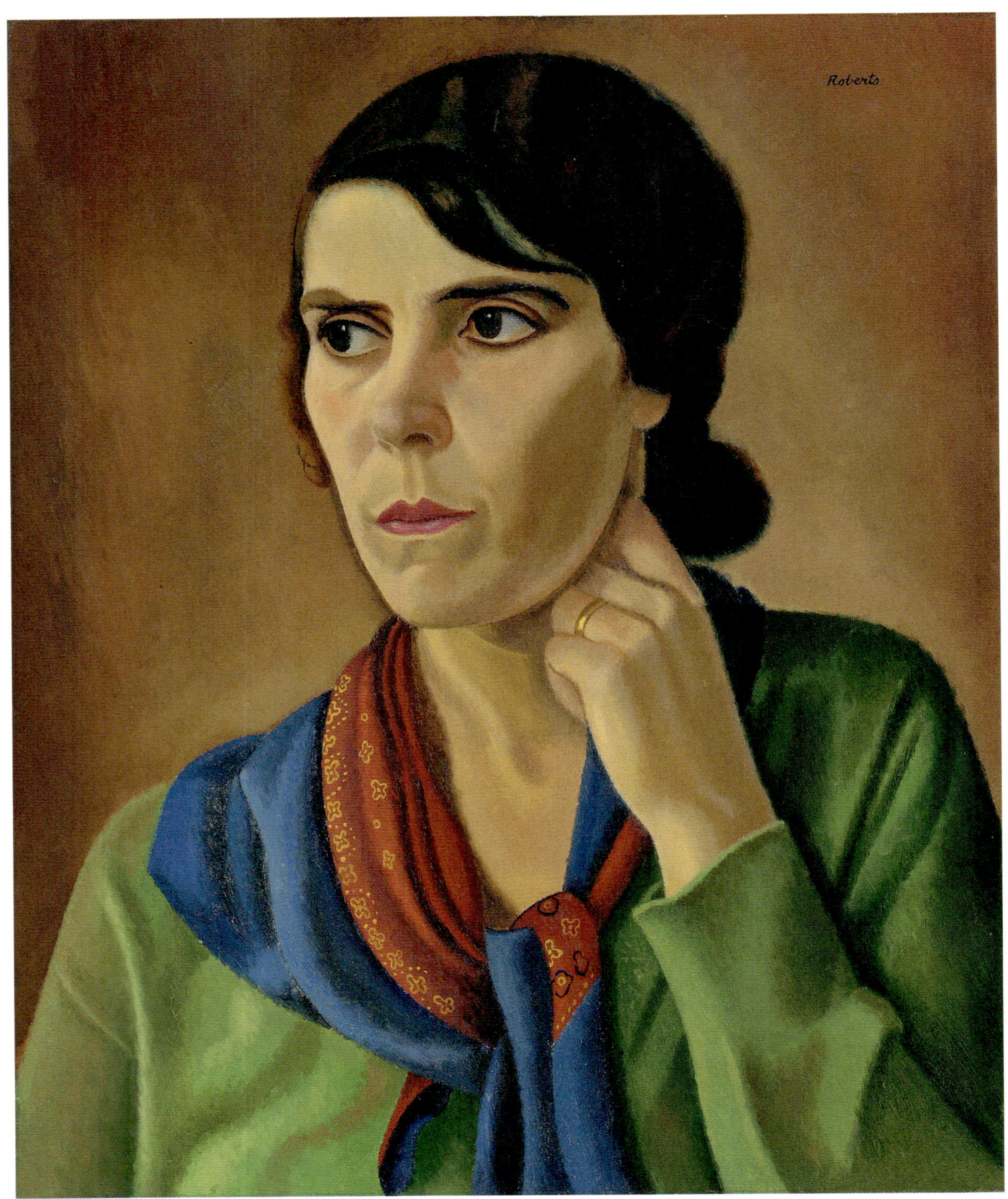
Roberts

William Roberts (1895-1980)

Portrait of May Berry, 1933

Oil on canvas, signed - 55.6 x 45.5 cm.

May Berry was a patron of Roberts, acquiring from him The Park Bench, painted in the same year as her portrait. May was married to Joe Berry, mentioned in a notebook of John Roberts as 'A civil servant, no children, which enabled him to collect modern firsts, signed and limited [..] His books lined a wall and more of his flat overlooking the Thames. We went over to see the Boat Race from his windows.' The Berrys, who lived at 48 Upper Mall, were neighbours of Eric Ravilious and Tirzah Garwood, who lived at No. 58.

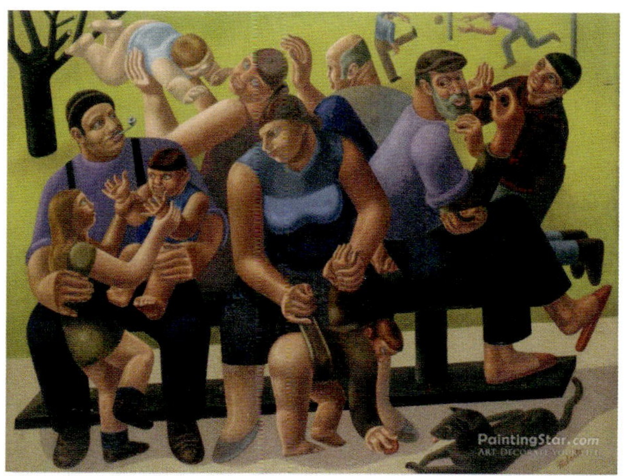

William Roberts, The Park Bench, 1933 owned by May Berry.

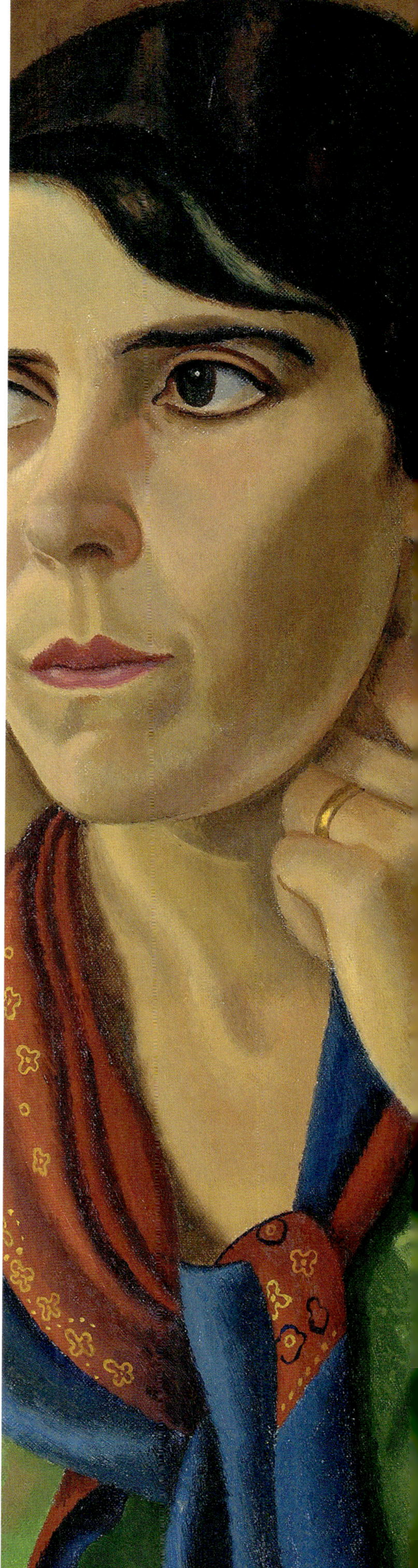

Kenneth Rowntree (1915-1997)

Putney Garden, 1960s

Acrylic on board - 61 x 61 cm.

Kenneth Rowntree and his family lived in Putney between 1950 and 1970. Diana Rowntree later recalled :

'We found a house on the Thames, upstream of Putney Bridge, and turned the attic into a studio. Its comfort permanently slowed Kenneth's working speed from the swift tempo demanded by one-day forays into distant landscapes.'

The Thames provided Rowntree with a steady stream of subjects : views from his window, paintings of Putney Reach, and night time scenes such as Putney Bridge, Nightpiece (an example of which is in the Government Art Collection), which, in a twentieth century modernist idiom, recall Whistler's night paintings.

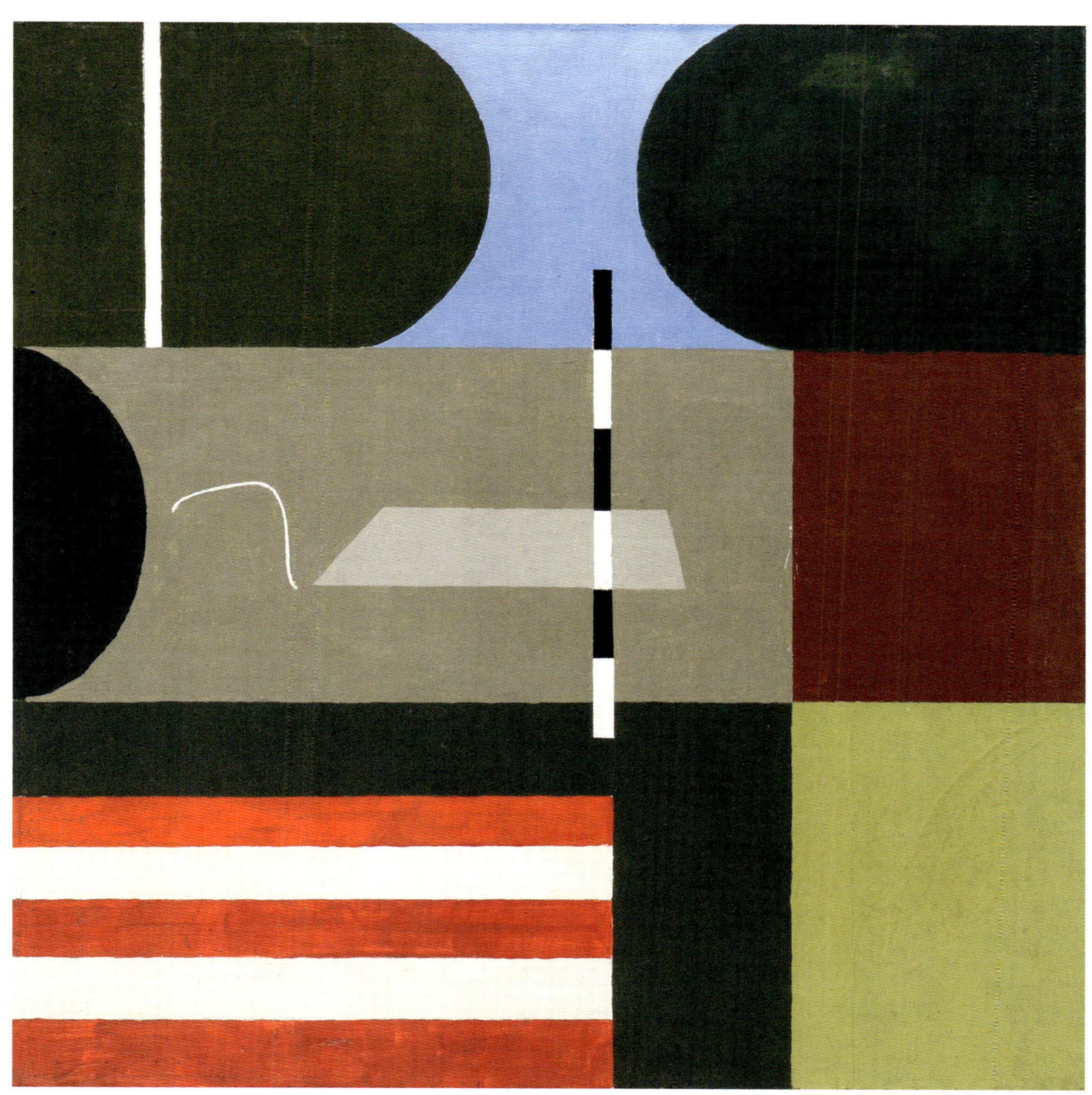

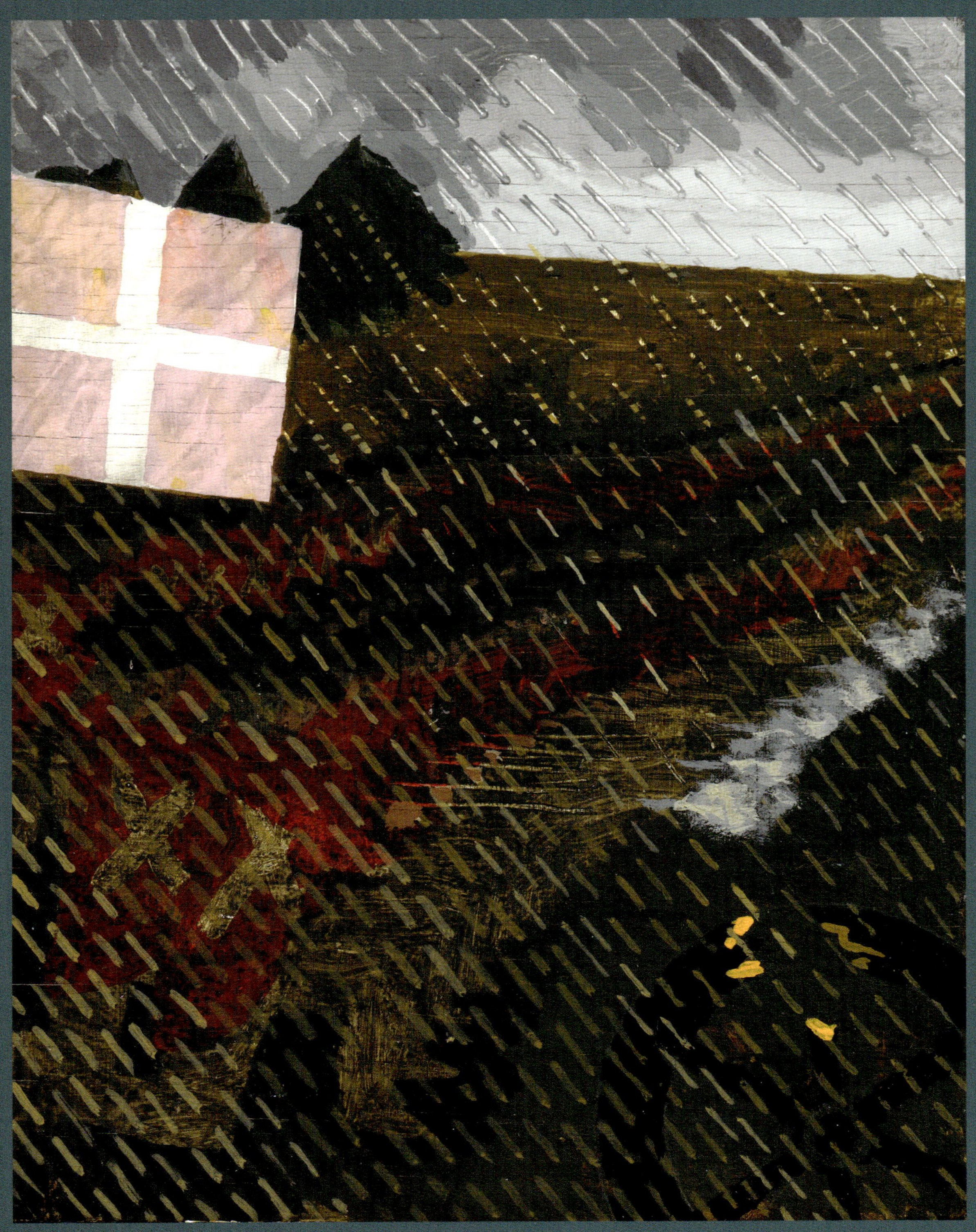

Kenneth Rowntree (1915-1997)

Falling Rain with Raised Flag

Acrylic on board - 32.5 x 25 cm.

As Professor of Fine Art in Newcastle (1959 -1980) Rowntree was at the epicentre of an important northern school of modernism that revolved around his friends Victor Pasmore (1908 -1988) and Richard Hamilton (1922- 2011). Even in retirement, his work, in its return to figuration from abstraction, displays his consistent qualities of humour and inventiveness. Rowntree's oeuvre is both influenced by and anticipates a wide variety of artistic styles, from Ravilious to David Hockney, from the Euston Road School to the Dadaism of Kurt Schwitters.

'One of the most appealing British artists of the mid-twentieth century, Kenneth Rowntree knew how to tease, please and baffle, how to communicate joy without complacency, how to charm without any hint of preciousness. His pictures of ordinary English streets and fields, back-rooms of pubs, churches in Mexico and weathervanes in Nantucket are deeply satisfying works of art which point out new things in the world. He had an unerring feel for strange yet satisfying compositions in which everything is idiosyncratically alive and at the same time settled, iconic, and complete.' (Alexandra Harris, A Strange Simplicity: Kenneth Rowntree, A Centenary Exhibition, Liss Llewellyn, 2015.

Rudolf Sauter (1895-1977)

Searchlights along the Thames Estuary, October 1940

Oil and pastel on board - 59.5 x 38 cm.

Searchlights relates in both time and subject to a body of work Sauter made in October 1940 in response to the Battle of Britain. Four of these semi-abstract watercolour drawings, recording aircraft vapour trails, are in the collection of the RAF Museum, Hendon. During World War II, Rudolf Sauter was an Army Welfare Officer under South Eastern Command. Although he was never an Official War Artist, the events he witnessed informed his work. Sauter produced imaginative compositions with prophetic titles inspired by events he had observed, but he was uninterested in attempting to portray a faithful account.

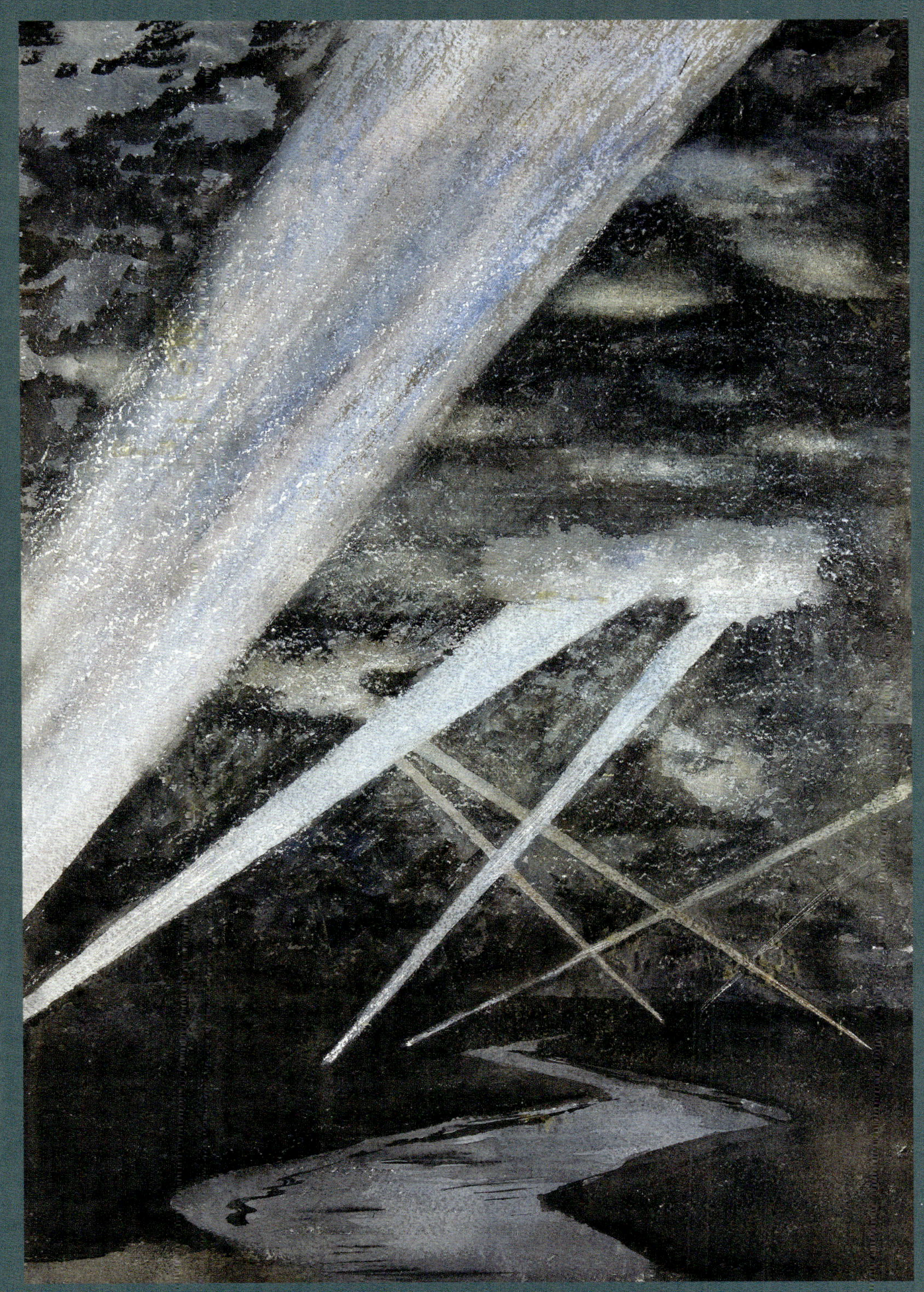

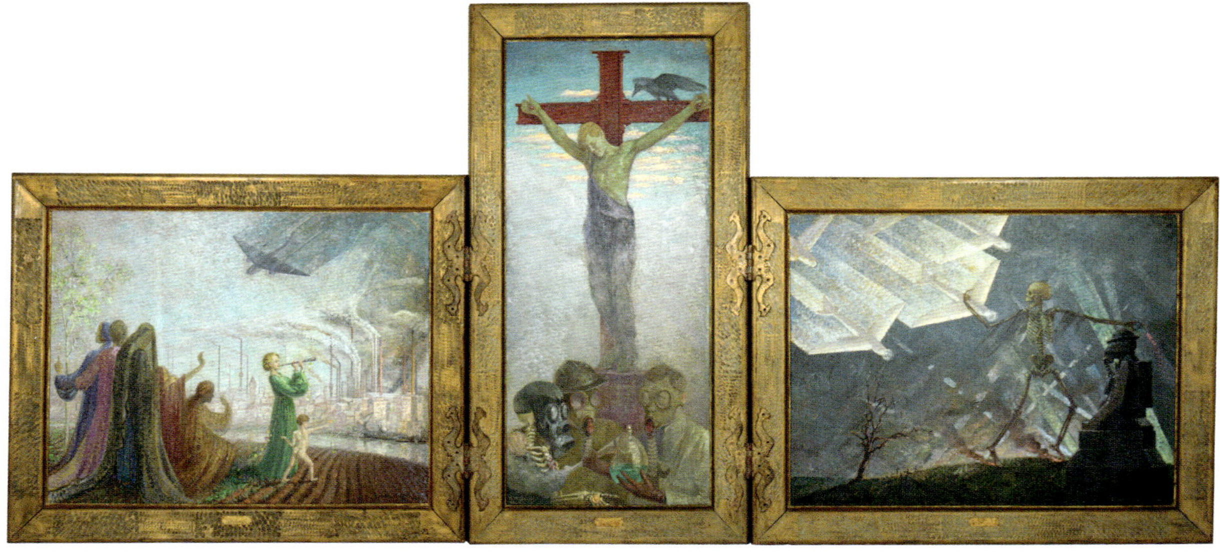

Rudolf Sauter (1895-1977)

Never More!

Tryptich, oil on canvas, signed and dated 1934-5 - 2 canvases 86 x 122cm / 1 canvas 138 x 62 cm.

Imbued with complex anti-war and religious imagery, Rudolf Sauter's *Never More!* (a modern Triptych) was displayed in London's Arlington Gallery, 3-13 March 1936. It was located in the section of the exhibition Mad New World, its center panel entitled The Reaping, left panel The Sowing, and right panel entitled The Harvest. As the Second World War approached, Sauter achieved several more exhibitions as part of a burgeoning career. However, none would be as timely and significant as the one in the Arlington Gallery, and none reflected so vividly the fatalism of this public triptych.

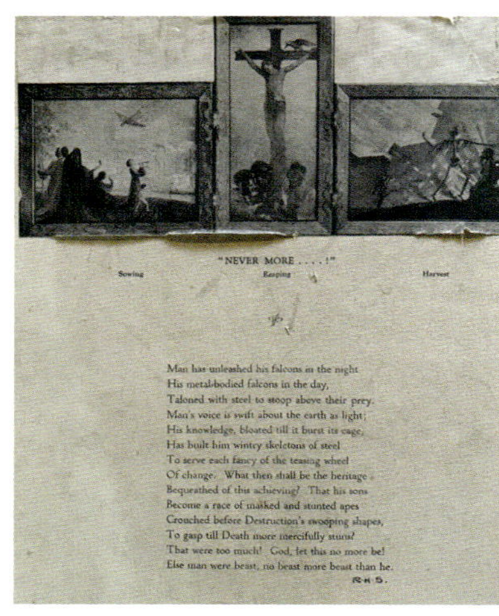

"NEVER MORE . . . . !"

Sowing — Reaping — Harvest

Man has unleashed his falcons in the night
His metal-bodied falcons in the day,
Taloned with steel to stoop above their prey.
Man's voice is swift about the earth as light;
His knowledge, bloated till it burst its cage,
Has built him wintry skeletons of steel
To serve each fancy of the teasing wheel
Of change. What then shall be the heritage
Bequeathed of this achieving? That his sons
Become a race of masked and stunted apes
Crouched before Destruction's swooping shapes,
To gasp till Death more mercifully stuns?
That were too much! God, let this no more be!
Else man were beast, no beast more beast than he.

R.H.S.

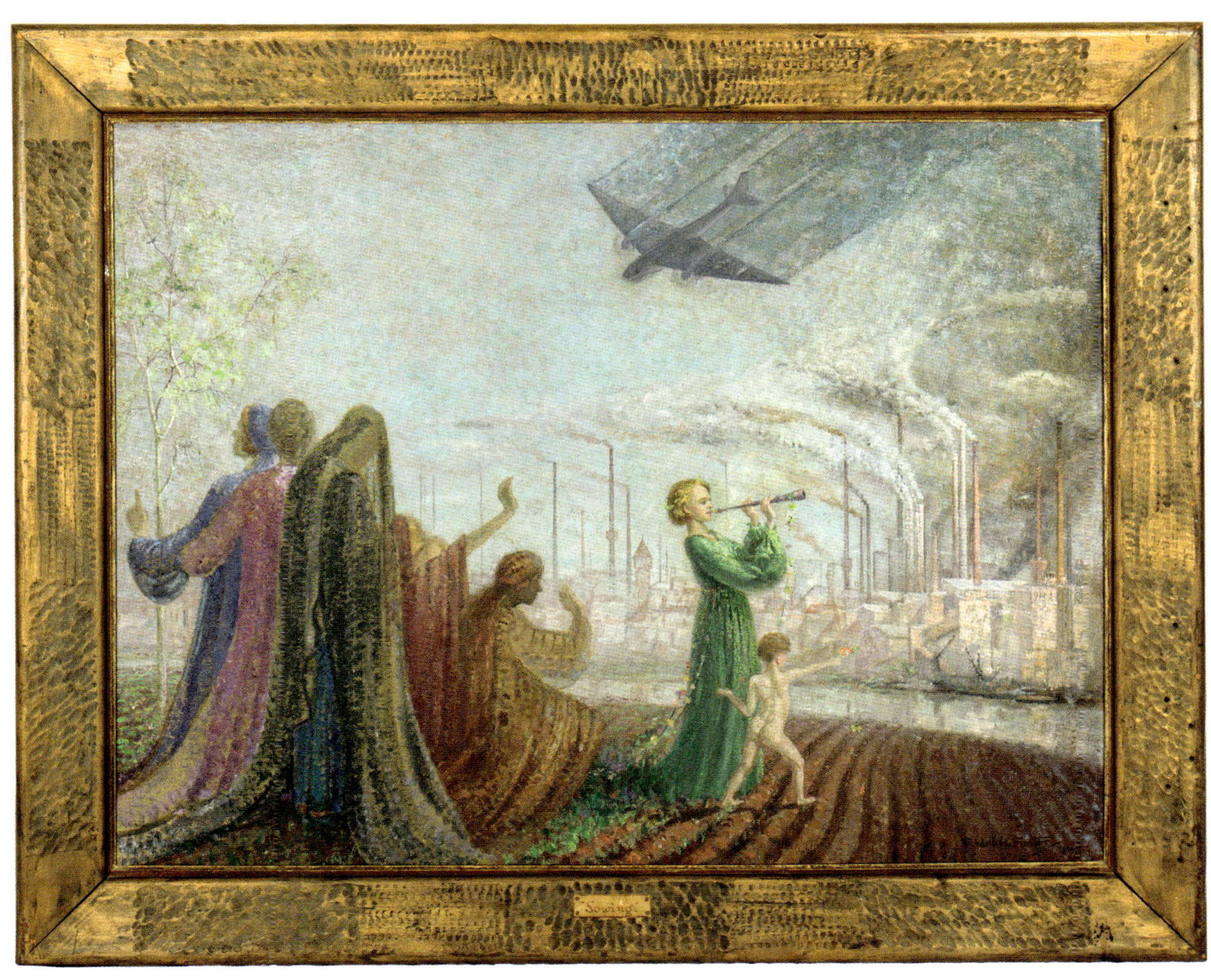
"Sowing"

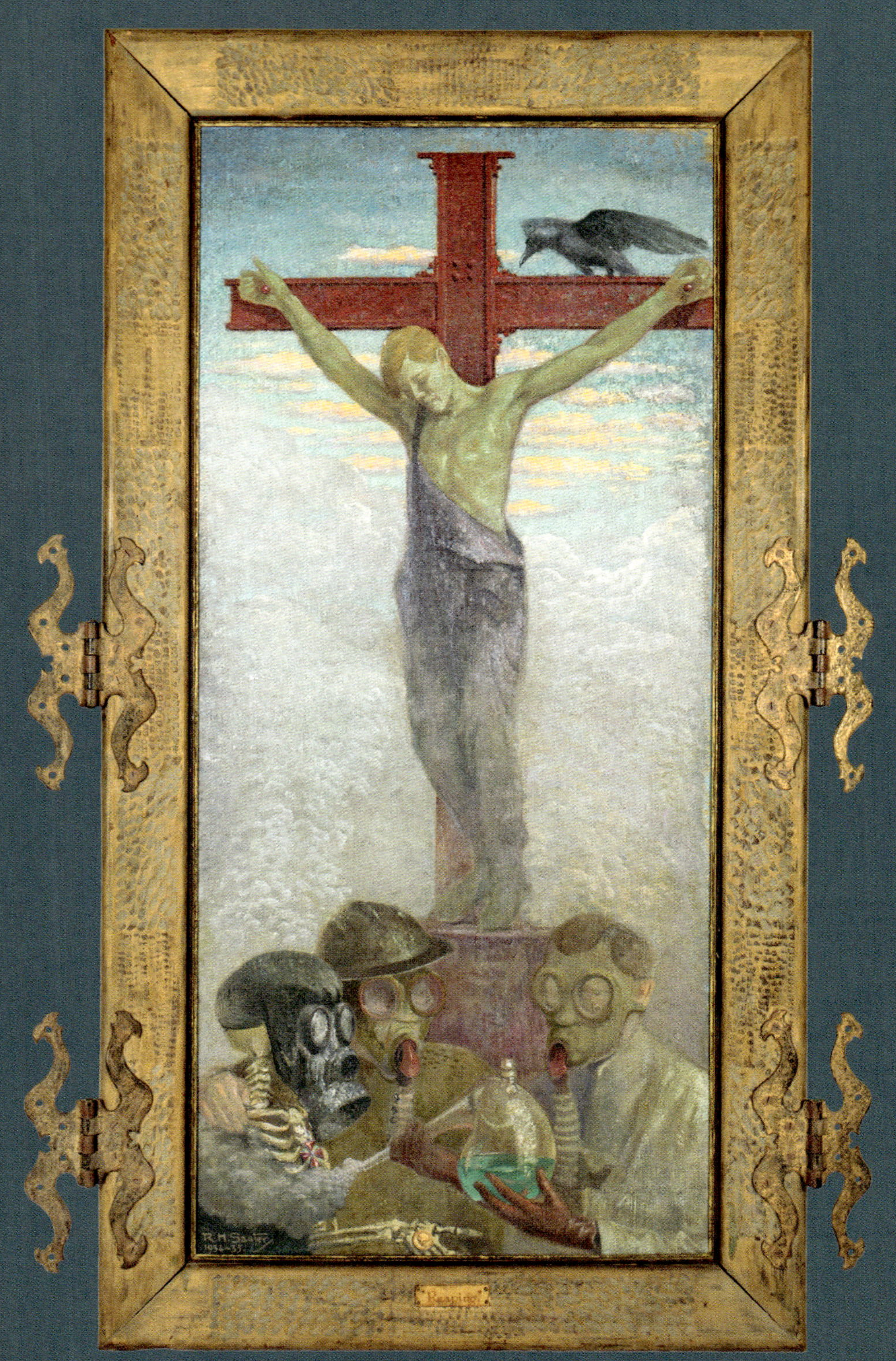

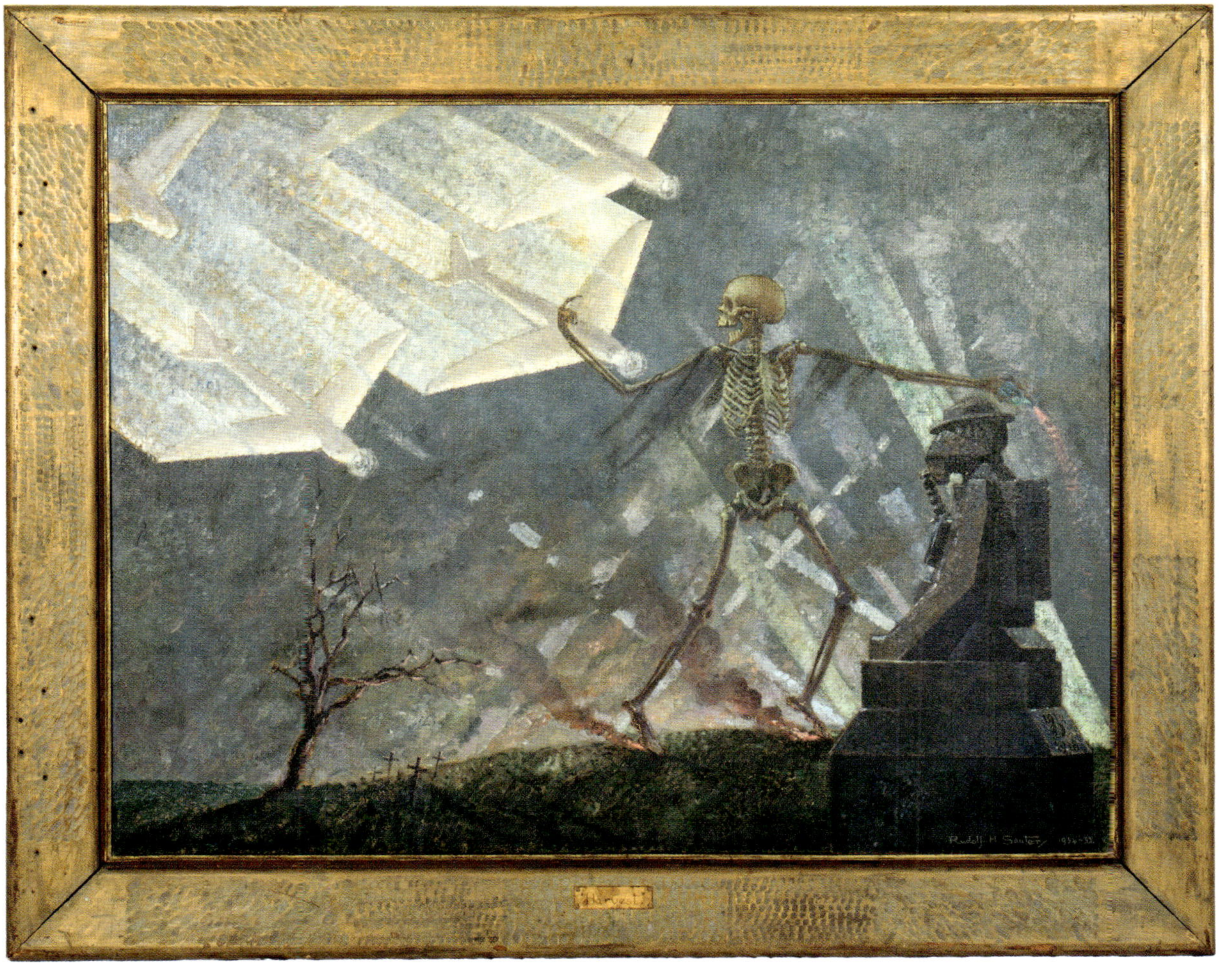

We are grateful to Jeffrey S. Reznick, author of the landmark study *War and Peace in the Worlds of Rudolf H. Sauter: A Cultural History of a Creative Life (Anthem Press, 2022).*

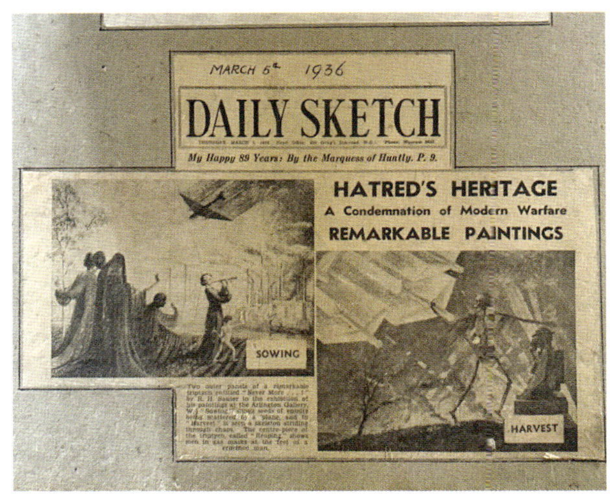

MARCH 5th 1936

DAILY SKETCH

My Happy 89 Years: By the Marquess of Huntly. P. 9.

HATRED'S HERITAGE

A Condemnation of Modern Warfare

REMARKABLE PAINTINGS

SOWING

HARVEST

Two outer panels of a remarkable triptych entitled "Never More . . . !" by R. H. Sauter to the exhibition of his paintings at the Arlington Gallery, W.1. "Sowing" shows seeds of enmity being scattered by a plane, and in "Harvest" is seen a skeleton striding through chaos. The centre-piece of the triptych, called "Reaping," shows men in gas masks at the feet of a crucified man.

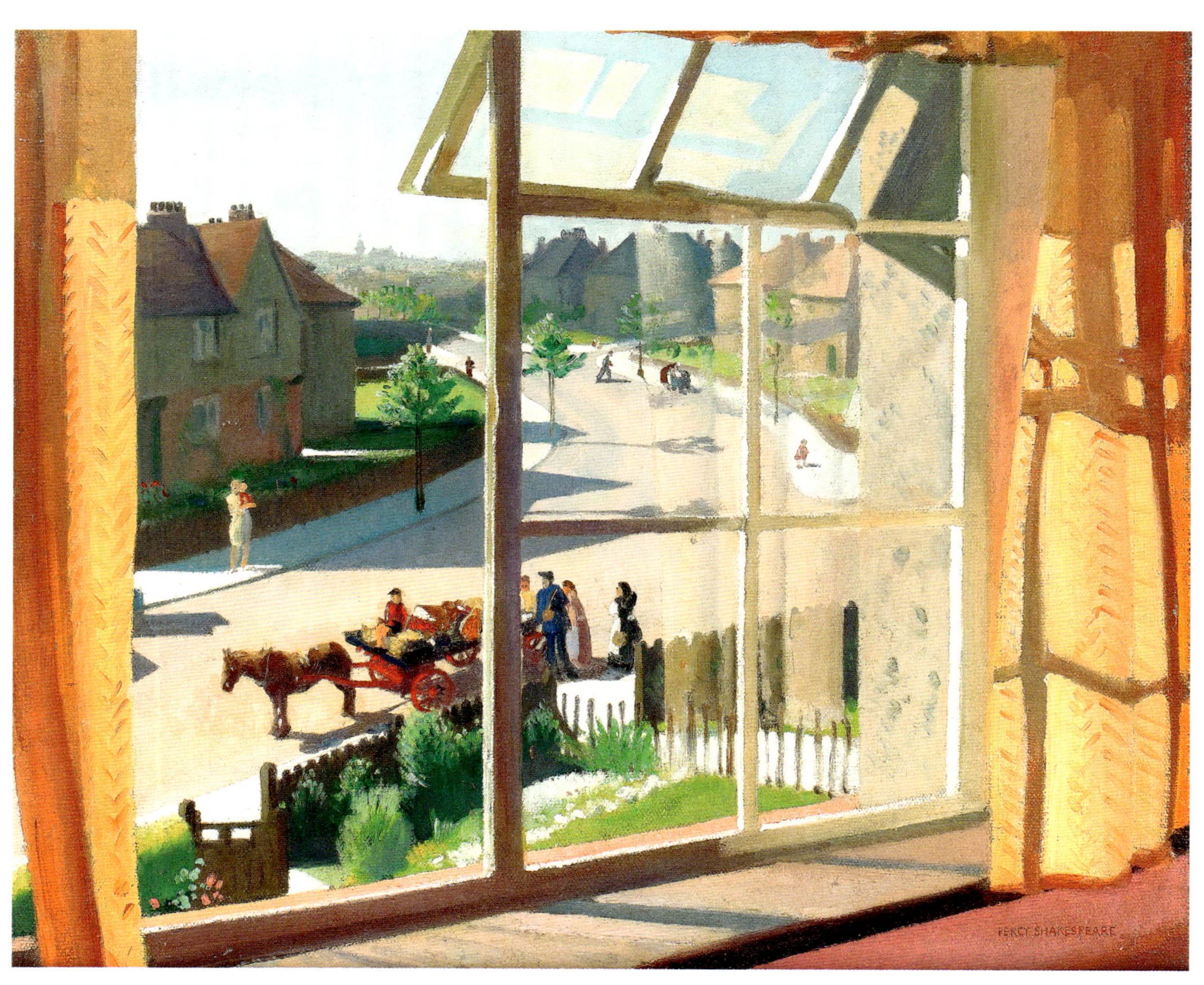
PERCY SHAKESPEARE

Percy Shakespeare (1906-1943)

View from the Artist's Bedroom, Wren's Nest, mid 1930's

Oil on canvas, signed - 52 x 62 cm.

This painting shows a view from the artist's bedroom, 12 Maple Road, Wren's Nest, Dudley. Wren's Nest – a famous geological site (and today a Nature Reserve) near Dudley – was a green oasis in the industrial Black Country. On its slopes Dudley built the first of its council houses. The Shakespeares (Percy was the fourth of eight children) were re-housed to Wren's Nest in the late 1920s, from the Dudley slums. As a painter he triumphed over the rigours of his environment to become a regular exhibitor at the Royal Academy and twice at the Paris Salon. The bedroom, which Percy shared with one of his three brothers, also doubled as his studio and served as the setting for his striking self-portrait, Morning Exercise, 1934.

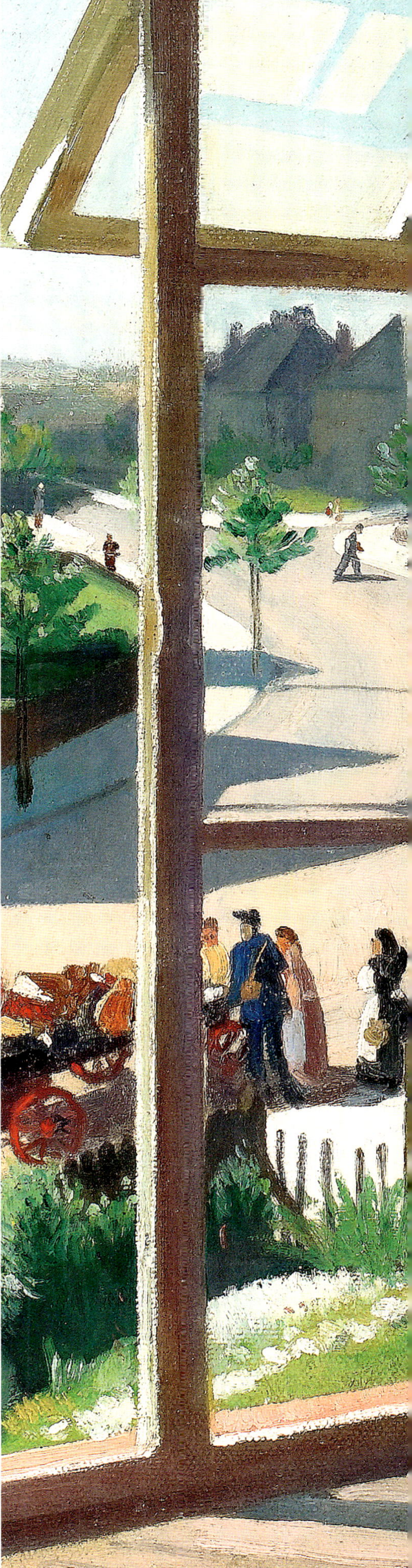

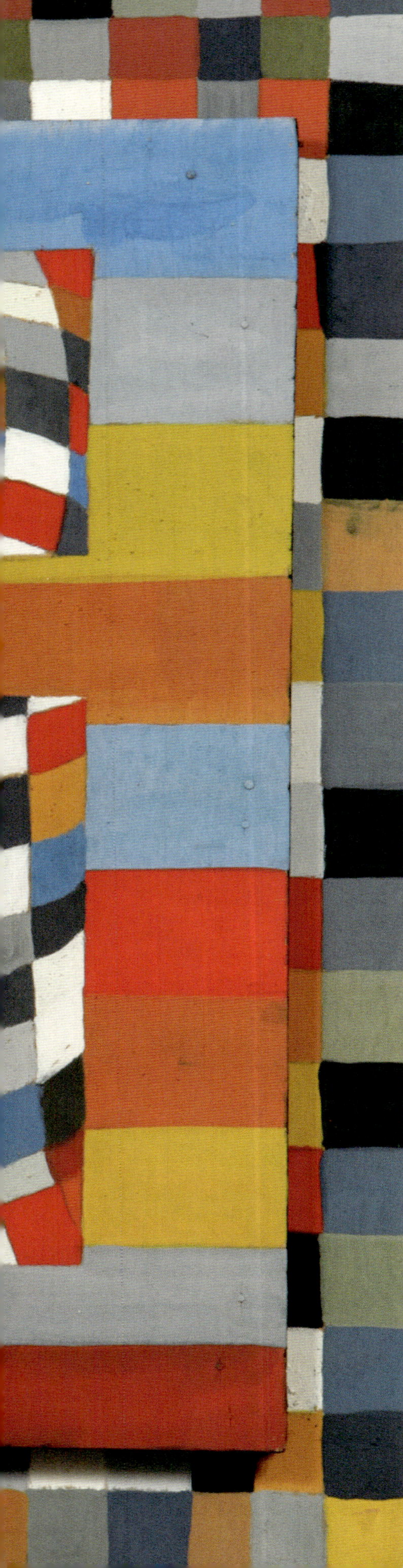

Jack Smith (1928-2011)

Painted Relief, 1962

Oil on board, signed 'Jack Smith', titled and dated on the reverse, with label from Matthiesen Ltd., London - 51 x 51 cm.

Jack Smith studied at Sheffield College of Art (1944-1946), Saint Martin's School of Art (1948-1950) and the Royal College of Art (1950-1953). At the RCA, Smith studied under John Minton, Ruskin Spear and Carel Weight. During the 1950s, Smith's early work was in a neo-realist style known as 'The Kitchen Sink School' featuring domestic subjects.

In the 1960s, Smith abandoned realism and adopted a brightly coloured, abstract style comparable to those of Wassily Kandinsky and Piet Mondrian, incorporating Constructivism and Biomorphism with elements of hieroglyphic and musical notation. 'Sometimes I like to confuse the spectator with different realities, so there's flatness, lots of flatness and suddenly there's something which maybe thought of as three-dimensional, so I may use shadow in that case, you know. But that's again in order to create a visual, a visual diversion if you like, or what might be considered a sudden foreign body in the work.'

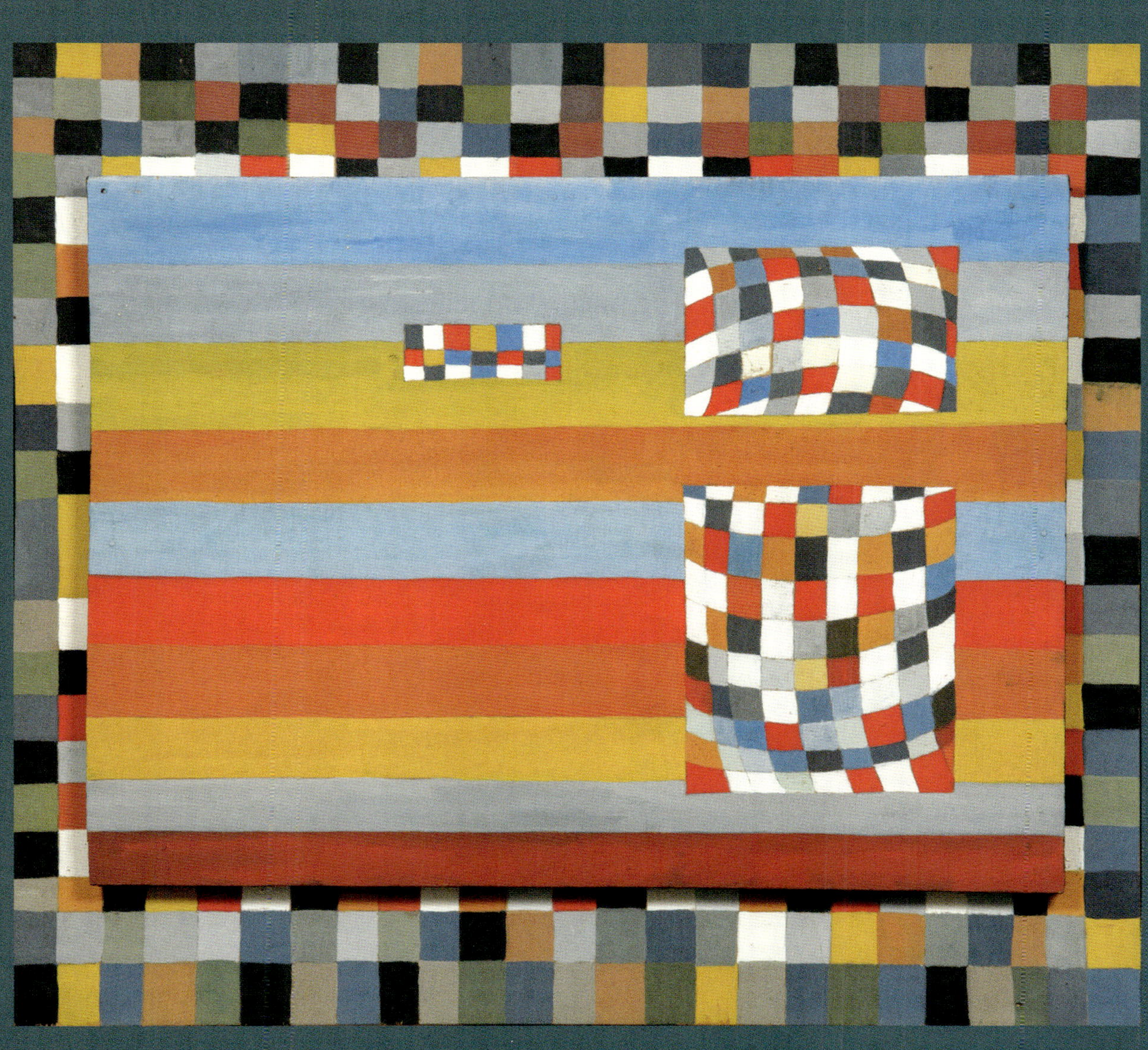

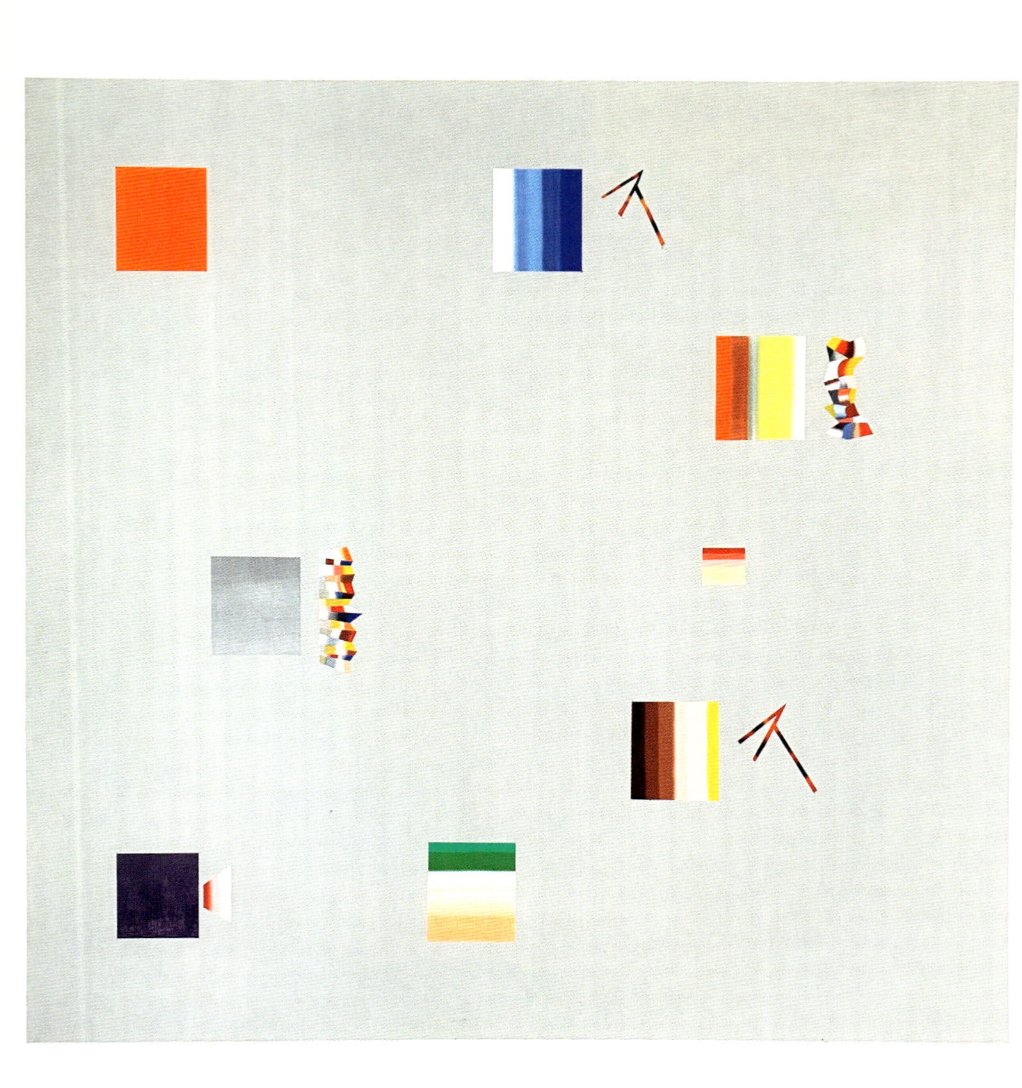

Jack Smith (1928-2011)

13 Elements on Grey (Sound + Silence), 1970

Oil on board - 107 x 107 cm.

A letter from the artist to the previous owner, dated 05 august '69, reads;
Dear S and D, Thank you so much for sending me the photographs of my work you have, what I consider to be some very important paintings and it gave me great pleasure to see them again. I hope that they will continue to fascinate and give you pleasure. Your choice is excellent. Regarding '13 ELEMENTS ON BLACK (SOUND + SILENCE)' it is not acrylic board but Oil paint on black acrylic. I think that is important. The provenance is Lord Strauss as you say. As you know he was a very active politician. It has been a fascinating experience for me to see these works again and to know that they belong to people who have knowledge of art. With best wishes to you both, Jack Smith
Of similar works from this period, now in the Tate collection : (Activities, Major and Minor (1972) and Sounds and Silences (1975) Smith commented : 'I think of my paintings as diagrams of an experience of sensation. The subject is very important. The sound of the subject, its noise or its silence, its intervals and its activity. When I talk about the sound or the music of the subject, I'm not always thinking in terms of a symphony, but groups of single notes. The closer the painting is to a diagram or graph, the nearer it is to my intention. I like every mark to establish a fact in the most precise, economical way. I have been consistently interested in light; between 1952-6 as an outside source and since then as a quality within the painting Light as a subject no longer interests me, but it's still essential that each painting contains it. This kind of remoteness I feel makes one more aware of certain aspects of a subject that cannot be visually explained without preconceived ideas getting in the way. There is silence in the earlier paintings though that is not the subject. Later on, that silence became the subject'.

(Conversation with Jack Smith, 5 April 1978, and a letter of 27 May 1978, Tate Archive)

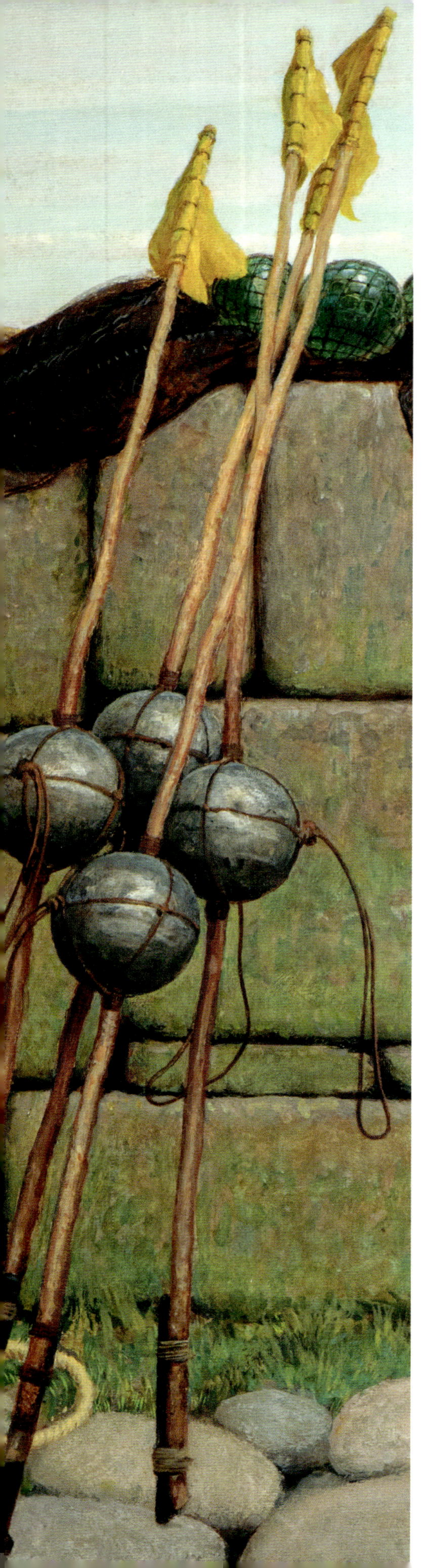

John Bulloch Souter (1890-1972)

Still Life of Fishing Nets and Floats by a Wall, c. 1930

Oil on board, signed - 40.5 x 30.5 cm.

Born in Aberdeen, Souter won the Byrne Travelling Scholarship awarded by the Scottish Education Department which enabled him to comfortably tour the European continent. During this continental tour, he was purportedly much impressed by Diego Velázquez, Johannes Vermeer and Jean-Baptiste-Siméon Chardin. Iconography of the still life is intriguing : the palette is a symphony of graduated earth colours, greens, blues and browns; and the carefully arranged motifs combine to give a surreal feel to the composition. It might be that Souter painted it purely for his own pleasure, as an antidote to painting the Society portraits for which he was much in demand. But equally he might have intended to imbue this still life with a deeper meaning : The Parable of the Fishing Net, in the gospel of Matthew, reveals that a day of judgment is coming when God will separate good from evil.

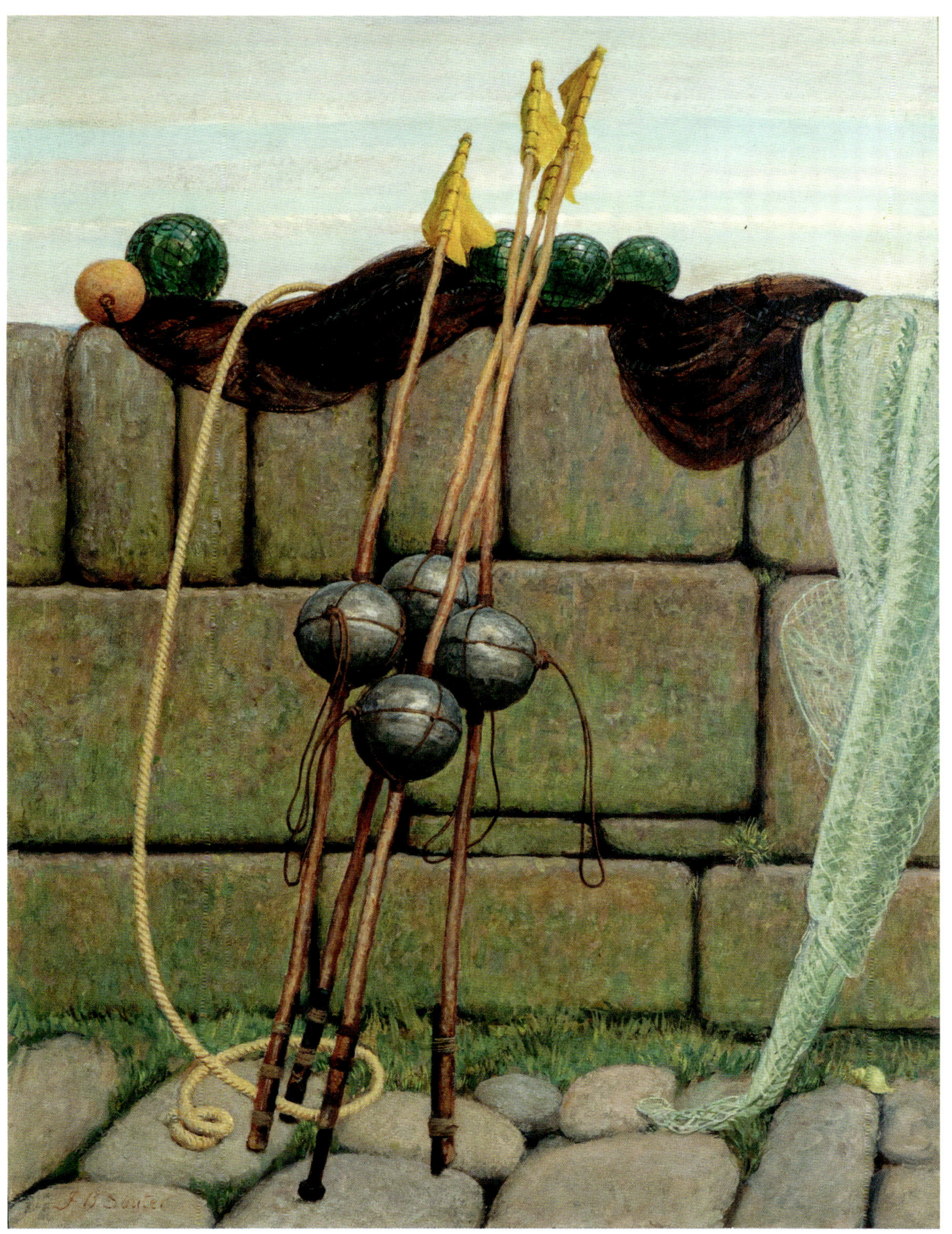

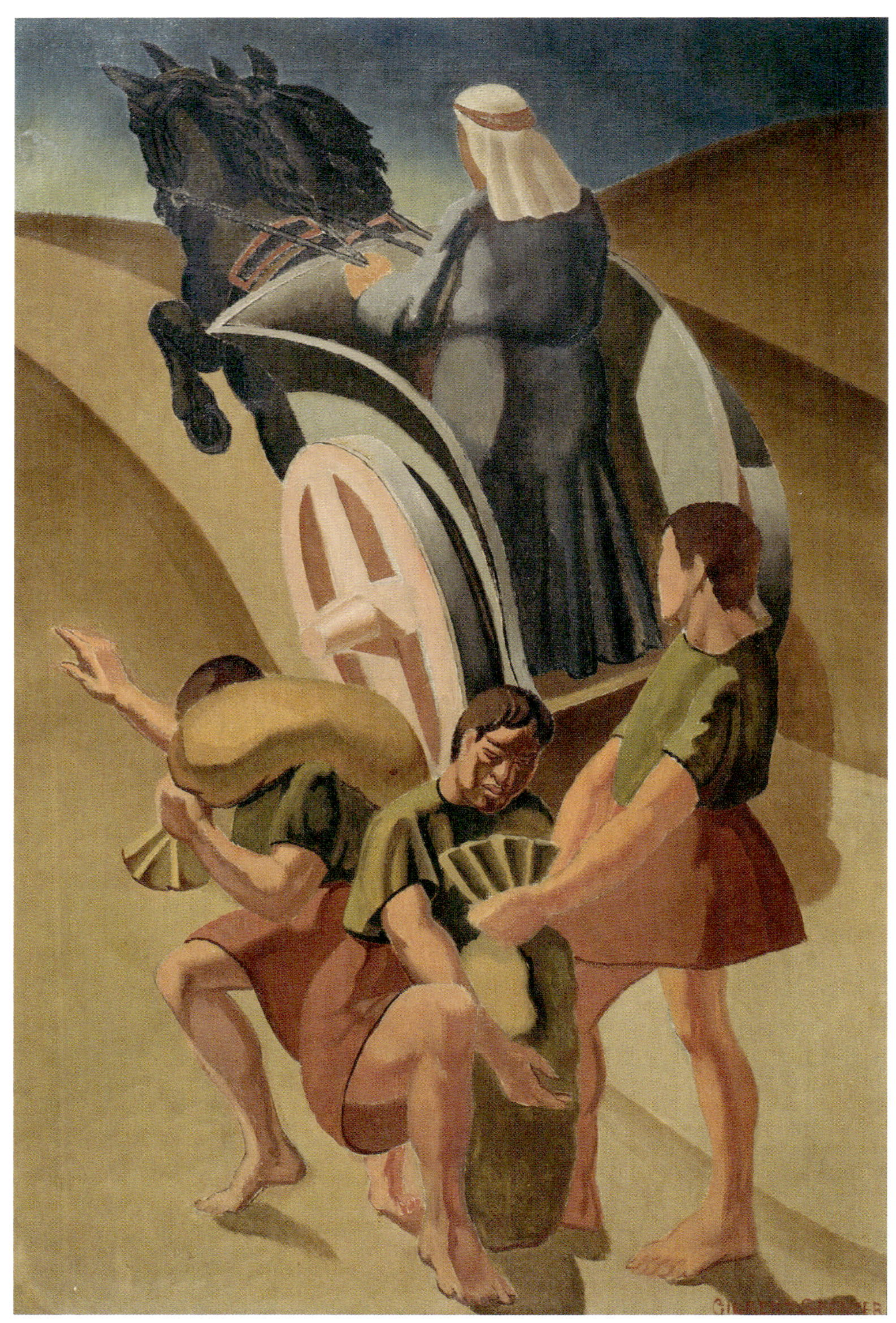

Gilbert Spencer (1892-1979)

Gehazi and Naaman, mid 1930s

Oil on canvas, signed - 86 x 60 cm.

Biblical subject matter featured heavily in Gilbert Spencer's early works. This seemed a natural concomitant from his training at the Slade, and the Summer Composition Competition, which frequently offered a Biblical or Classical theme for the artists' brief. Henry Tonks was the Professor of Art throughout Spencer's tenure. Tonks was particularly fond of setting Biblical topics for this Prize and demanded considerable skill of the artist tasked with both upholding this visual tradition, while revolutionising the format for a modern audience. Other religious paintings in Gilbert Spencer's early career include The Crucifixion (now in the collection of the Tate Gallery), which relocates this seminal scene to Cookham Meadow, as well as The Shepherds Amazed, 1920, from the Gospel of Luke, which belongs to Leeds Art Gallery. Spencer also produced a series of drawings to illustrate The Ten Commandments in 1934 (Mill House Press), and one of the illustrations was based upon the composition of Gehazi and Naaman.

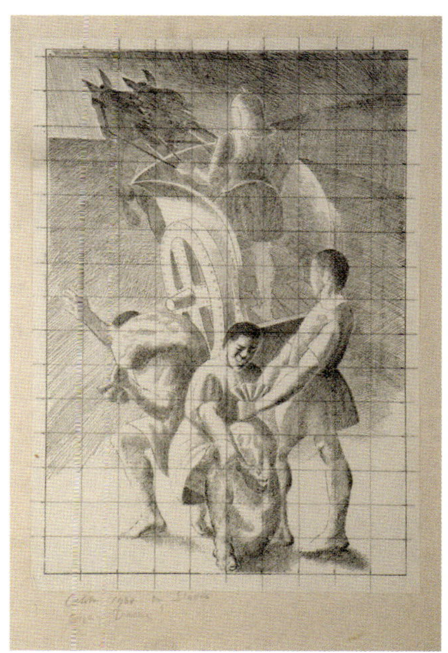

John Cecil Stephenson (1889-1965)

Clarabella, 1950

Tempera on board - 81.3 x 61 cm.

Clarabella is one of three variants for Stephenson's large mural commissioned by the Industry Building at the 1951 Festival of Britain. The exhibition was entitled Sixty paintings for 51. Works submitted were to be a minimum of 45 x 60 in. The oldest artist asked was W G Gillies (73 at the time), the youngest Lucian Freud (29). Other artists selected included John Armstrong, Edward Burra, Ivon Hitchens, L S Lowry, John Minton, William Scott, Keith Vaughan, Carel Weight and Rodrigo Moynihan.

Stephenson's finished mural was to employ luminous paints, newly developed by G.E.C. Industries. Although the commission was not always trouble-free, it was an opportunity for the artist's work to be seen on a large scale and by a huge audience. A related work, Painting: Design for the Festival of Britain, is in the Government Art Collection.

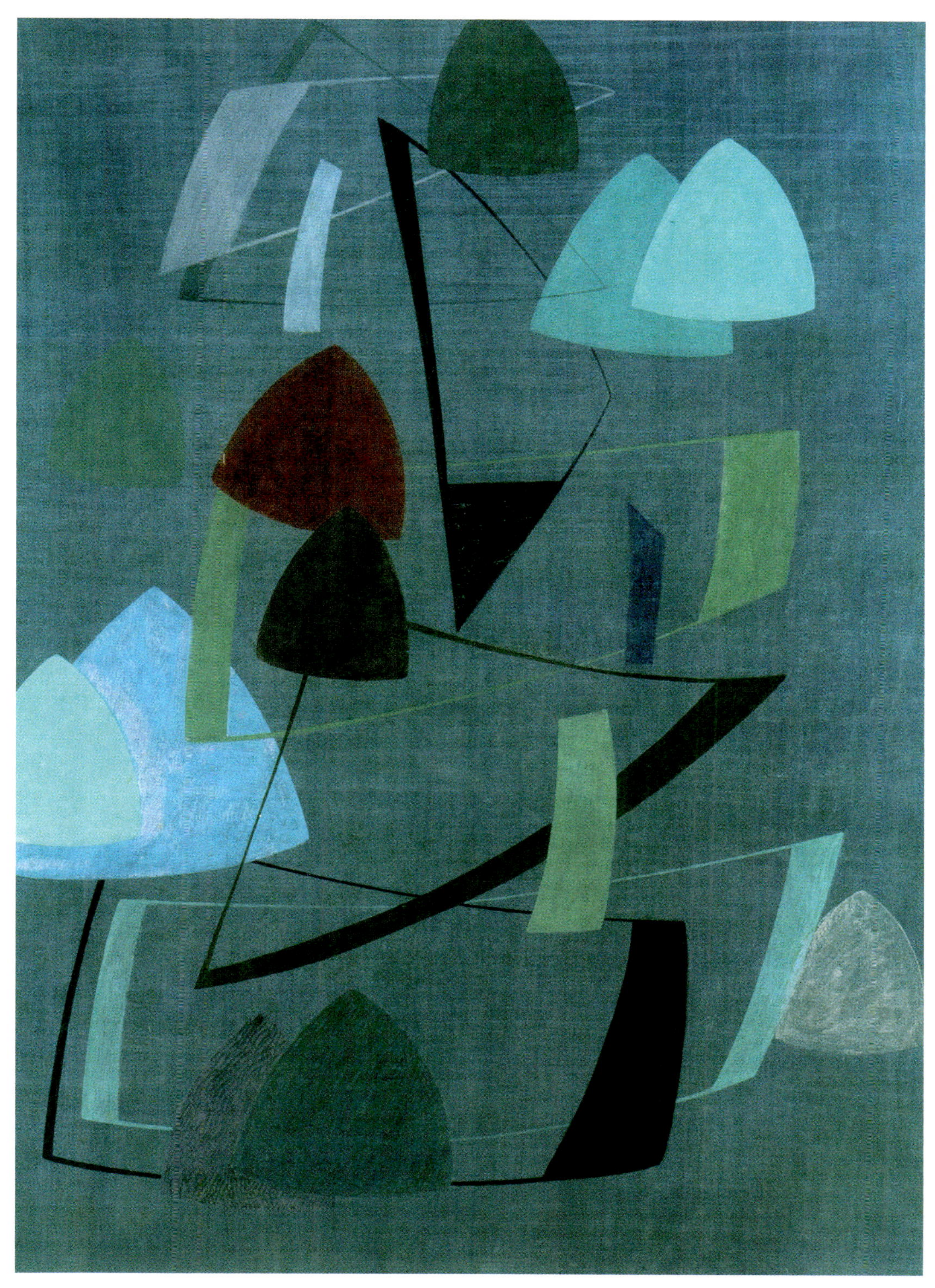

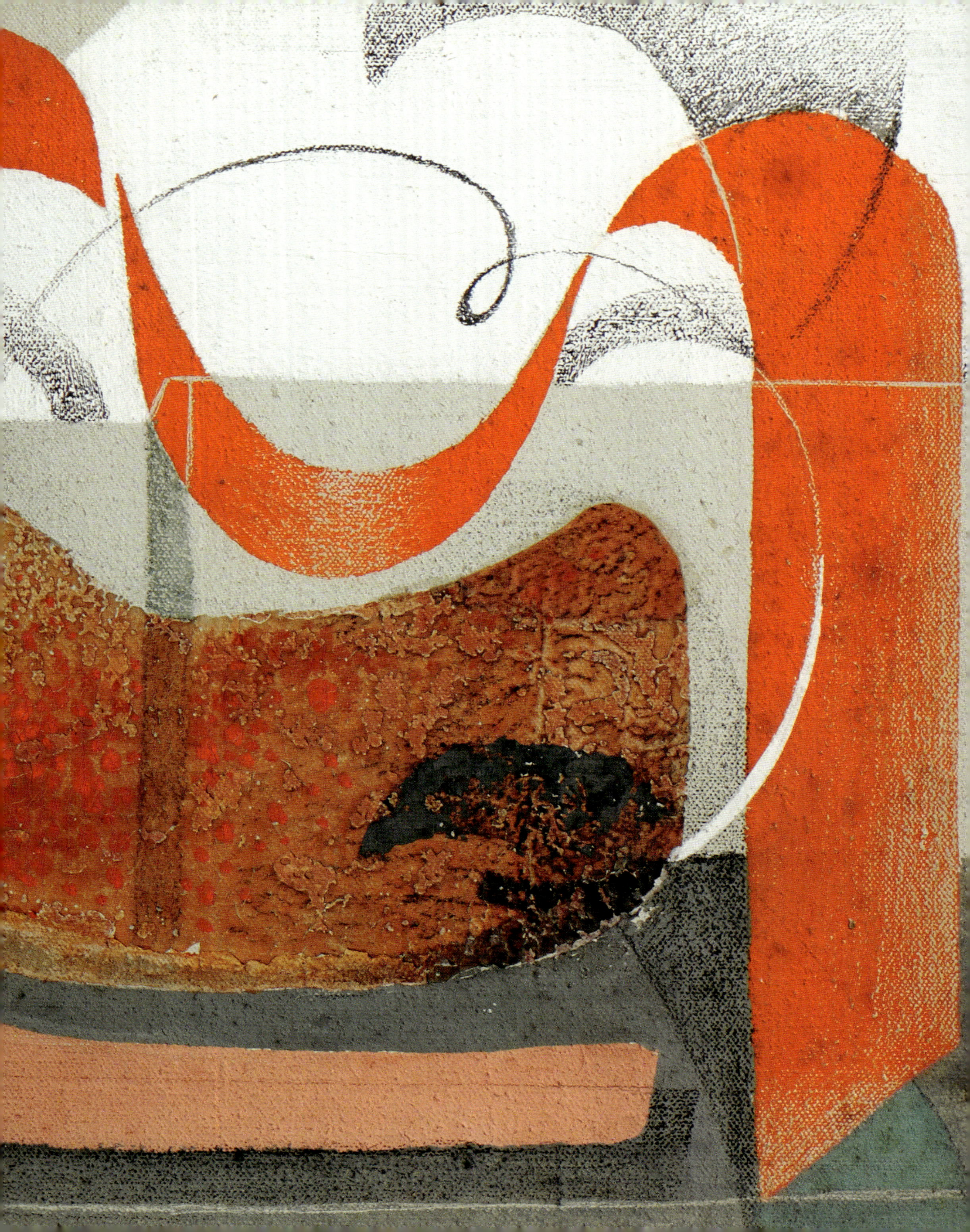

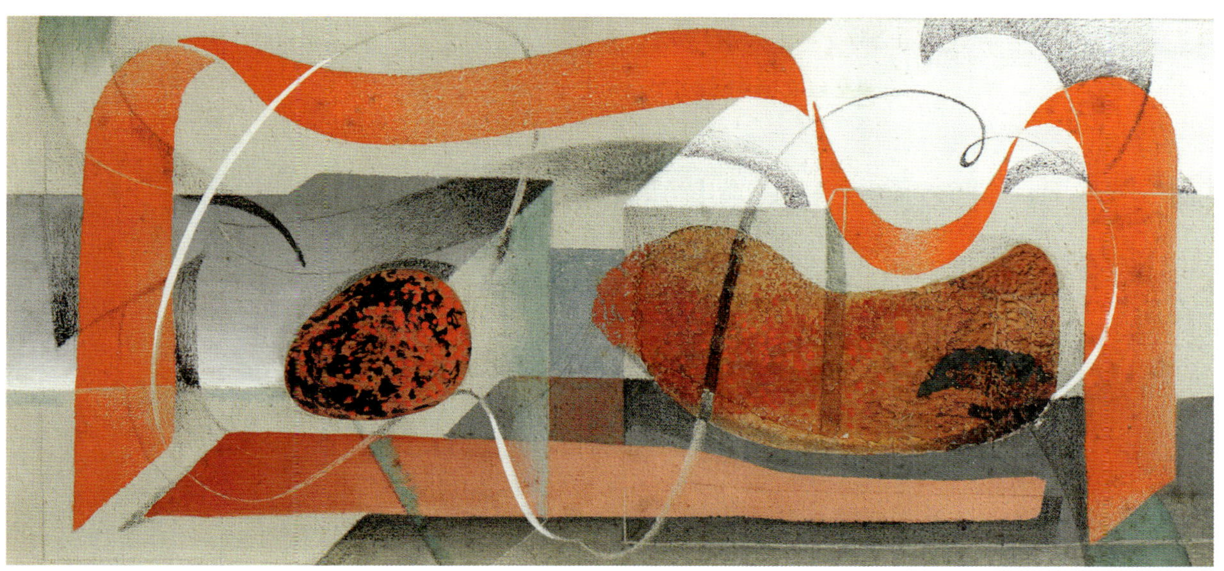

John Cecil Stephenson (1889-1965)

Abstraction, 1934

Oil, gouache, pencil and collage on canvas over panel, signed twice and incribed - 23 x 46 cm.

John Cecil Stephenson was one of the leading modernist artists working in Britain between the wars, moving, after the First World War, to The Mall, in Hampstead, London, where he would remain for the rest of his life. Referred to as 'the English Bateau-Lavoir' by Jean Hélion, the Mall Studios became the focal point of British Modernism in the 1930s. The 'nest of gentle artists' - Herbert Read's term - who resided here included Henry Moore, Barbara Hepworth, and Ben Nicholson, as well as international figures such as Naum Gabo, Alexander Calder, and Piet Mondrian. Stephenson was the mainstay, and very much at the core of this group. He was also highly rated by these contemporaries. Upon entering the nest himself, Herbert Read was quick to note that Stephenson was 'one of the earliest artists in this country to develop a completely abstract style', while his work was included in the groundbreaking Circle show of 1937.

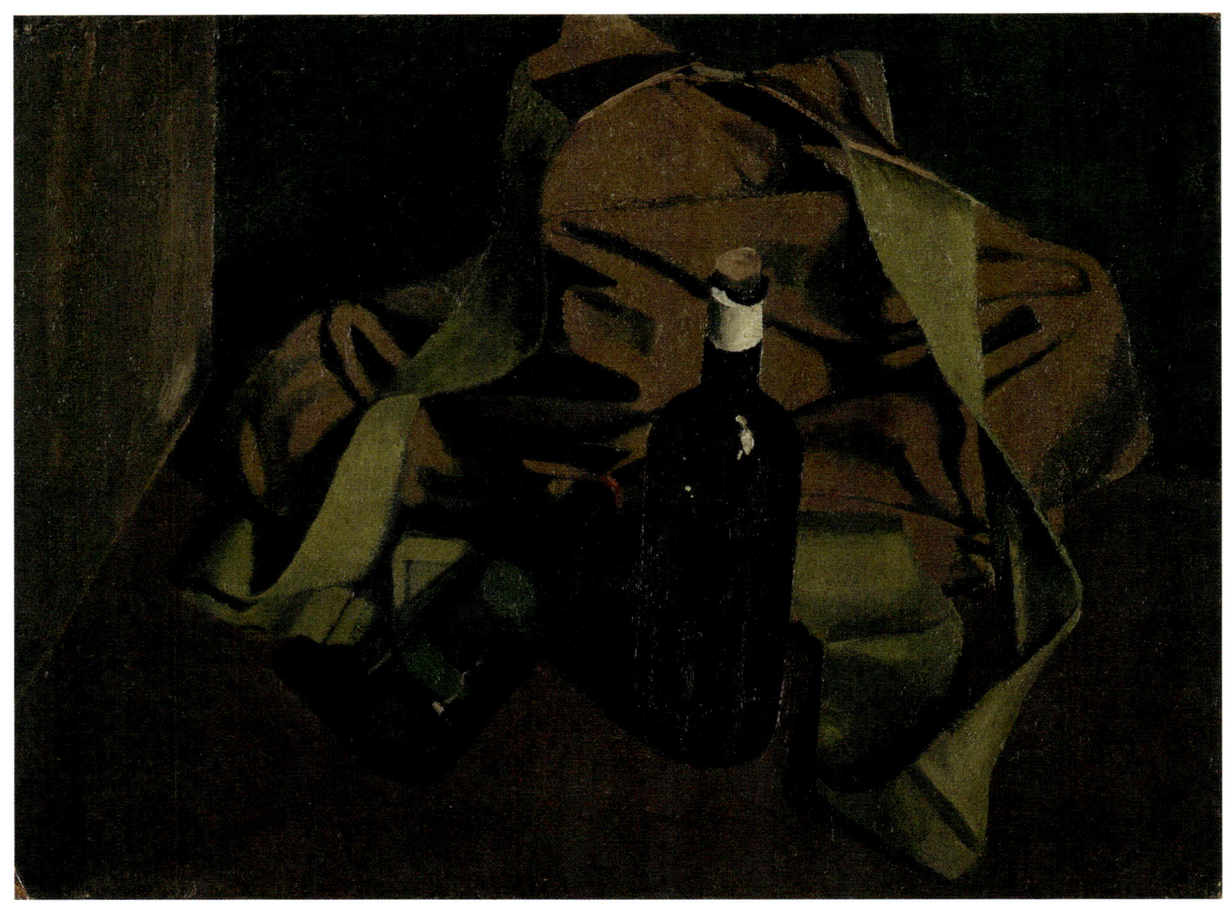

William S. Taylor (1920-2010)

Soldier's kit, 1940

Oil on board - 34 x 44 cm.

This still life dates to the period when the Royal College of Art evacuated from South Kensington in the autumn of 1940, taking over two hotels in Ambleside, the Queen's and the Salutation, for studios and accommodation. During this period Taylor set up his studio at Gale Cottage, in Old Lake Road in Ambleside : 'I stayed there for my post-graduate year. Candles and oil lamps were the source of artificial light; a small stove with a pipe through the roof was for heating; a tin wash basin for washing and a stove for cooking completed the facilities. Having been rejected on medical grounds by the armed forces, these years were for me, in spite of the slaughter going on in the real world, the halcyon days : my time was my own, with few responsibilities and only my painting to concern me.' (Letter to Paul Liss, 7 November 2001.)

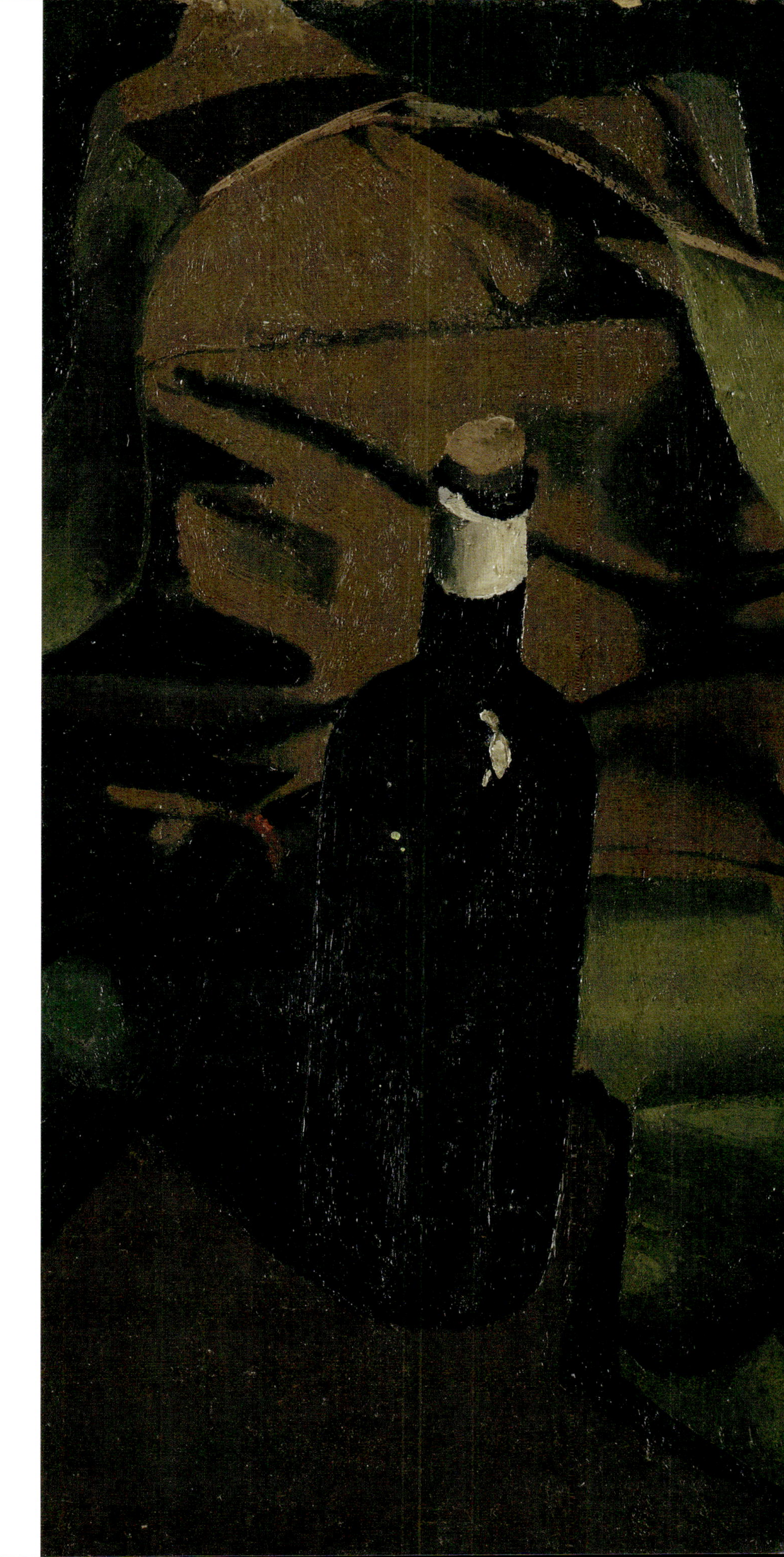

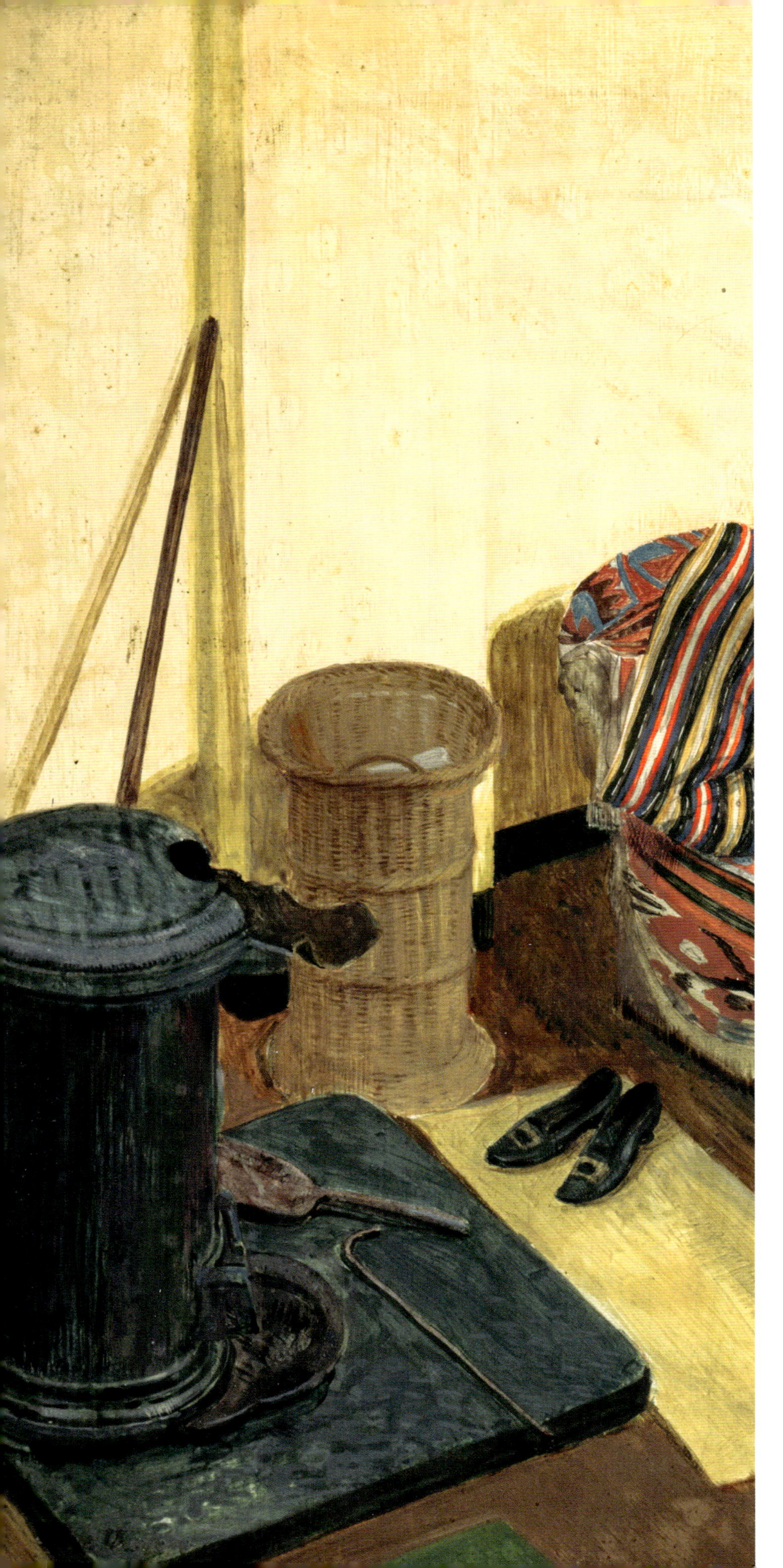

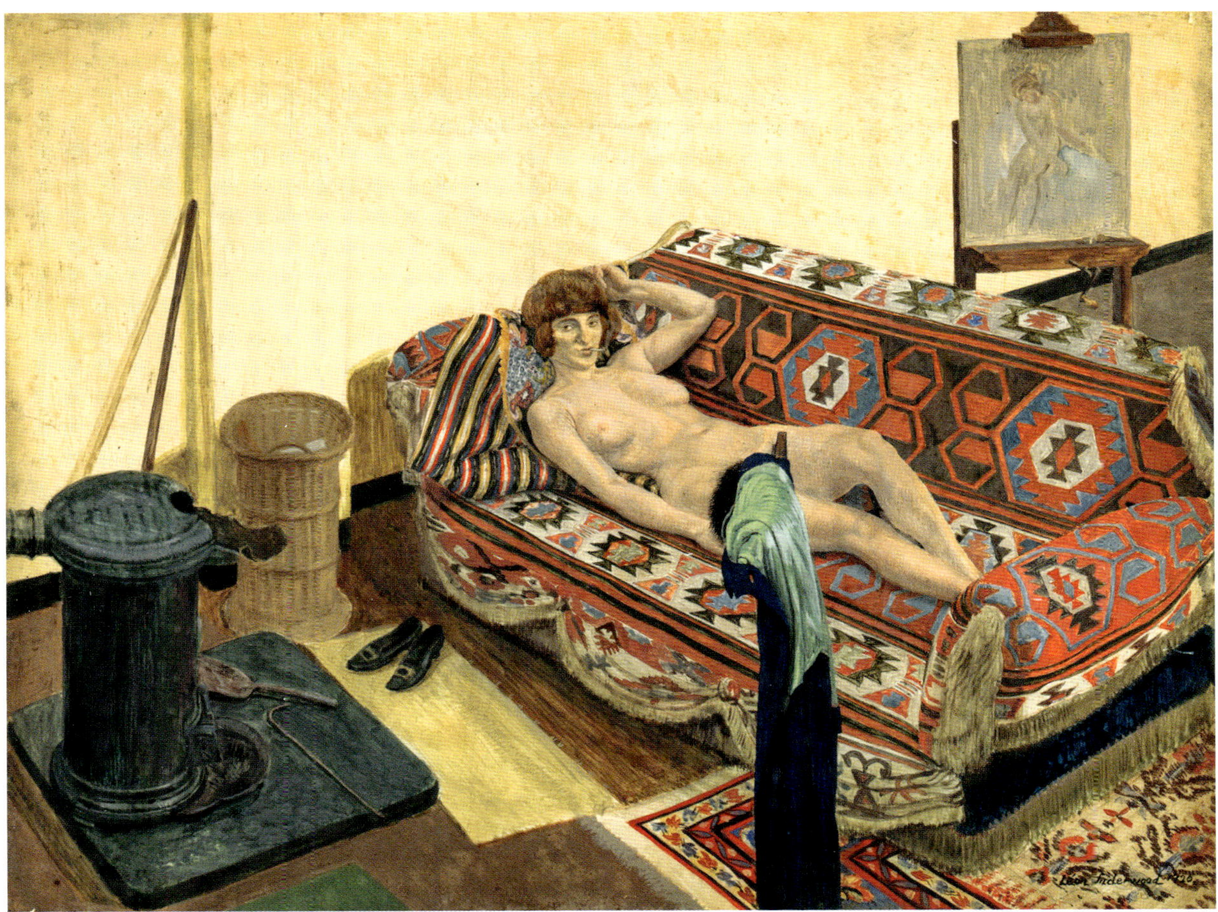

Leon Underwood (1890-1975)

Cecile on the Sofa, 1920

Tempera on panel - 29.5 x 38.5 cm.

1920, the year in which Underwood painted this studio scene, was a pivotal one for Underwood. Having served during WW1 as a Captain in the Camouflage Section of the Royal Engineers, Underwood attended the Slade School of Art for a year's refresher course and won a British Prix de Rome scholarship.

The setting for this painting might be his Hammersmith studio where he set up a private art school, the Brook Green School, which he ran, intermittently, until 1938. He also taught a life drawing class at the Royal College of Art from 1920 until 1923 when he resigned and travelled to Paris and Iceland.

Paule Vezelay (1892-1984)

Lines in Space, No. 11, 1950

Cotton and nylon thread box construction, signed in pencil on the stretcher bar, verso and with the artist's signed label verso. - 24 x 35 cm.

Paule Vézelay was a British-born artist who lived and worked in Paris from 1926 until 1939. There she changed her name from Marjorie Watson-Williams in order to obscure both her nationality and gender. Lines in Space was a series that spanned over 3 decades:

In 1964 Paule Vézelay recalled the genesis of such constructions:

When lines are drawn by a skilled and sensitive artist they are sometimes imbued with an almost celestial quality which miraculously endows them with 'Life'... I knew that any untrained hand guided by borrowed knowledge could, with a minimum of practice, make lines upon a two-dimensional surface in such a way that they create an illusion of three-dimensional space, but was there any reason why artists should continue to confine Living Lines to a two-dimensional surface while ordinary lines outside the Realm of Art enjoyed freedom in Space? ('Comments on Lines in Space', unpublished essay sent to Tate Gallery, Jan. 1964).

The articulation and definition of space was a common concern among many of the artists of Abstraction-Création, the international avant-garde group to which Vézelay belonged. While such artists as César Domela, Jean Gorin and Ben Nicholson extended painting's illusionistic space into the third dimension of the relief, others such as Alexander Calder, Naum Gabo and Katarzyna Kobro made sculptures in which actual space was an integral element. For them, an abstract art characterised by space and purity was an essential part of the new society for which they hoped and worked. Vézelay was not the only one among them who related the abstract qualities of her work to a spiritual level of reality. This was an art for a new society and a new consciousness.

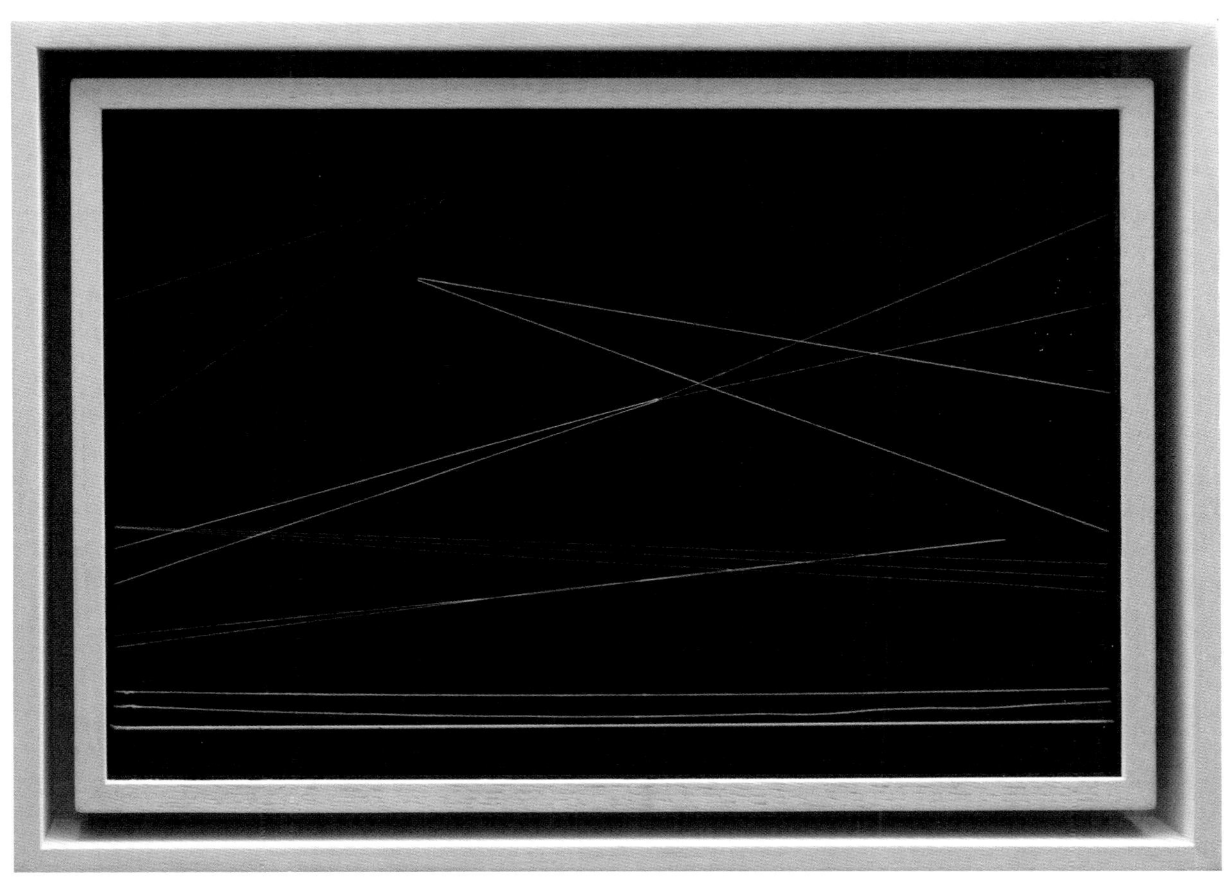

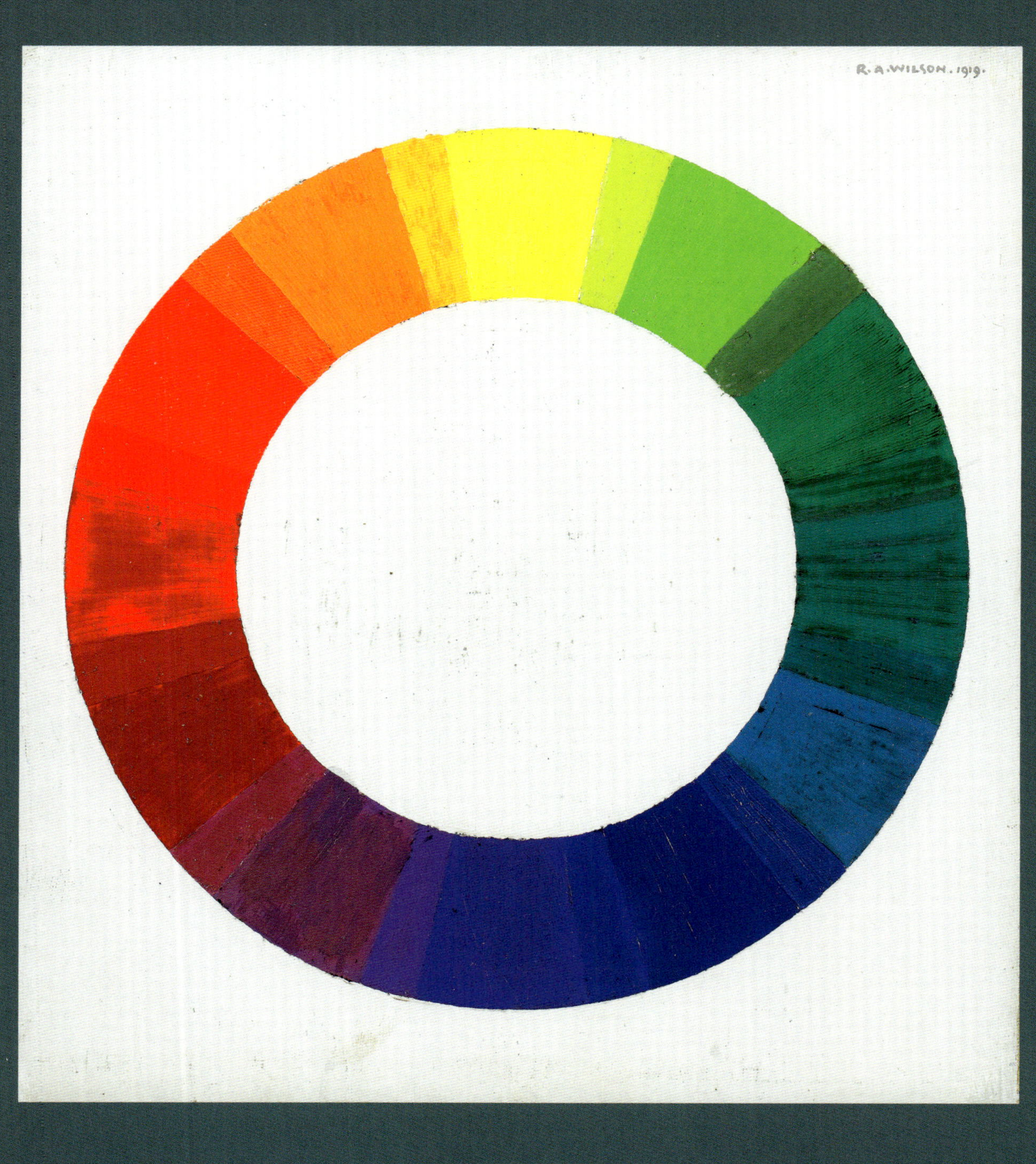
R. A. WILSON. 1919.

Robert Arthur Wilson (1884-1979)

Colour Wheel, 1919

Oil on canvas, signed and dated - 33 x 31 cm.

'Colour: its meaning and use, logic,mystery, symbolism and power' was the title of a BBC radio broadcast talk given by Wilson in May 1920. Although Colour Wheel shows an awareness of Chevreul's colour theories, its broader symbolism might equally relate to the void left by the war and the power of renewal as suggested by the continuous form of a circle.

His paintings were much studied by art students of the period, and were part of a wider discourse that was taking place at the time, led by intellectual luminaries such as James Wood.
Exploring colour harmony was central to Wilson's work and a subject on which he wrote and lectured.
In his introduction to R.A.Wilson's Exhibition of Paintings and Colour Studies, that took place at the Guild of Decorators' Syndicate, London, in May 1922, James Wood stated, somewhat prophetically: 'Great advances were made by the artists of the last generation in the treatment of form and colour; it is doubtful whether the twentieth century will not be marked by certain discoveries.'

Index

Acknowledgements

Nancy and Richard Balaban
Christopher Campbell-Howes
Francis Carline
Hermione Carline
Roland Carline
Bob Davenport
Nicholas Finney
Geoff Hassell of Artbiogs.co.uk
Dr Libby Horner
Ian Jack
Simon Lawrence
Ayla Lepine
Anton Liss
Eva Liss
Steven Maisel
Maudji
Chris Mees of ArtHistoryResearch.net
Momo
Dr Chloë Reddaway
Jeffrey Reznick
Anna Sampson
Jackie Setter
Robin Shaw
Richard Shillitoe
Abbie Sprague
Chris Stephens
Richard Thompson
Charles Tolkien-Gillett
Mark Wake
Tom Wheare

Photography:
Douglas Atfield
Glynn Clarkson
Evelina Llewellyn
Stéphane Pons